Maths Progress

International 11–14

Contributing editors: Dr Naomi Norman and Katherine Pate

7

P Pearson

Published by Pearson Education Limited, 80 Strand, London, WC2R 0RL.

www.pearsonschoolsandfecolleges.co.uk

Text © Pearson Education Limited 2020
Project managed and edited by Just Content Ltd
Typeset by PDQ Digital Media Solutions Ltd
Original illustrations © Pearson Education Limited 2020
Cover illustration by Robert Samuel Hanson

The rights of Nick Asker, Jack Barraclough, Sharon Bolger, Gwenllian Burns, Greg Byrd, Lynn Byrd, Andrew Edmondson, Keith Gallick, Sophie Goldie, Bobbie Johns, Catherine Murphy, Amy O'Brien and Katherine Pate to be identified as authors of this work have been asserted by them in accordance with the Copyright, Designs and Patents Act 1988.

First published 2020

24

15

British Library Cataloguing in Publication Data

A catalogue record for this book is available from the British Library.

ISBN 978 1 292 32715 0

Printed in Great Britain by Bell and Bain Ltd, Glasgow

Acknowledgements

The publisher would like to thank the following for their kind permission to reproduce their photographs:

123RF: Marek Uliasz 54, Comaniciu Dan Dumitru 63, klotz 77, serezniy 85, arekmalang 132, Brian Jackson 137, Krisztian Miklosy 200, solarseven 207, smn 227; **Alamy Stock Photo:** Alex Segre 27, YAY Media AS 158, Karen Fuller 205; **DK Images:** William Reavell 164; **Getty Images:** Wavebreakmedia Ltd 12, Chad Ehlers 37, Vladimir Rys Photography 39, alexeys 105, SDI Productions 135, majana 140, joannawnuk 160, nikonaft 184, suti 198, ugde 224; **Science Photo Library:** DETLEV VAN RAVENSWAAY 29, BRIAN BELL 233; **Shutterstock:** Toria 1, Warren Goldswain 4, maminez 35, agsandrew 57, Anton Balazh 59, STILLFX 80, Stephen VanHorn 83, Jiratthitikaln Maurice 88, Dmitry Kalinovsky 102, 5AM Images 108, Rehan Qureshi 111, Danai Deepeng 126, KK Tan 128, Alex Bogatyrev 130, sirtravelalot 155, VINCENT GIORDANO PHOTO 162, Wichudapa 177, Miao Liao 179, LanaG 182, Four Oaks 203, sommernambuler 210, Q Photographs 230, egd 248, Fotosenmeer 251.

All other images © Pearson Education

The publisher would like to thank Diane Oliver for her input and advice.

Note from the publisher

Pearson has robust editorial processes, including answer and fact checks, to ensure the accuracy of the content in this publication, and every effort is made to ensure this publication is free of errors. We are, however, only human, and occasionally errors do occur. Pearson is not liable for any misunderstandings that arise as a result of errors in this publication, but it is our priority to ensure that the content is accurate. If you spot an error, please do contact us at resourcescorrections@pearson.com so we can make sure it is corrected.

Contents

Maths Progress International

Confidence • Fluency • Problem-solving • Progression

Confidence at the heart

Maths Progress International is built around a unique pedagogy that has been created by leading educational researchers and teachers. The result is an innovative learning structure based around 10 key principles designed to nurture confidence and raise achievement.

Pedagogy – our 10 key principles

- Fluency
- Problem-solving
- Reflection
- Mathematical reasoning
- Progression
- Linking
- Multiplicative reasoning
- Modelling
- Concrete - Pictorial - Abstract (CPA)
- Relevance

This edition of Maths Progress has been designed specifically for international students and provides seamless progression into Pearson Edexcel International GCSE Mathematics (9–1), as well as complete coverage of the Pearson Edexcel iLowerSecondary Award and the UK National Curriculum.

Student books

The **Student books** are based on a single well-paced curriculum with built-in differentiation, fluency, problem-solving and reasoning so you can use them with your whole class. They follow the unique unit structure that has been shown to boost confidence and support every student's progress.

Workbooks

The **Workbooks** offer extra practice of key content. They provide additional support via guided questions with partially-worked solutions, hints and QR codes linking to worked example videos. Confidence checkers encourage students to take ownership of their learning, and allow them to track their progress.

This innovative 11–14 course builds on the first edition KS3 Maths Progress (2014) course, and is tailored to the needs of international students.

Take a look at the other parts of the series

ActiveLearn Service

The *Active*Learn service enhances the course by bringing together your planning, teaching and assessment tools, as well as giving students access to additional resources to support their learning. Use the interactive Scheme of Work, linked to all the teacher and student resources, to create a personalised learning experience both in and outside the classroom.

What's in *Active*Learn for Maths Progress International?

- ✔ **Front-of-class student books** with links to PowerPoints, videos and animations
- ✔ **Over 40 assessments and online markbooks,** including end-of-unit, end-of-term and end-of-year tests
- ✔ **Online, automarked homework activities**
- ✔ **Interactive Scheme of Work** makes re-ordering the course easy by bringing everything together into one curriculum for all students with links to resources and teacher guidance
- ✔ **Lesson plans** for every student book lesson
- ✔ **Answers** to the Student books and Workbooks
- ✔ **Printable glossaries** for each Student book contain all the key terms in one place
- ✔ **Student access to glossaries, videos, homework and online textbooks**

ActiveLearn Progress & Assess

The Progress & Assess service is part of the full *Active*Learn service, or can be bought as a separate subscription. This service includes:

- assessments that have been designed to ensure that all students have the opportunity to show what they have learned
- editable tests that mimic the style of Pearson Edexcel International GCSE exams
- online markbooks for tracking and reporting
- baseline assessments for Year 7 and both tiers of International GCSE.

Welcome to Maths Progress International
Student books

Starting a new course is exciting! We believe you will have fun with maths, while at the same time nurturing your confidence and raising your achievement. Here's how:

Learn fundamental knowledge and skills over a series of *Master* lessons.

Some questions are tagged as *Finance* or *STEM*. These questions show how the real world relies on maths.

Literacy hints explain unfamiliar terms and *Strategy hints* help with working out.

You can improve your ability to use maths in everyday situations by tackling *Modelling*, *Reasoning*, *Problem-solving* and *Real* questions. *Discussions* prompt you to explain your reasoning or explore new ideas with a partner.

Clear objectives show what you will cover in each lesson.

Why learn this? shows you how maths is useful in everyday life.

Improve your *Fluency* – practise answering questions using maths you already know.

The first questions are *Warm up*. Here you can show what you already know about this topic or related ones...

...before moving on to further questions, with *Worked examples* and *Hints* for help when you need it.

Key points explain key concepts and definitions where you need them.

Your teacher has online access to *Answers*.

A printable *Glossary* containing all the key mathematical terms is available online.

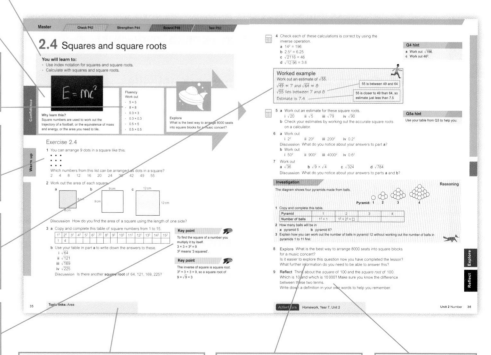

Topic links and *Subject links* show you how the maths in a lesson is connected to other mathematical topics and other subjects.

Explore a real-life problem by discussing and having a go. By the end of the lesson you'll have gained the skills you need to start finding a solution to the question using maths.

At the end of each lesson, you get a chance to *Reflect* on how confident you feel about the topic.

At the end of the Master lessons, take a **Check up** test to help you decide to Strengthen or Extend your learning. You may be able to mark this test yourself.

Choose only the topics in **Strengthen** that you need a bit more practice with. You'll find more hints here to lead you through specific questions. Then move on to *Extend*.

Extend helps you to apply the maths you know to some different situations. Strengthen and Extend both include Enrichment or Investigations.

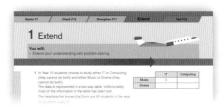

When you have finished the whole unit, a **Unit test** helps you see how much progress you are making.

STEM lessons

These lessons focus on STEM maths. STEM stands for Science, Technology, Engineering and Maths. You can find out how charities use maths in their fundraising, how engineers monitor water flow in rivers, and why diamonds sparkle (among other things!).

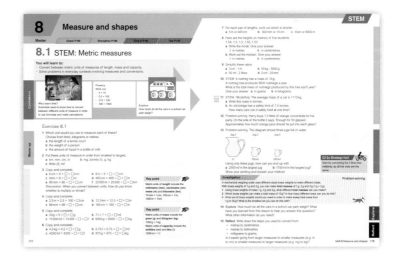

Further support

You can easily access extra resources that tie into each lesson by logging into *Active*Learn. Here you will find online homework clearly mapped to the units, providing fun, interactive exercises linked to helpful worked examples and videos.

The workbooks, full of extra practice of key questions, will help you reinforce your learning and track your own progress.

1.1 Averages and range

You will learn to:
- Find the mode, median and range of a set of data.
- Calculate and interpret the mean of a set of data.
- Compare sets of data using averages and range.
- Solve problems involving mean, mode, median and range.

Confidence

Why learn this?
Internet providers advertise the average speed of their broadband to help customers decide which service to use.

Fluency
Look at the numbers: 2, 3, 6, 3, 3, 1, 9.
- Which is the largest number?
- Which is the smallest number?
- Which number occurs most often?

Explore
What is the average number of computers per household in the country?

Exercise 1.1

Warm up

1 Look at these numbers:
102, 105, 107, 101, 119, 101, 118
   a Write the numbers in ascending order.
   b Which number is
      i in the middle
      ii the largest
      iii the smallest
      iv the 6th number in the list?

2 Write down the **mode** for each of these sets of **data**.
   a TV, phone, phone, computer, tablet, TV, TV, phone, tablet, phone, tablet, computer, phone
   b 4   7   2   2   4   5   3   9   4   3
   c 0.5   0.1   0.3   0.5   0.3   0.2   0.1   0.4   0.3

3 Work out the **range** for each set of values in Q2 where possible.
   Discussion Which set of data in Q2 does not have a range? Why not?

4 Problem-solving / Reasoning
   a Write down a set of data that has two modes.
   b Write down a set of data that has no mode.

5 Work out the **median** for each of these sets of numbers.
   a 5, 9, 3, 2, 7, 9, 7
   b 11, 12, 9, 8, 15, 17, 13, 20, 12

Key point
Data is a set of information. Each piece of information is called a **value**.

Key point
The **mode** is the most common value. It is also called the **modal** value.

Key point
The **range** is the difference between the smallest and largest values. The larger the range, the more spread out the values.

Key point
The **median** is the middle value when the data is written in order.

Worked example

Find the median of 4, 2, 6, 7, 2, 1, 3, 6, 6, 9

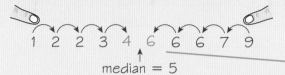

1 2 2 3 4 6 6 6 7 9

median = 5

> There are two middle values. The median is halfway between 4 and 6.

6 Work out the median for each of these sets of marks.

a 8, 3, 2, 2, 5, 9

b 6, 10, 7, 15, 8, 17, 11, 9

Discussion What fraction of the values are less than the median?

7 The numbers of children in the families of some Year 7 students are

4	3	2	2	1	2	3	4	3
2	1	2	1	6	2	3	3	4

Find the median.

Discussion What do you notice about the median for this set of values?

8 Copy and complete the calculations to find the **mean** of each of these sets of values.

a 1, 1, 4

$$\text{Mean} = \frac{1+1+4}{3} = \frac{\square}{3} = \square$$

b 9, 9, 2, 4

$$\text{Mean} = \frac{\cdots\cdots\cdots\cdots}{4} = \frac{\square}{\square} = \square$$

c 17, 17, 17, 17, 17

$$\text{Mean} = \frac{\cdots\cdots\cdots\cdots}{\square} = \frac{\square}{\square} = \square$$

> **Key point**
> The **mean** of a set of values is the sum of the values divided by the number of values.

9 Real / Reasoning Twenty Year 7 students recorded the number of times in a week that they visited Wikipedia for information.

10, 7, 4, 5, 6, 5, 9, 7, 6, 8, 7, 7, 5, 5, 6, 8, 8, 7, 10, 8

Find

a the mean

b the median

c the **modal** number of visits.

> **Key point**
> The **modal** value is another way of saying 'the mode'.

10 Real / Reasoning Two football players record the number of goals they score in 10 matches:

Player A: 0, 1, 1, 1, 3, 1, 2, 1, 1, 1

Player B: 0, 0, 5, 0, 0, 4, 3, 0, 0, 1

a For each player work out

  i the mean

  ii the median

  iii the modal number of goals scored.

b Calculate the range of the number of goals scored for each player.

c Who would you choose for your team? Explain your reasoning.

11 Sabeen is going on holiday. She does not like the rain.

She looks at the rainfall each day in two places over 7 days in July.

	Monday	Tuesday	Wednesday	Thursday	Friday	Saturday	Sunday
England	0.5 cm	0.7 cm	0.2 cm	0.7 cm	0 cm	0.1 cm	0.2 cm
St Lucia	0 cm	0 cm	0 cm	0 cm	0 cm	5.4 cm	0 cm

Work out the mean rainfall for each place.

Discussion Should Sabeen choose the place with the lower mean?
Explain your answer.

12 Problem-solving / Reasoning The mean of 3, 4, 11 and n is 6.
What is the value of n?

Q12 hint

First work out the sum of the four values.

13 Problem-solving / Reasoning Find a set of three numbers with
  a range = 0, mean = 3
  b median = 3, mean = 5
  c mode = 7, median = 7
  d mean = 5, mode = 4

Investigation   **Reasoning**

For a set of data:
• can the mode and median be the same
• can the mean and median be the same
• can the mode, mean and median be the same
• can the range be less than the mode?
Write down a simple set of data to show each answer, if it is possible.
The range of a set of data is 0. What can you say about the median, mode and mean?

---

14 Explore What is the average number of computers per household in the country?
Is it easier to explore this question now you have completed this lesson?
What further information do you need, to be able to answer this?

15 Reflect In this lesson you need several mathematical skills, for example ordering numbers. Write down a list of all the other mathematical skills you used for this lesson.
Copy and complete the sentence until you have listed them all:
I used _____ to work out the _____

1.2 More averages and range

You will learn to:
- Group discrete and continuous data.
- Draw and interpret grouped frequency diagrams.

Why learn this?
Grouping people's ages helps to show the age distribution in the UK.

Fluency
12, 20, 9, 19
- Which of these numbers are contained in the class 10–19?
- How can you tell the mode from a frequency diagram?

Explore
Estimate the percentage of the population that is able to vote.

Exercise 1.2

1 Write these values into a grouped frequency table like this:
7, 3, 8, 11, 2, 21, 15, 12, 4, 20, 13, 2, 15, 12, 4, 17

Class	Tally	Frequency
1–5		
6–10		

2 Real Harry measured the pulse rate (beats per minute) of some classmates.

Pulse rate	Frequency
70–79	1
80–89	8
90–99	7
100–109	3

a How many students had a pulse rate between 80 and 89?
b How many students had a pulse rate between 90 and 109?
c What is the **modal class**?

3 Is each set of data **discrete** or **continuous**?
a The maximum daily temperatures in May.
b The numbers of songs on some mp3 players.
c The masses of a batch (a quantity or group) of bread loaves.
d The data in Q2.
e Shoe sizes

Key point

The **modal class** is the one with the highest frequency.

Key point

Discrete data can only take particular values. For example, dress sizes can only be even numbers. For discrete data you can use groups like 1–10, 11–20 …
Continuous data is measured and can take any value. For example, length, mass and capacity. For continuous data there are no gaps between the groups.

4 A researcher measured the wingspans of some long-eared bats.
18 cm, 28 cm, 25 cm, 8 cm, 19 cm, 22 cm, 11 cm, 24 cm, 5 cm, 13 cm,
23 cm, 23 cm

a Copy and complete the grouped frequency table for the data.
Make the **classes** have equal widths.

Wingspan, w (cm)	Frequency
$0 \leqslant w < 10$	
$10 \leqslant w < \square$	
$\square \leqslant w < \square$	

b What is the modal class?

Investigation   Problem-solving

The data shows the times, in minutes, that some students spent intensely exercising in a day.
90, 15, 10, 0, 5, 0, 10, 20, 25, 50, 0, 0, 15, 8, 50, 45, 20, 30, 17, 10, 30, 70, 45, 25, 20

a **i** Make a frequency table for the data. Use 5 equal class intervals.
  ii Draw a frequency diagram for the data.
b Repeat part **a**. This time use 10 equal class intervals.
c Which diagram do you think shows the data best? Explain your answer.

Discussion Explain your choice of intervals.

---

5 Carla measured the heights, h cm, of some students in her class.
The grouped frequency table shows her results.

Height, h (cm)	Frequency
$120 \leqslant h < 130$	1
$130 \leqslant h < 140$	4
$140 \leqslant h < 150$	6
$150 \leqslant h < 160$	5
$160 \leqslant h < 170$	2

a Copy and complete the frequency diagram.

b Which is the modal class?

c How many students are at least 150 cm tall?

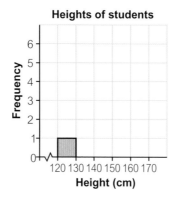

Heights of students

Q5a hint

For continuous data, there are no spaces between the bars.

6 **Explore** Estimate the percentage of the population that is able to vote.
Look back at the maths you have learned in this lesson.
How can you use it to answer the question?

7 **Reflect** Look back at the investigation. When do you think it is sensible to use grouped data? When would using grouped data look confusing?
Do you think it's always important to have equal class intervals for grouped data? Why or why not?

1.3 Two-way tables and bar charts

You will learn to:
- Use two-way tables.
- Interpret and draw dual bar charts and compound bar charts.

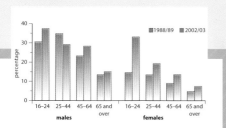

Why learn this?
Tables and charts are used by the Office of National Statistics to compare data.

Fluency
What are the next two numbers?
- 0, 5, 10, 15,...
- 20, 22, 24, 26,...
- 0, 50, 100, 150,…

Explore
What information does the Office for National Statistics display using dual bar charts?

Exercise 1.3

1 Chris drew this bar chart to show his classmates' favourite cold drinks.
   a How many students like squash best?
   b Which drink do four students prefer?
   c How many more students prefer fizzy drinks to juice?
   d How many students are in Chris's class?

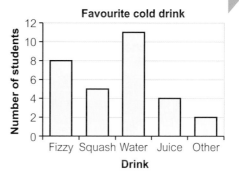

Favourite cold drink

2 Alan and Yolanda complete record sheets for their weekend press-up fitness exercises.

Name: Alan
Press-ups
Sat   20
Sun   22

Name: Yolanda
Press-ups
Sat   20
Sun   15

   a Copy and complete this **two-way table**.

	Sat	Sun	Total
Alan			
Yolanda			
Total			

   b Write Alan's data in the top row. Work out the total.
   c Write Yolanda's data in the second row.
   d Work out the total of each column.
   e Add the row totals together. Check by adding the column totals together.

Key point

A **two-way table** splits data into groups in rows across the table and in columns down the table. You can calculate the totals across and down.

3 The frequency table shows some recycling by the Sohal and Jenkins families for a month.

	Cans	Glass bottles	Plastic bottles	Cardboard boxes	Newspapers and magazines
Sohal	45	50	45	20	30
Jenkins	35	20	65	50	5

a Copy and complete the **dual bar chart**.

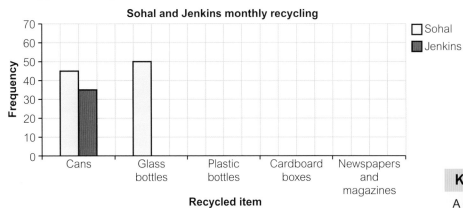

b How many cans did the Jenkins family recycle?

c Which item was recycled most by the Sohals?

d How many glass and plastic bottles were recycled altogether?

e Which family recycled more?

Key point

A **dual bar chart** compares two sets of data. The bars are drawn side by side.

Q3d hint

Include glass bottles and plastic bottles for both families.

4 The **compound bar chart** shows the photos Giselle uploaded to different websites.

a **i** How many photos of herself did Giselle upload to Facebook?

ii How many photos of places did Giselle upload to Facebook?

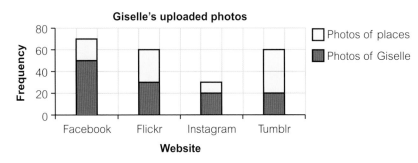

Key point

A **compound bar chart** combines different sets of data in one bar.

b Copy and complete the table.

	Facebook	Flickr	Instagram	Tumblr
Photos of Giselle				
Photos of places				

c Did Giselle upload more photos of herself than of places? Explain your answer.

5 Students from three different schools were asked which charity they would prefer to raise money for. The tally chart shows the results.

	Oxfam	Save the Children	RSPCA	Help the Aged
Grantham	卌	卌 l	卌 l	lll
Chilbrook	ll	卌 llll	卌 ll	llll
Oakmead	lll	llll	卌 卌	lll

a Copy and complete the compound bar chart.

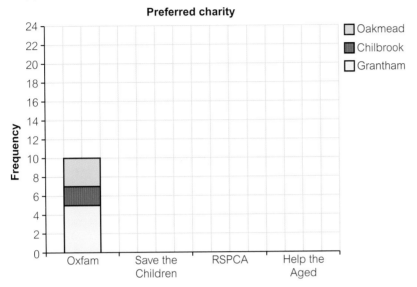

b How many students at Chilbrook answered the questionnaire?
c At which school did the RSPCA receive the most votes?
d Which charity received the most votes overall?

6 **STEM** Hugh counted the butterflies and bees that were attracted to different colours of flowers in his garden.

	White	Yellow	Red	Blue	Green
Bees	7	15	2	18	1
Butterflies	7	10	8	3	3

a How many butterflies and bees visited blue flowers?
b Which are the most attractive colours for bees?
c Hugh says, 'Bees and butterflies are equally attracted to white.' Is he correct? Explain your answer.
d Write a sentence about how bees and butterflies
  i differ in their colour preferences
  ii are similar in their colour preferences.

7 **Explore** What information does the Office for National Statistics display using dual bar charts?
Look back at the maths you have learned in this lesson. How can you use it to answer this question?

8 **Reflect** In this lesson you compared data using dual bar charts and compound bar charts. Which type of chart did you find easier to interpret? Why?
When would it be more useful to use a compound bar chart?
When would it be more useful to use a dual bar chart?

1.4 More graphs and tables 1

Confidence

You will learn to:
- Interpret and draw line graphs.
- Recognise when a graph is misleading.

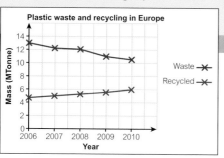
Plastic waste and recycling in Europe

Why learn this?
Line graphs can be used to predict future outcomes.

Fluency
Which graph shows the temperatures
- increasing
- decreasing
- staying the same?

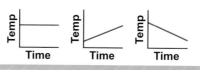

Explore
How can line graphs show the worst and best scenarios?

Exercise 1.4

Warm up

1 The line graph shows how the volume of air in a scuba tank changed during a dive.
  a How much air was in the tank
    i at the start of the dive
    ii after 20 minutes?
  b How long did it take for the volume of air to drop to 7 litres?
  c How much air did the diver use during the last 20 minutes of the dive?
  d When was the diver the most active during the dive? Explain your answer.

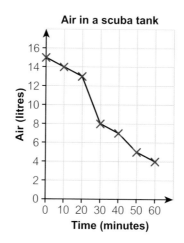
Air in a scuba tank

Q1 Literacy hint

A scuba tank is a container of air that is part of an underwater breathing apparatus.

Key point

When a line graph shows changes over time, put time on the horizontal axis.

2 **Modelling** The table shows the daily maximum wind speed in knots in the Hebrides in one week.

Day	Mon	Tue	Wed	Thu	Fri	Sat	Sun
Speed (knots)	31	33	41	41	42	57	60

  a Copy the axes. Plot the points using crosses. Join the points with a ruler.
  b Callum says this is a good model for predicting the wind speed for the next few months. Explain why he is wrong.

Discussion Does every point on the line graph mean something?

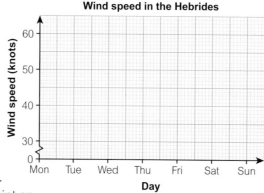
Wind speed in the Hebrides

Q2a hint

The zig-zag shows there's a break in the axis scale.

Q2b hint

'Explain' means write a sentence:
This is not a good model because…

3 Real The graph shows the predicted and recorded heights of the sea tide at Lowestoft during a winter storm in 2013.

   a **i** What time was the highest recorded tide?

      ii What height was the highest recorded tide?

     iii How much higher was the recorded tide than the predicted tide at 4 pm?

   b What time is the lowest recorded tide?

   c Write a sentence to compare

      i the predicted and recorded tide times

     ii the predicted and recorded heights.

Tide heights at Lowestoft

(Line graph with y-axis "Height (m)" from 0 to 5, x-axis "Time" from 8 am to 8 pm; lines labelled Recorded and Predicted)

Q3 hint

Were the predicted high and low tide times correct?

4 Real The table gives the mean monthly temperatures (°C) in Canberra and London over one year.

	Jan	Feb	Mar	Apr	May	Jun	Jul	Aug	Sep	Oct	Nov	Dec
Canberra	20	21	17	13	9	6	5	7	9	12	15	18
London	10	4	4	6	8	12	15	17	17	14	10	7

   a Draw a line graph to show both sets of temperatures.
      Put the months on the horizontal axis.
      Choose a suitable scale for the vertical axis.

   b Which are the coldest three months in

      i Canberra

     ii London?

   c Write two sentences about your graph, comparing the temperatures in Canberra and London.
      You could use some of these words: warmer, colder, maximum, minimum, range.

Q4c hint

Compare maximum, minimum and range.

5 Reasoning Apasra drew these two line graphs to show the sales of digital tablets and personal computers.

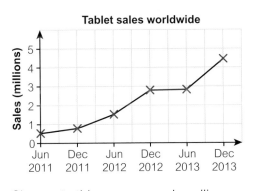

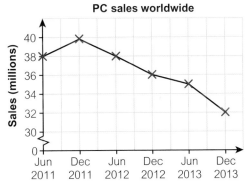

She wrote this newspaper headline:
'Huge rise in tablet sales. Massive decline in PC sales.'

   a Explain why Apasra's line graphs are misleading.

   b Draw the PC sales graph using the axis for the tablet sales graph.

   c Write a more accurate newspaper headline.

Q5a hint

Look at the vertical scale of each graph.

6 The bar chart and table show the decrease in CD sales of music singles between 1997 and 2003 in the UK.

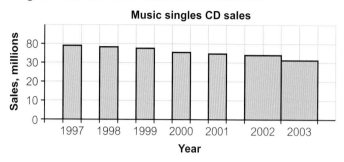

Music singles CD sales

Year	Sales (millions)
1997	78
1998	74
1999	71
2000	56
2001	51
2002	44
2003	31

a Give two reasons why the bar chart is misleading.

b Draw an accurate bar chart.

Discussion How would you need to change the axes of the bar chart again if you included sales up to today?

Q6b hint

Do you need to start the sales axis at 0?

7 The table shows the weather for Lerwick, Scotland.

	Jan	Feb	Mar	Apr	May	Jun	Jul	Aug	Sep	Oct	Nov	Dec
Max temp (°C)	5	5	6	8	11	13	14	14	13	10	8	6
Rainfall (mm)	109	97	69	68	52	55	72	71	87	104	111	118

Copy these axes.

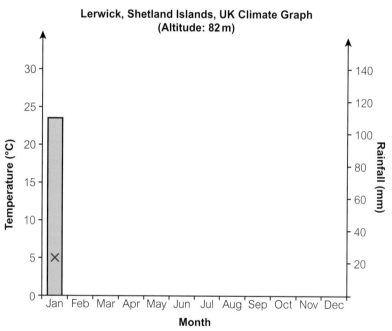

Lerwick, Shetland Islands, UK Climate Graph (Altitude: 82 m)

Q7 hint

Plot the temperature in the middle of each month.

a Draw a bar chart for rainfall (mm).

b On the same graph, draw a line graph for maximum temperature (°C).

c Write two sentences describing how the weather changed during the year.

8 Explore How can line graphs show the worst and best scenarios? Is it easier to explore this question now you have completed the lesson? What further information do you need to be able to answer this?

9 Reflect List five ways that graphs can mislead you. You could begin with 'It is misleading when different scales are …'

Reflect   Explore

1.5 More graphs and tables 2

You will learn to:
- Analyse and present data using spreadsheets in a computer software program.
- Choose the most appropriate graph to represent data and solve problems.
- Draw, read and interpret tables, bar charts, pie charts, bar-line graphs and line graphs.

Confidence

Fluency
Find the mode, median, mean and range for this set of data.
11, 7, 12, 12, 8, 6, 11, 12, 9, 8

Why learn this?
Computers are much faster than humans at processing data.

Explore
In what ways can a spreadsheet be used to interpret and display large amounts of data to make it easier to interpret the data?

Exercise 1.5

1 Look at this part of a spreadsheet.
a What is the number in cell B2?
b Which cell is the number 81 in?

	A	B
1	81	16
2	54	25

Warm up

Key point

A **spreadsheet** is a page of rows and columns of **cells**.
Each cell can contain a number or text.

2 Follow these instructions to input the number 14 into cell A1.
Click on cell A1.
Type 14.
Press Enter or the Down Arrow key.
You are now ready to enter data into cell A2.

3 If you make a mistake, click the Undo button.
Try it and see what happens.

4 **Real** The data shows the numbers of weeks the ten most popular UK singles stayed in the Top 10 in 2011.
14, 10, 12, 16, 10, 11, 11, 13, 12, 10

a Input the data into column **A** of the spreadsheet, starting at cell **A1**.
b Rearrange the numbers from smallest to largest.
   i Select the cells **A1** to **A10**.
   ii Use the sort feature to sort the data from **Smallest to Largest**.
c Find the mode.
   i Type the word **Mode** in cell **A11**.
   ii In cell **B11**, type exactly **=mode(**
   iii Select all of the numbers and press **Enter** to put the mode into cell **B11**.
d Find the median.
   i Type the word **Median** in cell **A12**.
   ii In cell **B12**, type exactly **=median(**
   iii Select the data and press **Enter** to put the median into cell **B12**.

Q4 Strategy hint

Everyone makes mistakes. This is called human error. Check you have entered the data correctly.

Q4b ii hint

After sorting, check that the numbers in column A are in the order you expect.

Q4c ii hint

Typing = tells the spreadsheet to calculate something.

e Find the mean.

  i Type the word **Mean** in cell **A13**.

  ii In cell **B13**, type exactly **=average(**

  iii Select the data and press **Enter** to put the mean into cell **B13**.

f Find the range.

  i Type the word **Range** in cell **A14**.

  ii In cell **B14**, type exactly **=A10-A1**

  iii Press **Enter** to put the range into cell **B14**.

Discussion Experiment to find out what happens to the mode, median, mean and range if you change the value in cell **A1**. You will need to press **Enter** each time you change **A1**.

Q4e ii hint

Spreadsheets use the word 'average' instead of 'mean'.

Q4f ii hint

You don't need to type capital letters. Just type **=a10-a1**

5 Lauren kept a record of the amounts of time she spent playing on a computer game.

Day	Mon	Tues	Wed	Thur	Fri	Sat	Sun
Time (minutes)	30	45	45	15	70	120	60

  a Copy the table onto a new spreadsheet, starting at cell **A1**.

  b Draw a line graph for the data. Follow these steps.

  i Select the whole table.

  ii Click the **Insert** tab on the top menu.

  iii Select **Chart** and then **the first line graph** from the list.

Discussion Right-click on the graph line and select **Format Data Series …**

Experiment to see how the options change the style of the line.

  c Look at the graph. Read off the modal time Lauren spent playing on the computer game.

  d Use the method in Q4 to calculate

  i the mean

  ii the mode

  iii the median

  iv the range

  of the length of time Lauren played on her computer each day

Q5a hint

Click on the **Sheet 2** tab at the bottom of the screen to select a new spreadsheet.

Investigation

Reasoning

Experiment with the different types of graph you can draw of the data in Q5. Use the 'Recommended Charts' option.

• Which graphs show the data in a way that is meaningful?

• Which graphs are not useful?

• From which graphs is it easy to read

  i the mode **ii** the range?

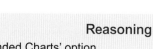

6 Anita asked 25 girls in Year 7 which musical instrument they liked the most.

Instrument	Girls
clarinet	3
violin	8
piano	5
saxophone	4
drum	5

  a Copy the table onto a new spreadsheet, starting at cell **A1**.

  b Draw a bar chart for the data.

  i Select the whole table.

  ii Click the **Insert** tab.

  iii Click Column and select the first 2D column bar chart.

  iv Give your bar chart a title and label the axes.

Discussion Make the chart box smaller.

What do you notice about the vertical scale?

Q6b hint

Select the whole chart by clicking on its border. Click the **Layout** tab on the top menu. Use the **Chart Title** and **Axis Titles** buttons.

Topic links: Mode, Median, Range, Bar charts, Line graphs, Pie charts

7 Use the data in Q6a.

 a Draw a pie chart for the data. Follow these steps.
   i Select the whole table.
   ii Click the **Insert** tab.
   iii Select **2D pie**.
   iv Experiment with other types of pie chart. Which is your favourite?

 b Use your pie chart to work out the mode.

 c Can you work out any other averages from the pie chart?

 d Do you think the pie chart or the bar chart displays the data more clearly? Explain.

8 Bassi made a table to show the lengths of tracks on his favourite CD.

Track length (seconds)	Frequency
50–99	3
100–149	11
150–199	6
200–249	2
250–299	3

Q8 hint

You must close the gaps between the bars because the data values are times (in seconds), which is continuous data and can be measured as accurately as you choose. Right-click on a bar and select **Format Data Series...**

 a Copy the table onto a new spreadsheet, starting at cell **A1**.

 b Draw a bar chart for the data.

 c Use the **Format Data Series...** option to colour the bars yellow and give them a black border.

9 Two groups of 100 people, A and B, were asked how they travelled to work in the morning. The results are shown below.

Key point

A **bar-line graph** is very similar to a bar chart except the bars are drawn as lines.

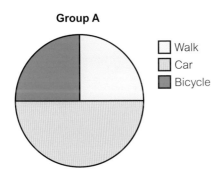

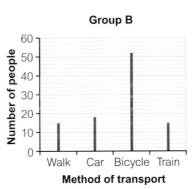

 a Which was the modal method of transport for
   i Group A
   ii Group B?

 b In which group did the largest number of people walk?

 c How many more people travelled by car in Group A than Group B?

 d Which type of graph displays the data more clearly? Explain.

10 **Explore** In what ways can a spreadsheet be used to interpret and display large amounts of data to make it easier to interpret the data? Is it easier to explore this question now you have completed the lesson? What further information do you need to be able to answer this?

11 **Reflect** You have now calculated averages with and without the help of a spreadsheet. Did the spreadsheet make it easier or more difficult to calculate each average? Explain your answers.

1 Check up

Averages and range

1 Hayley recorded the distances, in km, pupils live from School A.
0.5, 1, 1, 1, 2, 2, 7, 3, 0.5, 2

  a **i** Find the median distance.

    ii Work out the mean distance.

    iii Work out the range.

  b Hayley says, 'The median is the best average to use for this data.'
Is she correct? Explain your answer.

  c Hayley also recorded distances, in km, from School B.
She calculated the same statistics.

Median	Mean	Range
3 km	3.63 km	11 km

Choose the correct letter to complete this statement.
Students live closer to School ____, on average.

Charts and tables

2 The two-way table shows the meal choice of passengers on an aeroplane.

	Chicken	Fish	Vegetarian
Fruit	17	33	4
Chocolate brownie	12	18	16

  a How many passengers chose

    i chicken and chocolate brownie

    ii vegetarian

    iii fruit?

  b How many passengers are on the aeroplane?

3 80 boys and 60 girls chose their favourite topics in maths.
The bar chart shows the results for the boys.

  a What is the boys' favourite topic?

  b Copy and complete the two-way table.

	Number	Algebra	Statistics	Geometry
Boys				
Girls	20	10	20	10

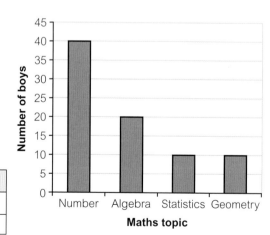

  c Draw a dual bar chart for the two sets of data.

4 This frequency diagram shows the heights of wheat stalks (main stems).

a What is the modal class?

b How many stalks are in the class $120 \leqslant h < 125$?

c How many stalks are at least 120 cm tall?

d Marcia says, 'This graph shows there are more than double the number of stalks in class $125 \leqslant h < 130$ than in $120 \leqslant h < 125$.' Explain why she is wrong.

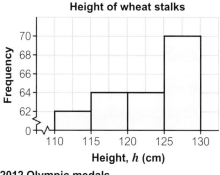

Height of wheat stalks

5 The bar chart shows the medals received by four countries at the 2012 Olympics.

a Which country won the fewest silver medals?

b How many more gold medals did Kazakhstan win than Jamaica?

c A third of the medals won by one country were bronze. Which country?

d Which kind of medal was won by these countries the most?

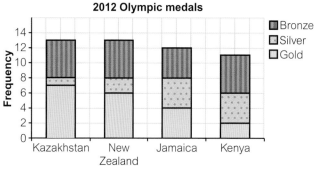

2012 Olympic medals

Line graphs and spreadsheets

6 The line graphs show the depth of snow at two ski resorts at the end of each month.

a What was the depth of snow at Winter Park in April?

b Which ski resort had snow earlier?

c In which months did Winter Park have more snow than Avoriaz?

d At which ski resort did the snow start melting first? How can you tell?

e What was the difference in depth of snow between the two resorts in February?

Ski resort snow depth

7 Look at this part of a spreadsheet.
Decide whether each statement is true or false. If a statement is false, rewrite it to make it true.

a The value in cell B2 is 11. b The median age is 10.

c The modal age is 12. d The mean age is 11.

e The range is 8.

◢	A	B	C
1	Name	Age	
2	Ami	12	
3	Ben	11	
4	Charlie	12	
5	Denis	10	
6	Ed	11	
7	Fred	12	
8	Gill	10	
9			

8 How sure are you of your answers? Were you mostly

😠 Just guessing 😐 Feeling doubtful 🙂 Confident

What next? Use your results to decide whether to strengthen or extend your learning.

Challenge

9 a Write down three numbers whose range is 2.

b Write down three numbers whose median is 8.

c Write down three numbers whose mean is 5.

10 a The numbers 4, 2, 7, ☐ have a mode of 2. What is the missing number?

b The numbers 4, 2, 5, ☐ have a mean of 4. What is the missing number?

c The numbers 20, 70, 10, ☐ have a range of 80. What is the missing number?

d The numbers 8, 4, 6, ☐ have a median of 5. Write down a possible value of the missing number.

1 Strengthen

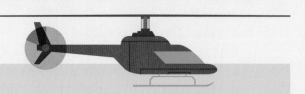

You will:
- Strengthen your understanding with practice.

Averages and range

1 Here are marks for three rounds of a quiz.
Jo: 6, 5, 7   Karl: 12, 1, 6

  a Whose results are the more consistent?

  b Work out the range for Jo and for Karl.

  c Write the missing word from this sentence.
    Choose from 'greater' or 'smaller'.
    The _____ the range, the more consistent the results.

  d Who would you like on your team, Jo or Karl? Explain why.

> **Q1a hint**
>
> Whose results are more or less the same every time?

 2 Fiona recorded the number of times she used her smartphone each hour one Sunday evening: 3, 0, 1, 2, 7

  a **i** Work out the mean.
     ii Work out the range.

  b Work out the mean and range for Monday evening: 2, 1, 1, 2, 3

  c Write down the missing word for each sentence. Choose from 'more' or 'less'.
    On average, Fiona used her smartphone _____ on Sunday.
    The data for Sunday is _____ consistent than the data for Monday.

> **Q2a i hint**
>
> Work out the total. Divide the total by the number of values.

 3 Rob records the number of hours he works over 10 days:
8, 11, 7, 0, 0, 10, 12, 13, 9, 12.5

  a Write the data in order from smallest to largest.

  b Put a ring around the two data values in the middle of your list.

  c Work out the median. Sum the two values and divide by 2.

  d Work out the mean.

  e What is the mode?

  f Which average should Rob use to estimate how many hours he works each day? Explain your answer.

> **Q3b hint**
>
> There are an even number of data values, so the median will be between the two middle values.

Charts and tables

1 The table shows some dentist appointments on one day.

Type of appointment	Fillings	Cleaning	Dentures	Extraction
Dentist A	8	11	5	3
Dentist B	10	4	1	3

The blue bar shows Dentist A had 8 appointments for fillings.

  a How many appointments did Dentist B have for fillings?

  b Copy and complete the dual bar chart for the data.

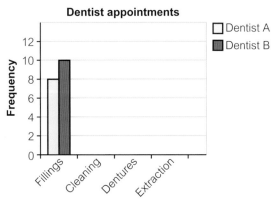

Dentist appointments

2 Ollie asked some Year 7 students what they like reading most.

	Fiction	Graphic novels	Non-fiction	Magazines
Boys		7	6	5
Girls		5	4	6

He started to draw a compound bar chart for the data.

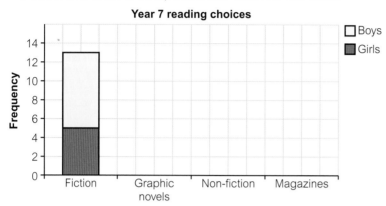

a How many girls prefer fiction?

b How many boys prefer fiction?

c Copy and complete the bar chart.

Q2b hint

Look at the Frequency axis. Count up from the top of the Girls part to find the height of the Boys part.

Q2c hint

Draw the Girls bars first. Then draw the Boys bars on top.

3 Two students are neighbours. They compared their travel times (in minutes) to school by bus and by car.

Bus	15	22	19	18	21	19	20	17	21	19
Car	7	16	28	15	21	17	29	9	24	20

a **i** Work out the median travel time by bus.

  ii Work out the median travel time by car.

  iii **Reasoning** Use the medians to compare the travel times by bus and by car.

   Travelling by car is _____ than by bus on average because the median time by bus is _____ than by car.

b **i** Work out the range of travel times by bus.

  ii Work out the range of travel times by car.

  iii Use the ranges to compare the travel times by bus and by car.

   Travel times by car differ _____ than by bus because the range of car travel times is _____ than the range of bus travel times.

Q3a iii hint

Complete the sentence using the words 'quicker' or 'slower', 'less' or 'greater'.

Q3b iii hint

Complete the sentence using the words 'more', 'less', or 'greater'.

4 Solhail uses a table to record the number of hours people in his class spend on homework each night.

Hours	Frequency
$0 \leq h < 1$	16
$1 \leq h < 2$	7
$2 \leq h < 3$	6

a Solhail has forgotten to include his own data. He spends 1.5 hours per night on his homework.
  In which group should he include his data?

b How many people are in his class?

c What is the modal length of time spent on homework?

Q4b hint

Find the sum of the frequencies. Don't forget to include Solhail.

Q4c hint

Which group has the highest frequency?

5 Darren recorded the distance, d km, he travelled each day.
0, 0, 0, 1, 1, 2, 2, 2, 2, 3, 3, 4, 5, 7, 7, 8, 9, 9, 10, 12, 12, 15, 18, 19, 21, 23

Travel each day

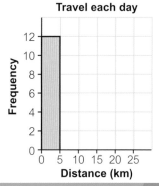

Distance, d (km)	Tally	Frequency
$0 \leqslant d < 5$	卌 卌 ‖	12
$5 \leqslant d < 10$		
$10 \leqslant d < 15$		
$15 \leqslant d < 20$		
$20 \leqslant d < 25$		

a Copy and complete the tally chart.

b Which is the modal class?

c Copy and complete the frequency diagram for this data.

Q5a hint

Where should you record the value '5'?

Line graphs and spreadsheets

1 The line graph shows the money, in £, John gave to two charities.

a How much was given to each charity in January?

b In which month was £50 given to Oxfam?

c In which month was more money given to the MSF than Oxfam?

d How much more money was given to Oxfam than the MSF in May?

e Fill in the missing word. Choose from 'increased' or 'decreased'.

  i Between April and June, the amount donated (given) to the MSF ___.

  ii Between April and June, the amount donated to Oxfam ___.

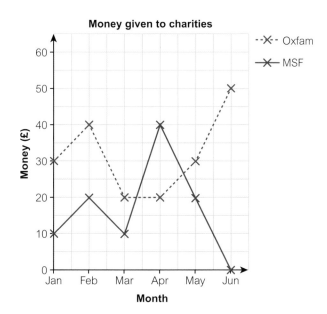

2 The spreadsheet shows information about the first language of some employees.

◢	A	B
1	Language	Number of employees
2	Arabic	123
3	English	111
4	German	98
5	Spanish	141
6		

Cell B2 shows that 123 people have Arabic as their first language.

a Which cell shows how many people have:

  i English

  ii Spanish?

  as their first language?

b How could you use the spreadsheet about employees' first languages to work out the total number of employees?

c What is the modal language?

Q2c hint

Which language is the first language of the greatest number of people?

3   Leo recorded his best javelin throw at a competition each year.
    He drew two graphs to show his results.

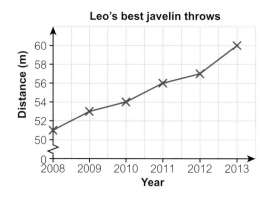

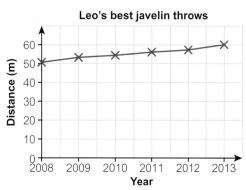

Which graph makes Leo look better? Why?

Q3 hint

Leo looks better in graph ☐ because...

Enrichment

1   Amad and her friend Munir travel by bus to E.
    Amad gets on at C, and Munir gets on at B.
    a   How much longer is Munir on the bus than Amad?
    b   How much time are they on the bus together?

Bus timetable for route 464

A	11 33	11 48	12 03	12 18	12 33	12 48
B	11 41	11 56	12 11	12 26	12 41	12 56
C	12 02	12 17	12 32	12 47	13 02	13 17
D	12 07	12 22	12 37	12 52	13 07	13 22
E	12 48	13 03	13 18	13 33	13 48	14 03

2   **Reflect**   For these Strengthen lessons, copy and complete these
    sentences:
    I found questions _____ easiest. They were on _____ (list the
    topics)
    I found questions _____ most difficult. I still need help with
    _____ (list the topics)

Reflect

1 Extend

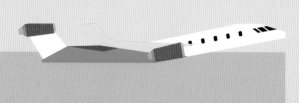

You will:
- Extend your understanding with problem-solving.

1 In Year 10 students choose to study either IT or Computing (they cannot do both) and either Music or Drama (they cannot do both).

The data is represented in a two-way table. Unfortunately, most of the information in the table has been lost.

	IT	Computing
Music	5	
Drama		

The headteacher knows that there are 60 students in the year.

20 students study IT.

12 students study Drama and Computing.

Copy and complete the table using this information.

2 A station manager recorded the number of minutes late for all trains in one hour.

18, 1, 0, 3, 2, 11, 4, 9, 42, 11, 12, 0, 0, 23, 25, 2, 15, 13

a Design a grouped frequency table for the data.
   The classes in your table must have equal widths.
   Write the inequality for each class.

b Write a sentence about the lateness of the trains.

3 **Reasoning** The line graph shows the numbers of full-time and part-time workers in the USA.

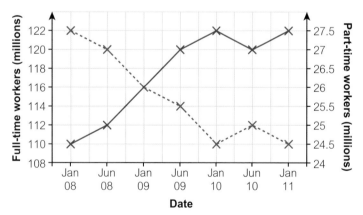

a How many part-time workers were there in June 2010?

b How many full-time workers were there in January 2011?

c A magazine used this caption with the graph:
   'Fall in full-time jobs matched by rise in part-time jobs.'
   Explain why the caption is wrong.

Discussion Does the point where the graphs cross mean anything?

> **Q4 hint**
>
> Read the values on each graph.

4 a Here are the masses, in kg, of the rowers in the 2012 Oxford University rowing team.
77.8, 82.4, 91.6, 93.6, 91.2, 94.6, 79.6, 96.8
  i What is their median mass?
  ii Work out the range.
  iii Calculate their mean mass.

b The table below shows some statistics about the masses of the 2012 Cambridge University rowers.

Mean	Median	Range
96.3	94.5	17.8

Write two sentences comparing the masses of the rowing teams.

c Reasoning The cox is an extra member of the rowing team. The Oxford cox has a mass of 49.6 kg.
  i Which statistic does this extra value change the most?
  ii What is the most suitable average to use for the mass of the team?

5 Reasoning The chart shows the number of generators hired out each day by a company.

a What is the modal number of generators hired per day?

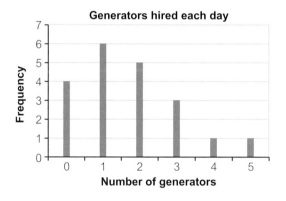

b On how many days were more than 2 generators hired out?
c Draw a frequency table for the data in the chart.
d Work out the mean number of generators hired per day.

6 Real The emergency response times, t minutes, for ambulances in a town were recorded for a week.
8.2, 4.2, 16.1, 5.3, 7.3, 9.6, 6.9, 19.3, 12.7,
13.6, 4.9, 6.1, 5.8, 7.3, 3.5, 8.8, 11.1

a Tally the times into a grouped frequency table. Use five equal classes.

Time, t (minutes)	Frequency
$0 \leqslant t < 4$	
$4 \leqslant t < \square$	

b What is the modal class?
c Reasoning The government target is to respond within 8 minutes.
  i How many ambulances achieved this target?
  ii How many did not?
d Draw a frequency diagram for the data.
e Here are the first few emergency response times for the next week.
  4.2, 7.8, 5.1, 6.0, 9.7, 7.3, 8.4, 8.9
  i What is unusual about this data? Give a possible reason for it.
  ii Work out the mode, median and mean for this data.
  iii Reasoning Which one of these three averages best represents the data?

7 This dual bar chart shows the percentage of electrical energy generated by different sources for two energy companies.

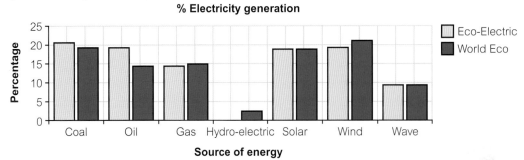

% Electricity generation

Legend: Eco-Electric, World Eco

a Which company produces the greater proportion of electricity using renewable sources?

b Eco-Electric produces 150 000 GWh of electricity. How many GWh does it produce using

   i wind power   **ii** gas?

c Write one or two sentences comparing how the two companies generate their electricity, explaining which company you think is more environmentally conscious.

Q8a hint

Hydro-electric, solar, wind and wave are all renewable sources.

8 **Real / Modelling** A mountain lion was tracked using an electronic tag. She travelled a distance, d miles, each day.

a Jamal has started a tally chart.

6.8, 5.7, 6.4, 3.6, 12.1, 9.4, 8.0, 9.2, 2.8, 3.7, 9.4, 5.6, 13.0, 6.0, 5.5, 14.2, 3.2, 4.2, 8.0, 3.8, 17.3, 8.8, 3.8, 8.7, 11.8, 8.7, 3.4, 10.1, 14.1, 19.4

   i Copy and complete the tally chart.

   ii What is the modal class?

   iii On how many days did the lion travel at least 10 miles?

b Jamal thinks that there should be five equal classes instead of four.

   i Make a new tally chart for the data using five equal classes.

   ii Write down the new modal class.

   iii What would happen if you kept increasing the number of classes?

Distance, d (miles)	Tally	Frequency
$0 \leqslant d < 5$	I	
$5 \leqslant d < 10$	III	
$10 \leqslant d < 15$	I	
$15 \leqslant d < 20$		

c The lion crossed the Grand Canyon during the day. The line graph shows her height above sea level, in metres, every 2 hours.

   i When did the lion reach the bottom of the Grand Canyon?

   ii How far above sea level is the bottom of the Grand Canyon?

   iii How high did the lion ascend?

   iv Compare the lion's descent and ascent.

   v Estimate the height of the lion above sea level at 7.30 am.

   vi Is this line graph a good model for predicting how other lions cross the Grand Canyon? Give reasons for your answer.

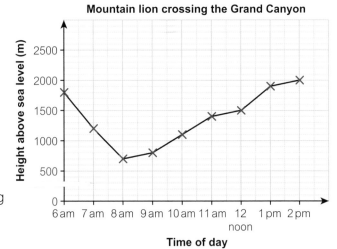

Mountain lion crossing the Grand Canyon

9 The table shows the heights, h cm, of a class of Year 7 students.

	$135 \leqslant h < 140$	$140 \leqslant h < 145$	$145 \leqslant h < 150$	$150 \leqslant h < 155$	$155 \leqslant h < 160$	Total
Boy	3	7	3	4	0	
Girls	2	2	6	4	1	
Total						

  a Copy and complete the table.
  b How many girls are shorter than 150 cm?
  c How many students are at least 145 cm tall?
  d Compare the average height of the girls and the boys.

Investigation   Reasoning

1 Work out the mean of these numbers: 2, 2, 2, 6, 8
2 a Add 1 to each of the numbers and work out their mean again.
  b How has the mean changed?
3 a Multiply each of the numbers in part **1** by 3 and work out their mean again.
  b How has the mean changed?
4 a What do you think would happen to the mean if you divided the numbers in part **1** by 2?
  b Try it and see if your prediction is correct.

Worked example

Find the mean of 100, 97, 98, 105 and 103 using an **assumed mean**.

Key point

The **assumed mean** is a sensible estimate for the mean.

$$
\begin{array}{cccccc}
 & 100 & 97 & 98 & 105 & 103 \\
\text{Differences from 100} & 0 & -3 & -2 & +5 & +3 & = 3
\end{array}
$$

The values are all close to 100, so assume the mean is 100. Work out the differences from 100.

$3 \div 5 = 0.6$

$100 + 0.6 = 100.6$

Add up the 5 differences and **divide** by 5 to find the mean difference.

Add the mean difference to the assumed mean.

10 Finance / Reasoning A consumer watchdog (monitor) recorded the prices a supermarket charged for a box of cereal each week.
Here are the results.
£2.90, £3.50, £3.00, £3.20, £3.70
Use an assumed mean of £3 to calculate the mean price.

11 Reflect List all the different ways you have learned for displaying data. Which way to display data do you find:
  • Easiest to read and understand? Why?
  • Hardest to read and understand? Why?
  • Easiest to draw? Why?
  • Hardest to draw? Why?

1 Unit test

1 The table shows the sizes of parcels delivered by a postman and a courier on Monday.

	Small	Medium	Large
Postman	15	10	5
Courier	10	15	20

a Work out the number of parcels the postman delivered on Monday.

b Work out how many large parcels were delivered in total.

c Calculate the number of parcels delivered altogether.

d The compound bar chart shows the deliveries made on Tuesday.

   i Work out how many large parcels were delivered by the courier on Tuesday.

   ii Work out how many more small parcels did the postman deliver on Tuesday than on Monday.

   iii Calculate the total number of medium parcels delivered on both days.

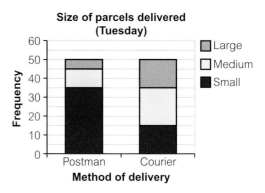

2 The table shows the distances jumped in the men's large hill ski jumping individual qualifying round at the Sochi Winter Olympics.

Distance (m)	131	130	130	129	128	127	127	126	126	125

Work out the mean distance jumped.

3 Leonda surveys a group of adults and a group of children about their favourite types of film. She records the data in a spreadsheet.

◢	A	B	C
1	Genre	Children	Adults
2	Sci-Fi	5	27
3	Comedy	69	39
4	Action	18	11
5	Thriller	8	23
6			

a Work out how many more children than adults chose comedy.

b Work out how many children and adults were surveyed.

c Draw a dual bar graph for the data.

4 Two students each played a video game many times.
The table shows some information about their scores.

	Mean	Range
Oscar	75	80
Venus	70	20

a Write two sentences comparing the performances of the students.

b Which student would you like on your team?
Give a reason for your answer.

5 Two pans of hot water were left to cool to room temperature. One pan had a lid. The graph shows the recorded temperatures.

   a Write down the temperature of the water in the pan with the lid after 20 minutes.

   b Write down the temperature of the room.

   c Compare the times it took the pans to reach room temperature.

   d Work out the difference in the temperatures after 30 minutes.

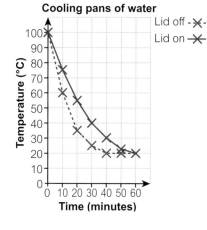

Cooling pans of water

Lid off - ✕ -
Lid on — ✕

6 Here are the masses of some calves (young cows) on a farm:
   37 kg, 58 kg, 49 kg, 42 kg, 38 kg, 57 kg, 44 kg, 40 kg, 51 kg, 48 kg, 38 kg, 40 kg, 46 kg, 50 kg, 41 kg

   a Copy and complete the tally chart for the data.

Mass, m (kg)	Tally	Frequency
$35 \leqslant m < 40$		
$40 \leqslant m < 45$		
$45 \leqslant m < 50$		
$50 \leqslant m < 55$		
$55 \leqslant m < 60$		

Calf mass

   b Write down the modal class.

   c Copy and complete the frequency diagram for the data.

Challenge

7 The table shows the music albums sold monthly by two bands.

	Jan	Feb	Mar	Apr	May	Jun	Jul	Aug
The Breakers	1200	1300	1350	1500	1700	1750	1700	1600
Tempest	500	550	500	600	700	850	850	950

   a Draw a misleading line graph that suggests The Breakers are improving sales quicker than Tempest.

   b Draw a misleading bar chart that suggests that Tempest is improving sales quicker than The Breakers.

Q7 hint

You can decide the scale, where the scale starts and how much data to show.

8 Reflect Think back to when you have struggled to answer a question in a maths test.

   a Write two words that describe how you felt.

   b Write two things you could do when you struggle to answer a question in a maths test.

   c Imagine you have another maths test and you do those two things you wrote in your answer to part **b**. Would you feel the same as you answered in part **a**? Explain.

Reflect

2.1 Rules of divisibility

You will learn to:
- Use rules for divisibility by 2, 3, 4, 5, 9 and 10.

Why learn this?
It is useful to know when a whole number is divisible by another, when working out which is the best deal in shops.

Fluency
Work out
- 2 × 10
- 4 × 5
- 3 × 9

Explore
How many students should you have in a class if you want to be able to split the class into many different equal sized groups?

Confidence

Exercise 2.1

Warm up

1 Write down the next three numbers in each sequence.
   a 2, 4, 6, 8, 10, …   b 3, 6, 9, 12, 15, …
   c 4, 8, 12, 16, 20, ….   d 5, 10, 15, 20, 25, …
   e 9, 18, 27, 36, 45, …   f 10, 20, 30, 40, 50, …

2 Is 12 divisible by
   a 2   b 3   c 4   d 5   e 6   f 7?

3 **Problem-solving** A bag contains 20 sweets.
   Can they be shared equally between
   a 2   b 3   c 4   d 5 people

4 a Write down the numbers in the cloud that are divisible by 2.

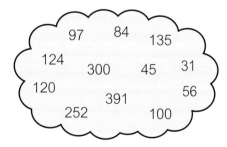

   b How can you tell when a number is divisible by 10?
   c How can you tell when a number is divisible by 5?
   d Write down the numbers in the cloud that are divisible by
      i 10   ii 5

Key point

9 can be divided by 1, 3 and 9 without leaving a remainder.
9 is **divisible** by 1, 3 and 9.

Key point

All even numbers are divisible by 2. A number is divisible by 2 if it ends in 0, 2, 4, 6 or 8.

Q4b hint

What do all the numbers in the 10 times table end in?

Q4c hint

What do all the numbers in the 5 times table end in?

5 Reasoning Yosef thinks he has found a way to decide if a number is divisible by 3.

He finds the sum of the digits in the number and checks if that is a multiple of 3.

For example:

225   2 + 2 + 5 = 9

9 is a divisible by 3 therefore 225 is divisible by 3.

a Use a calculator to check whether 225 is divisible by 3.

b Use Yosef's method to decide whether each of these numbers is a multiple of 3.

Check your answers on a calculator.

    i 96   **ii** 103   **iii** 133   **iv** 150

Investigation   **Reasoning**

Here are the numbers in the 9 times table:

9, 18, 27, 36, 45, 54, 63, 72, 81, 90

1 Find the sum of the digits in all the 2-digit numbers. What do you notice?

Here are the next few numbers:

99, 108, 117, 126, 135, 144, 153, 162, 171, 180

2 Find the sum of the digits. If the answer has 2 digits, find the sum of these digits. What do you notice?

3 Explain how to work out if a number is divisible by 9.

> **Hint**
>
> 99 9 + 9 = 18 1 + 8 = 9

---

6 Reasoning Leah says, 'To multiply by 4 you double and double again. Therefore, to divide by 4 you should halve and halve again'.

a Do you agree with Leah?

Noam says, 'All even numbers are divisible by 4'.

b Do you agree with Noam?

c **i**   Write down the first 10 even numbers.

   ii Circle those that are divisible by 4.

  iii Halve each of these numbers.

     What do you notice?

d Copy and complete this statement.

A number is divisible by 4 if, when you halve it, the answer is

_____ .

> **Q6a hint**
>
> Test Leah's method on the numbers 124, 888 and 1248 and check your answer on a calculator.

> **Q6b hint**
>
> Test Noam's method on the numbers 8, 10 and 12.

> **Q6c hint**
>
> When you halve a number that is divisible by 4, is the answer odd or even?

7 Real / Problem-solving A factory produces chocolate bars.

It then packs them into boxes of 4.

One day it produces 2856 chocolate bars.

After the bars are packed into boxes of 4, are there any remaining?

8 Problem-solving In a class, there are 30 students.

Without leaving anyone out, can the teacher group them evenly into groups of

a i 2   **ii** 3   **iii** 4   **iv** 5   **v** 9   **vi** 10?

b What is the smallest number of students who could be split into groups of 2 and into groups of 9?

9 Explore How many students should you have in a class if you want to be able to split the class into many different equal sized groups?

10 Reflect Write your own instructions to explain how to decide whether a number is divisible by

a 2   **b** 3   **c** 4   **d** 5   **e** 9   **f** 10.

Reflect

2.2 Factors, multiples and primes

You will learn to:
- Understand the difference between multiples, factors and primes.
- Find all the factor pairs of any whole number.
- Find the HCF and LCM of two numbers.

Why learn this?
Astronomers use the LCM to work out when planets are going to be in line.

Fluency
What are the missing numbers?
- 6 × ☐ = 36
- ☐ × 4 = 36
- 12 × ☐ = 36
- ☐ × 18 = 36
- 1 × ☐ = 36

Explore
How many rows of bricks and how many rows of large cinder blocks would you need to make walls the same height?

Exercise 2.2

1 Look at these numbers.
2, 3, 4, 5, 8, 12, 15, 18, 20, 24, 30
Which are
a **multiples** of 3   **b** **multiples** of 5   **c** **factors** of 40?

Q1 hint

A **multiple** of 3 is a number in the 3 times table.
A **factor** of 10 is a whole number that divides exactly into 10.

2 Look at these numbers.
4, 6, 8, 12, 16, 18, 20, 24, 28, 30, 32, 36
a Which are multiples of
   i 4   **ii** 6   **iii** 4 and 6?
b Copy and complete this **Venn diagram** using the numbers in the list.
Write each number in the correct section.

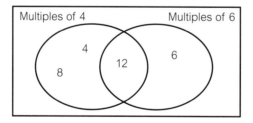
Multiples of 4   Multiples of 6
4
8   12   6

Q2b Literacy hint

A **Venn diagram** shows sets of items.

3 Here is a list of numbers.
2, 3, 6, 9, 11, 14, 17, 21, 25
Which are **prime numbers**?
Discussion Is a prime number always an odd number? Is an odd number always a prime number?

Key point

A **prime number** has exactly two factors, 1 and itself.

4 a Write down all the factors of 28.
b Write down all the **prime factors** of 28.

Key point

A **prime factor** is a factor of a number that is also a prime number.

Subject links: Technology (Q13, Q15)

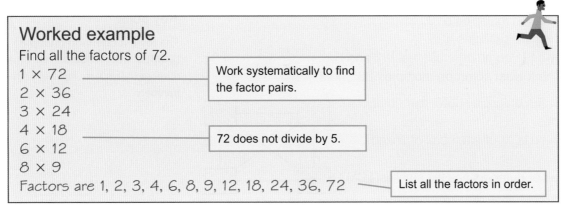

Worked example

Find all the factors of 72.

1 × 72
2 × 36
3 × 24
4 × 18
6 × 12
8 × 9

Work systematically to find the factor pairs.

72 does not divide by 5.

Factors are 1, 2, 3, 4, 6, 8, 9, 12, 18, 24, 36, 72 — List all the factors in order.

5 Find all the factors of
   a 48   **b** 56   **c** 104   **d** 100   **e** 36
   Discussion What type of number has an odd number of factors?

6 **Problem-solving** Hayley finds all the factors of a number.
   This is her list.
   1, 2, 3, 4, □, 9, 12, 13, □, □, 36, 39, □, 78, □, 156, 234, 468
   What are the missing numbers?

7 **a** Write down all the factors of 8.
   b Write down all the factors of 12.
   c Write down the common factors of 8 and 12.
   d What is the **highest common factor** of 8 and 12?

Q7c Literacy hint

What factors do 8 and 12 have in common?

Key point

The **highest common factor (HCF)** of two numbers is the largest number that is a factor of both numbers.

8 **a** Copy and complete this Venn diagram to show the factors of 15 and 18.

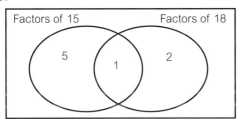

   b What is the HCF of 15 and 18?

9 Find the HCF of each pair of numbers.
   a 6 and 9   **b** 20 and 24   **c** 6 and 18
   Discussion Is the HCF always one of the numbers?

10 **Problem-solving / Reasoning** In this number wheel, the HCF of opposite numbers is equal to the number in the middle.
   Use the numbers from the cloud to copy and complete the wheel.
   Explain how you worked out your answers.

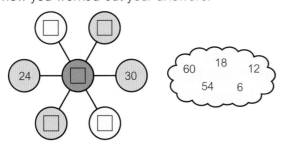

11 a List the first ten multiples of 3.
  b List the first six multiples of 5.
  c Write down the common multiples of 3 and 5.
  d What is the **lowest common multiple** of 3 and 5?

Key point

The **lowest common multiple** (**LCM**) of two numbers is the smallest number that is a multiple of both numbers.

12 Reasoning The diagram shows four numbers linked by lines.
  a Work out the LCM of each pair of linked numbers.
  b Which pair of numbers has the smallest LCM? Explain why.
  c Which pairs of numbers have the same LCM? Explain why.

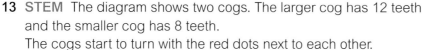

13 STEM The diagram shows two cogs. The larger cog has 12 teeth and the smaller cog has 8 teeth.
The cogs start to turn with the red dots next to each other.
What is the smallest number of turns each cog must make before the red dots are next to each other again?

14 Problem-solving Sita draws this Venn diagram to work out the LCM of two numbers.

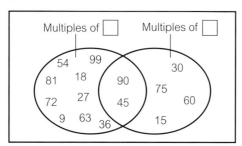

Copy and complete Sita's statement.
The LCM of ☐ and ☐ is ☐

Investigation   Problem-solving / Reasoning

A red light flashes every 6 seconds.
A blue light flashes every 8 seconds.
Work with a partner to answer these questions.
1 Both lights flash at the same time. How many seconds until they flash at the same time again?
2 Explain how you can work out all the times when the lights flash together.
3 A purple light flashes every 7 seconds and a yellow light flashes every 9 seconds.
Which pair of lights will flash together most within 1 minute?

15 Explore How many rows of bricks and how many rows of large cinder blocks would you need to make walls the same height?
Is it easier to explore this question now you have completed the lesson? What further information do you need to be able to answer this?

16 Reflect Write your own short definition for each of these mathematical words:
highest   lowest   common   factor   multiple
Now use your definitions to write (in your own words) the meaning of:
highest common factor   lowest common multiple

2.3 Positive and negative numbers

You will learn to:
- Compare and order positive and negative numbers.
- Add and subtract positive and negative numbers.

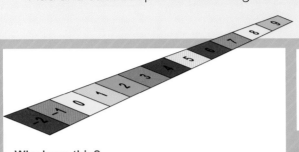

Why learn this?
The number line extends equally in the positive and negative directions – infinitely.

Fluency
Which is colder?
- 3°C or −2°C
- −4°C or −1°C

Explore
What is the difference between the average temperatures on different planets in the Solar System?

Confidence

Exercise 2.3

1 What are the missing numbers on the thermometer?

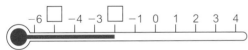

−6 ☐ −4 −3 ☐ −1 0 1 2 3 4

2 a The temperature is 6°C. It gets 8 degrees colder.
What is the new temperature?

    b The temperature is −7°C. It gets 5 degrees warmer.
What is the new temperature?

3 Use the number line to decide which sign, < or >, goes between each pair of numbers.

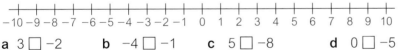

−10 −9 −8 −7 −6 −5 −4 −3 −2 −1 0 1 2 3 4 5 6 7 8 9 10

    a 3 ☐ −2   **b** −4 ☐ −1   **c** 5 ☐ −8   **d** 0 ☐ −5

Q3 hint

The further left on the number line the lower the number.

4 Write these numbers from smallest to largest.
    a 0, −3, 2   **b** 1, −4, 5, −2
    c 2, −2, 3, −3   **d** −10, −7, 8, 0, −1, −5

5 Real / Problem-solving Here are four thermometers showing the average temperature in December.
    a Which place is the coldest in December?
    b Los Angeles' average temperature is 19°C warmer than Moscow's. What is the average temperature of the two cities?
    c Oslo's average temperature is 30°C colder than Yaounde's. What is the temperature in Yaounde?

Yaounde

Moscow

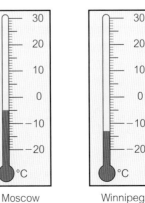

Winnipeg

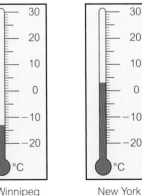

New York

Warm up

d What is the difference in temperature between Moscow and New York?

Key point

The difference between two values is always given as a positive number.

Q5d hint

Draw a number line and mark on the temperatures in Moscow and New York. Work out how many you need to 'jump' to get to zero and then how many to jump to 3.
Add together these values.
You can use only one jump but make sure you count carefully.

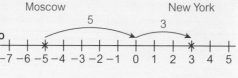

e What is the difference in temperature between
  i Yaounde and Moscow
  ii Moscow and Winnipeg
  iii Winnipeg and New York?

6 Use the number line to work these out.

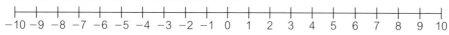

  a −6 + 3   **b** −6 − 3   **c** −3 − 6   **d** −3 + 6
  e −5 + 2   **f** −5 − 2   **g** 2 − 5   **h** 5 − 2

Investigation   Reasoning

Thato says, 'There is an easy way to find the difference between a positive number and a negative number. Add together the positive values of the numbers'.
For example to find the difference between −3 and 4 work out 3 + 4 = 7.
1 Do you agree with Thato? Try some differences to check his method.
2 Does Thato's method work for
  a two positive numbers   **b** two negative numbers?

7 a Copy and complete these patterns.
  i   2 + 3 = 5   **ii** 2 − 3 = −1
      2 + 2 = ☐   2 − 2 = ☐
      2 + 1 = ☐   2 − 1 = ☐
      2 + 0 = ☐   2 − 0 = ☐
      2 + −1 = ☐   2 − −1 = ☐
      2 + −2 = ☐   2 − −2 = ☐
      2 + −3 = ☐   2 − −3 = ☐

  b **Reasoning** Which sign, + or −, is missing from each statement?
    i 2 + −3 is the same as 2 ☐ 3.
    ii 2 − −3 is the same as 2 ☐ 3.
  c Copy and complete these rules:
    replace + + with +   replace + − with ☐
    replace − + with ☐   replace − − with ☐

Q7b hint

Numbers without a sign in front of them are positive.
2 − 3 is 2 − +3

8 Work out
  a 11 + − 3   **b** 11 − +3   **c** 11 − −3   **d** 11 + +3
  e −11 + −3   **f** −11 − +3   **g** −11 − −3   **h** −11 + +3

9 Work out
  a 8 + −6   **b** −4 + 9   **c** −12 + −3   **d** −3 − −7

Q9a hint

8 + −6 = 8 − 6 = ☐

10 **STEM** The table shows the melting point and boiling point of four compounds.

a What is the difference between the melting point and the boiling point of
  i nitric acid   **ii** sulfur dioxide?

b Work out the range of the melting point temperatures.

c Work out the range of the boiling point temperatures.

Compound	Melting point (°C)	Boiling point (°C)
nitric acid	−42	83
nitrogen chloride	−40	71
nitrogen oxide	−163	−152
sulfur dioxide	−75	−10

11 **Problem-solving** Here are some number cards:

a Which cards make the calculation
  i with the highest possible answer
  ii with the lowest possible answer?

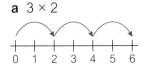

b Which cards make the calculation
  i with the highest possible answer
  ii with the lowest possible answer?

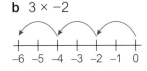

12 Work out

a 3×2

b 3×-2

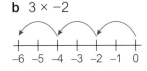

c 4×1 **d** 4×-1
e 2×5 **f** 2×-5
g 2×3 **h** 2×-3
i 6×8 **j** 6×-8

13 Work out

a 3×-4 **b** 7×-2
c 5×-8 **d** 9×-3
e 6×-1

14 **Problem-solving** The answer to a calculation is −8.

a Write three different calculations that give the answer −8.

b Now write three different calculations using a different operation, choosing from +, −, × in each one.

15 **Explore** What is the difference between the average temperatures on different planets in the Solar System?
Is it easier to explore this question now you have completed the lesson?
What further information do you need to be able to answer this?

16 **Reflect** Mia and Ali discuss what is different or the same about negative and positive numbers.
Mia says, 'Negative numbers get lower the further you get from zero, but positive numbers get higher'.
Ali says, 'When you add a negative number you are actually subtracting'.
Look back at what you have learned in this lesson about negative numbers.
What else is different about working with positive and negative numbers?
What else is the same?

Explore

Reflect

2.4 Squares and square roots

Confidence

You will learn to:
- Use index notation for squares and square roots.
- Calculate with squares and square roots.

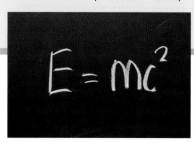

Why learn this?
Square numbers are used to work out the trajectory of a football, or the equivalence of mass and energy, or the area you need to tile.

Fluency
Work out
- 5 × 5
- 8 × 8
- 0.3 × 3
- 0.3 × 0.3
- 0.5 × 5
- 0.5 × 0.5

Explore
What is the best way to arrange 8000 seats into square blocks for a music concert?

Exercise 2.4

Warm up

1 You can arrange 9 dots in a square like this.

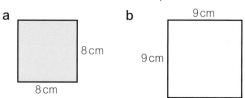

Which numbers from this list can be arranged as dots in a square?
2   4   8   12   16   20   24   36   42   49   55

2 Work out the area of each square.

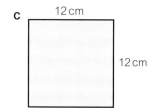

a — 8 cm × 8 cm

b — 9 cm × 9 cm

c — 12 cm × 12 cm

Discussion How do you find the area of a square using the length of one side?

3 a Copy and complete this table of square numbers from 1 to 15.

1^2	2^2	3^2	4^2	5^2	6^2	7^2	8^2	9^2	10^2	11^2	12^2	13^2	14^2	15^2
1	4													

b Use your table in part **a** to write down the answers to these.
  i $\sqrt{64}$
  ii $\sqrt{121}$
  iii $\sqrt{169}$
  iv $\sqrt{225}$

Discussion Is there another **square root** of 64, 121, 169, 225?

Key point

To find the square of a number you multiply it by itself.
$3 \times 3 = 3^2 = 9$
3^2 means '3 squared'.

Key point

The inverse of square is square root.
$3^2 = 3 \times 3 = 9$, so a square root of
$9 = \sqrt{9} = 3$

Topic links: Area

4 Check each of these calculations is correct by using the inverse operation.

a $14^2 = 196$

b $2.5^2 = 6.25$

c $\sqrt{2116} = 46$

d $\sqrt{12.96} = 3.6$

Q4 hint

a Work out $\sqrt{196}$.

c Work out 46^2.

Worked example

Work out an estimate of $\sqrt{55}$.

$\sqrt{49} = 7$ and $\sqrt{64} = 8$

$\sqrt{55}$ lies between 7 and 8

Estimate is 7.4

> 55 is between 49 and 64

> 55 is closer to 49 than 64, so estimate just less than 7.5

5 a Work out an estimate for these square roots.

i $\sqrt{20}$ ii $\sqrt{5}$ iii $\sqrt{79}$ iv $\sqrt{90}$

b Check your estimates by working out the accurate square roots on a calculator.

Q5a hint

Use your table from Q3 to help you.

6 a Work out

i 2^2 ii 20^2 iii 200^2 iv 0.2^2

Discussion What do you notice about your answers to part **a**?

b Work out

i 50^2 ii 900^2 iii 4000^2 iv 0.6^2

7 Work out

a $\sqrt{36}$ b $\sqrt{9} \times \sqrt{4}$ c $\sqrt{324}$ d $\sqrt{784}$

Discussion What do you notice about your answers to parts **a** and **b**?

Investigation Reasoning

The diagram shows four pyramids made from balls.

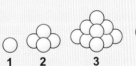

Pyramid: 1   2   3   4

1 Copy and complete this table.

Pyramid	1	2	3	4
Number of balls	$1^2 = 1$	$1^2 + 2^2 = \square$		

2 How many balls will be in

a pyramid 5   b pyramid 6?

3 Explain how you can work out the number of balls in pyramid 12 without working out the number of balls in pyramids 1 to 11 first.

8 **Explore** What is the best way to arrange 8000 seats into square blocks for a music concert?

Is it easier to explore this question now you have completed the lesson?

What further information do you need to be able to answer this?

9 **Reflect** Think about the *square* of 100 and the *square root* of 100.

Which is 10 and which is 10 000? Make sure you know the difference between these two terms.

Write down a definition in your own words to help you remember.

Explore

Reflect

2.5 More power and roots

Confidence

You will learn to:
- Carry out calculations involving squares, cubes, square roots and cube roots.
- Use factorising to work out square roots and cube roots.
- Solve word problems using square roots and cube roots.

Why learn this?
Scientists can use square roots to estimate how long an object takes to fall.

Fluency
Work out
- 5^2
- $\sqrt{36}$

Explore
For how long are you falling in a bungee jump (jump from an elasticated rope) from the Sidu River Bridge in China?

Warm up

Exercise 2.5

1 Work out
   a $5 \times 5 \times 5$
   b $3 \times 3 \times 3$

2 Work out
   a $7 + 5 \times 9$
   b $14 - \frac{8}{2}$
   c $3 \times 4 + 7 \times 5$

3 Write these calculations using **index notation**.
   a $3 \times 3 \times 3 \times 3 = 3^{\square}$
   b $2 \times 2 \times 2 \times 2 \times 2$
   c $7 \times 7 \times 7$

4 Match each **cube** number in the cloud to a number written in index notation in the other cloud.

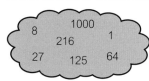
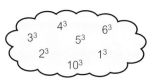

5 Work out these **powers** of 10.
   a 10^3
   b 10^5
   c 10^4
   d 10^6

6 Work out these **cube roots**.
   a $\sqrt[3]{27}$
   b $\sqrt[3]{125}$
   c $\sqrt[3]{1000}$
   d $\sqrt[3]{1}$
   e $\sqrt[3]{-8}$
   f $\sqrt[3]{-64}$

7 Work out the missing numbers.
   a $\sqrt[3]{216} = \sqrt[3]{8} \times \sqrt[3]{27} = 2 \times \square = \square$
   b $\sqrt[3]{8000} = \sqrt[3]{64} \times \sqrt[3]{125} = \square \times \square = \square$
   c $\sqrt[3]{1728} = \sqrt[3]{27} \times \sqrt[3]{64} = \square \times \square = \square$

Key point

You can use **index notation** to write a number to a **power** or **index**. The power tells you how many times the number is multiplied by itself.
$2^3 = 2 \times 2 \times 2$
2^3 is '2 to the power 3'.
3 is the power.

Key point

To find the **cube** of a number, multiply it by itself and then multiply by the number again.
2 cubed = $2 \times 2 \times 2$

Key point

The inverse of cube is **cube root**.
$2^3 = 8$, so the cube root of 8 is $\sqrt[3]{8} = 2$.

Q6e hint

$\square \times \square \times \square = 8$
$\square \times \square \times \square = -8$

Subject links: Science (Q12)

8 Work out

a $4^2 - 12$ **b** $3 + 9^2$ **c** $4 \times 3^2 + 5$

d $\dfrac{6^2}{4} - 15$ **e** $\sqrt{49} + 5 \times 8$ **f** $\dfrac{\sqrt{100}}{2} + 10^2$

9 Work out

a 3×2^3 **b** $10^3 \times 5$ **c** $\dfrac{10^3}{500}$

d $\dfrac{40}{2^3}$ **e** $4 \times \sqrt[3]{64}$ **f** $\dfrac{24}{\sqrt[3]{8}}$

10 Work out

a $50 - 3^3$ **b** $4^3 + 6^2$ **c** $6 \times 2^3 - 18$

d $4 \times \sqrt[3]{1000} - 35$ **e** $\dfrac{20}{\sqrt[3]{125}} - 2^2$

11 Use a calculator to work out

a $7^3 + 27$ **b** $2 \times 8^3 - 624$ **c** $6 \times 10^3 - 4 \times 9^3$

d $4 \times \sqrt[3]{729} + 4$ **e** $\dfrac{\sqrt[3]{1728}}{6} - 2$ **f** $4 \times \sqrt[3]{216} - 5^2$

12 STEM / Modelling You can estimate the time it will take an object to fall using this flowchart.

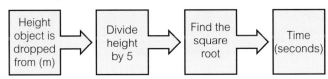

Work out the time it will take a ball to drop from these heights.

a 80 m   **b** 125 m   **c** 405 m

13 Problem-solving / Reasoning One number is missing from this list.

$\sqrt{49} \times 40$ 30^2 10×5^2 $\dfrac{800^2}{1000}$ ☐

The range of the numbers is 800.

a Work out the missing number.

b Is there only one possible answer to part **a**? Explain why.

14 Work out

a $\sqrt[3]{8}$ **b** $8\sqrt[3]{27}$ **c** $8\sqrt[3]{8 \times 27}$

What do you notice?

15 Problem-solving Work out $\sqrt[3]{512}$.

16 Problem-solving $\boxed{13\,824 = 8 \times 27 \times 64}$

Use this fact to work out $\sqrt[3]{13\,824}$.

17 Explore For how long are you falling in a bungee jump from the Sidu River Bridge in China?
Is it easier to explore this question now you have completed the lesson? What further information do you need to be able to answer this?

18 Reflect The $\sqrt{}$ root symbol began as the letter r in the 16th Century. You could remember r for root! List the mathematics notation used in this lesson, and ways you might remember it.

Key point

Squares, cubes, square roots are indices or powers.
The priority of operations is
- Brackets
- Indices or Powers
- Multiplication and Division
- Addition and Subtraction

Q11 hint

Use the $\boxed{\sqrt[3]{}}$ and $\boxed{x^y}$ buttons on your calculator.

Q15 hint

Work out which two cube numbers multiply to give 512.

Q18 hint

'Notation' means the signs and symbols you use.

Explore

Reflect

2.6 Calculations

Confidence

You will learn to:
- Estimate answers to complex calculations.
- Carry out calculations involving brackets.

Why learn this?
Brackets help to split a calculation up into separate parts. For example, when working out the speed of a car.

Fluency
Which of these numbers are
- square numbers
- cube numbers
- neither?

81 10 27 125 15 64 9 24

Explore
How can you calculate all the numbers from 1 to 20 using only the number 4?

Exercise 2.6

Warm up

1 Round each number to the nearest whole number.
   a 6.7   b 3.2   c 9.1   d 5.5

2 Round each number to the nearest 10.
   a 27   b 43   c 75   d 56

3 Work out
   a $5 + 3 \times 8$ b $\frac{18}{3} - 10$ c $7 \times 2 + \frac{20}{5}$

   d $5^2 + 6$ e $3^3 - 3$ f $4^2 + 2^3$

4 Write these values in **ascending** order.
   $\sqrt{9} + 12$ $\sqrt[3]{64} - 8$ $\sqrt{36} - \sqrt[3]{27}$

> **Q4 Literacy hint**
> Numbers in **ascending** order go from smallest to largest.

5 a Estimate the answer to each calculation.

   i $22 + 5.2 \times 41 \approx 20 + 5 \times \square = \square$ ii $65 \times 32 - 24 \times 73$

   iii $9.2 \times 4.6 \times 1.8 - 48.9$ iv $32.5 - \frac{51}{4.7}$

   v $\frac{46.7}{6.15} + 3.2 \times 4.9$ vi $\frac{63}{8.1} - \frac{29}{8.7}$

> **Q5a hint**
> Round numbers less than 10 to the nearest whole number. Round larger numbers to the nearest 10.

   b Use a calculator to work out the accurate answers to the calculations in part **a**.
   Use your estimates to check your answer.

6 **Problem-solving** Su wants to order this take-away meal.
   She has £25.
   Does she have enough?

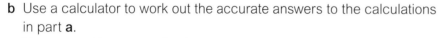

Satay chicken	£4.80	Boiled rice	2 × £1.10
Crispy duck	£6.10	Chow mein	2 × £2.90
Thai beef	£5.20	Spring rolls	3 × £1.85

Topic links: Area   **Subject links:** Science (Q8)

Worked example

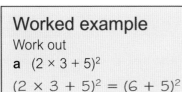

Work out

a $(2 \times 3 + 5)^2$

> Work out the value inside the brackets first. Start with $2 \times 3 = 6$

$(2 \times 3 + 5)^2 = (6 + 5)^2$

> Now add the 6 and 5.

$= 11^2$

$= 121$

> Finally work out 11^2.

b $\sqrt{27 - \dfrac{6}{3}}$

> The square root sign acts like brackets. Work out the value inside it first.

$\sqrt{27 - \dfrac{6}{3}} = \sqrt{27 - 2}$

> Now work out $27 - 2$.

$= \sqrt{25}$

> Finally work out the square root of 25.

$= 5$

Key point

The priority of operations is
- Brackets
- Indices or Powers
- Mutiplication and Division
- Addition and Subtraction

7 Work out

a $4(6 - 1)$

b $(10 - 8)^2$

c $(1 + 2 \times 4)^2$

d $(\frac{28}{4} - 4)^2$

e $\sqrt{21 - 5}$

f $(-2)^3$

g $\sqrt{50 + 2 \times 7}$

h $\sqrt{\dfrac{12}{4} + 6}$

Q7f hint

$-2 \times -2 \times -2$

 8 **Real / Modelling** Sally works out the speed of a zorb at the bottom of slopes of different heights. She uses the rule

$$\text{speed} = \sqrt{12 \times \text{height of slope}}$$

Speed is measured in metres per second.

height

Height is measured in metres.
Work out the speed of the zorb when the height of the slope is

a 5 m   **b** 35 m   **c** 57 m

Q8a hint

speed $= \sqrt{12 \times 5} = \square$

Investigation

Reasoning

The diagram shows two squares.

3 cm   4 cm

1 Work out the area of each square.
2 Work out the total area of the two squares.
3 Sita writes: $3^2 + 4^2 = (3 + 4)^2$
    Is Sita correct? Explain.
4 Is Sita's statement true for different size squares?

9 Work out these calculations. Check your answers using a calculator.

a $3 \times (\sqrt{81} - 7)$

b $(2^2 + \sqrt{9})^2$

c $10^2 - (45 + \sqrt{25})$

d $(5 \times 6 - 26)^3$

e $5^3 + (4 - 2)^3$

f $2 \times 3^3 + 10$

Q9 hint

Use the (and) buttons on your calculator.

10 Work out

a $\dfrac{8 + 22}{7 - 2}$

b $\dfrac{6 + 4^2}{2}$

c $\dfrac{3^3 - 3^2}{2 \times 3}$

d $\dfrac{\sqrt{81}}{12 - 9}$

e $\dfrac{\sqrt{144} - 2}{5}$

f $\dfrac{6^2 - 6}{\sqrt[3]{27}}$

Q10 hint

The dividing line of the fraction acts like a bracket.
$\dfrac{8 + 22}{7 - 2} = (8 + 22) \div (7 - 2)$

11 Problem-solving

a Match each calculation card with the correct answer card.
Check your answers using a calculator.

 $\sqrt{3^3 + 3^2}$  $13 - (\sqrt[3]{125} + 3)$ $8 \times (11 - \sqrt[3]{1000})$ $\sqrt[3]{40 + 24}$

 4   5   6   7   8

b There is one answer card left over. Write a calculation card to go with this answer card.
The calculation must include a cube root or a square root.

12 Work out

a $3 \times (7 + 8)^2$

b $3^2 \times (7 + 8)$

c $(3 \times (7 + 8))^2$

13 Write the answers to these calculations in descending order.

$\sqrt{25} + 2^2$ 3×2^2 $2^3 - 1$ $\sqrt{64} + \sqrt[3]{8}$ $\sqrt{5^2 - 4^2}$

14 Reasoning Rewrite each calculation using only the brackets that are needed.

a $(3 \times (2 \times 5)^2)$

b $(3 \times (2 \times 5))$

15 Explore How can you calculate all the numbers from 1 to 20 using only the number 4?
Look back at the maths you have learned in this lesson.
How can you use it to answer this question?

16 Reflect In this lesson you were asked to estimate.
Suzie says, 'Estimating is the same as guessing.'
Do you agree with Suzie?
Write down a definition of how you 'estimate' in maths.
How might estimating be used in other subjects and in everyday life?

2 Check up

Working with numbers

1 Look at these numbers.
   28   35   40   123   198
   Write down all the numbers from the list that are divisible by
   a 2   **b** 3   **c** 4   **d** 5   **e** 9   **f** 10

2 **a** Write down all the factors of 12.
   b Write down all the factors of 18.
   c Which of the factors of 12 are prime numbers?
   d What is the highest common factor of 12 and 18?

3 What is the lowest common multiple of 6 and 8?

4 Work out the difference between
   a -2 and 4   **b** -17 and -12 **c** -30 and -18

5 Work out
   a $12 - -4$ **b** $3 + -7$ **c** $-2 + 8$
   d $-15 + -4$ **e** $-2 - -5$ **f** $-8 - -12$

6 Work out an estimate for these calculations.
   a $31 + 2.9 \times 28$ **b** $10 + 31 \div 11$

Powers and roots

7 Work out
   a 10^4 **b** 2^3 **c** 7^2 **d** $\sqrt{36}$
   e $\sqrt[3]{125}$ **f** $\sqrt{64}$ **g** $\sqrt[3]{-125}$

8 Write down two square roots of 81.

9 Write down an estimate for $\sqrt{38}$.

10 Work out
   a 10×3^3 **b** $\frac{8^2}{2}$

11 Work out
   a $8 \times 2^3 - 4$ **b** $\frac{80}{2^3} - 2^2$

   c $10 \times \sqrt[3]{27} - 14$ **d** $\frac{\sqrt[3]{125}}{5} + 7 \times 5$

12 $576 = 16 \times 36$
   Use this fact to work out $\sqrt{576}$.

13 $3375 = 27 \times 125$
   Use this fact to work out $\sqrt[3]{3375}$.

Working with brackets

14 Work out

a $7(6 - 2)$

b $(3 \times 2 + 4)^2$

c $\sqrt{50 - 14}$

d $2 \times (\sqrt{4} + 9)$

e $(3^2 - \sqrt{16})^2$

f $4^3 - (8 - 5)^3$

15 Work out these. Give your answers to 2 decimal places.

a $28.3 - \frac{58}{6.1}$

b $\frac{34}{7.2} - \frac{37}{8.7}$

16 Work out

a $\frac{45 - 5}{2 + 6}$

b $\frac{36 - 8}{2^2}$

c $\frac{\sqrt{100}}{12 - 7}$

d $\frac{\sqrt[3]{125} + 13}{3^2}$

17 Work out

a $(3 + 1) \times 5^2$

b $(3 + 1)^2 \times 5$

c $((3 + 1) \times 5)^2$

18 **How sure are you of your answers? Were you mostly**

😞 Just guessing 😐 Feeling doubtful 🙂 Confident

What next? Use your results to decide whether to strengthen or extend your learning.

Challenge

19 a Work out the HCF of 48 and 56.

b Write down three other pairs of numbers that have the same HCF as your answer to part **a**.

20 Here are some number cards.

$\boxed{-5}\ \boxed{-4}\ \boxed{-3}\ \boxed{-2}\ \boxed{-1}\ \boxed{0}\ \boxed{1}\ \boxed{2}\ \boxed{3}\ \boxed{4}\ \boxed{5}$

What number cards can you use so that

a $\square + \square$ is smallest

b $\square + \square$ is largest

c $\square - \square$ is smallest

d $\square - \square$ is largest

e $- \square + \square$ is smallest

f $- \square + \square$ is largest

g $- \square - \square$ is smallest

h $- \square - \square$ is largest

Reflect

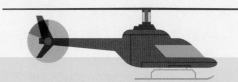

2 Strengthen

You will:
- Strengthen your understanding with practice.

Working with numbers

1 Copy and complete the sentences using the phrases in the box.
  a A number is divisible by 2 if it _____ .
  b A number is divisible by 4 if when you _____ it is even.
  c A number is divisible by 5 if it _____ .
  d A number is divisible by 10 if it _____ .

> ends in 0
> ends in 5 or 0
> is even
> halve it

2 a Check whether 123 is divisible by 3 by following these steps:
  i Add together the digits: $1 + 2 + 3 = \square$
  ii Is your answer a multiple of 3?
  iii Is 123 a multiple of 3?

> **Q2a iii hint**
>
> If your answer is a multiple of 3 the original number is divisible by 3.

  b Copy and complete to find out if these numbers are divisible by 3.
   i 47   **ii** 150   **iii** 171
     $4 + 7 = \square$ $1 + 5 + 0 = \square$ $1 + \square + \square = \square$
     47 _____ divisible by 3.   150 _____ divisible by 3.   171 _____

3 a Check whether 369 is divisible by 9 by following these steps:
  i Add together the digits: $3 + 6 + 9 = \square$
  ii Is your answer a multiple of 9?
  iii Is 369 a multiple of 9?

> **Q3a iii hint**
>
> If your answer is a multiple of 9 the original number is divisible by 9.

  b Are these numbers divisible by 9?
   i 124
   ii 297
   iii 333

4 List all the numbers from 1 to 30.
  Cross out 1
  Cross out all the multiples of 2 (apart from 2)
  Cross out all the multiples of 3 (apart from 3)
  Continue like this.
  The numbers left should all be **prime**.
  Check that they are.

> **Q4 hint**
>
> A **prime number** only divides exactly by 1 and itself.
> 1 is not a prime number.

5 Steve is finding the **common factors** of 16 and 20.
  a Copy and complete his working.
    Factors of 16: 1, 2, $\square$, $\square$, $\square$
    Factors of 20: 1, 2, $\square$, $\square$, $\square$, $\square$
    Common factors: 1, $\square$, $\square$
  b What is the highest common factor of 16 and 20?

> **Q5a hint**
>
> Circle the numbers that are the same in both lists. These are the **common factors**.

6 Find the highest common factor of 24 and 30.

> **Q6 hint**
>
> Follow the same steps as Q5.

Unit 2 Number   44

7 a Copy and complete this list of multiples of 3 that are less than 40.

3, 6, 9, ☐, ☐, ☐, ☐, ☐, ☐, ☐, ☐, ☐, ☐

b Copy and complete this list of multiples of 4 that are less than 40.

4, 8, 12, ☐, ☐, ☐, ☐, ☐, ☐

c Write down the **common multiples** of 3 and 4 that are less than 40.

d Write down the lowest common multiple of 3 and 4.

Q7c hint

Circle the numbers that are the same in both lists. These are the **common multiples**.

8 Find the lowest common multiple of 6 and 10.

Q8 hint

Follow the same steps as Q7.

9 Follow these steps to work out the difference between −7 and 2.

a Draw the number line from −7 to 2.

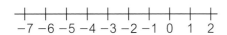

b Put a cross on the point −7 and draw a loop up to 0.

c What is the difference between −7 and 0?

d Draw another loop from 0 to 2.

e What is the difference between 0 and 2.

f Add together your answers to parts **c** and **e**.

10 Use the method in Q9 to work out the difference between

a −3 and 6

b −2 and 4

c −1 and 7

d −4 and 3

11 Eleri sets out her additions and subtractions with negative numbers like this:

7 ⊕ −4 = 7 ⊖ 4 = 3   (replace + − with −)

9 ⊖ −6 = 9 ⊕ 6 = 15   (replace − − with +)

Work out these. Set out your work like Eleri.

a 4 + −2   **b** 10 − −5   **c** −10 + −6

d −9 − −10   **e** −8 − 7   **f** −3 − 11

Q11a hint

Circle the two signs in the middle.
Replace different signs with −.
Replace the same signs with +.

Q11e hint

Start at −8, count back 7.

12 Estimate the answer to each calculation.

a $\frac{73}{8.7}$ **b** $\frac{52}{6.9}$ **c** $19.2 - \frac{61}{8.8}$ **d** $\frac{29}{6.4} + \frac{38}{5.1}$

Q12a hint

Round the 'bottom' number.
8.7 ≈ 9
Then round the 'top' number to a multiple of 9.

Powers and roots

1 Work out the missing numbers.

a $8^2 = 8 \times \square = \square$ **b** $3^3 = 3 \times \square \times \square = \square$

c $\square^{\square} = 7 \times 7 = \square$ **d** $\square^{\square} = 5 \times 5 \times 5 = \square$

e $\square^{\square} = 9 \times \square = \square$ **f** $\square^{\square} = 2 \times \square \times \square = \square$

Q1 hint

4^3 ← index
The index tells you how many 4s are multiplied together.
$4^3 = 4 \times 4 \times 4$

2 a Copy and complete this number line.

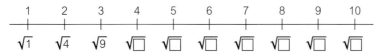

b Use the number line to estimate a value for these square roots.

i $\sqrt{45}$ **ii** $\sqrt{18}$ **iii** $\sqrt{95}$

Q2b i hint

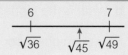

3 Work out these calculations.

  a $5 \times 2^3 = 5 \times \square \times \square \times \square = \square$

  b $3^2 \times 6$

  c $\frac{4^2}{2}$

  d $\frac{250}{5^3}$

Q3a hint

Work out numbers with an index before multiplication or division.

4 Work out these calculations.
Parts **a** and **c** have been started for you.

  a $13 + 3^3 = 13 + 3 \times \square \times \square = \square$

  b $4 \times 3^2 - 22$

  c $\frac{16}{2^3} + 4^2 = \frac{16}{\square} + \square \times \square = \square + \square = \square$

  d $8 \times \sqrt[3]{64} - 12$

  e $\frac{\sqrt[3]{27}}{3} + 4 \times 9$

  f $\frac{45}{\sqrt[3]{125}} - 5^2$

Q4 hint

Work out multiplication or division before addition or subtraction.

Q4d hint

Work out $\sqrt[3]{64}$ first. Then do the multiplication. Finally the subtraction.

5 a Copy and complete these square roots.

  $\sqrt{4} = 2$ $\sqrt{9} = 3$ $\sqrt{16} = \square$ $\sqrt{25} = \square$

  $\sqrt{36} = \square$ $\sqrt{49} = \square$ $\sqrt{64} = \square$ $\sqrt{81} = \square$

  b Complete the working to calculate $\sqrt{729}$.
  Use the fact that $729 = 9 \times 81$.

  $729 = 9 \times 81$
  $\sqrt{729} = \sqrt{9} \times \sqrt{81}$
  $\quad\quad = 3 \times \square$
  $\quad\quad = \square$

  c $1764 = 36 \times 49$

  Use this fact to work out $\sqrt{1764}$.

  d $2025 = 25 \times 81$

  Use this fact to work out $\sqrt{2025}$.

Q5c hint

$\sqrt{1764} = \sqrt{36} \times \sqrt{49} = \square \times \square = \square$

6 a Complete these cube roots.

  $\sqrt[3]{8} = 2$ $\sqrt[3]{64} = \square$ $\sqrt[3]{125} = \square$ $\sqrt[3]{1000} = \square$

  b Complete the working to calculate $\sqrt[3]{64\,000}$.
  Use the fact that $64000 = 64 \times 1000$.

  $64\,000 = 64 \times 1000$
  $\sqrt[3]{64\,000} = \sqrt[3]{64} \times \sqrt[3]{1000}$
  $\quad\quad = 4 \times \square$
  $\quad\quad = \square$

  c $8000 = 8 \times 1000$ Use this fact to work out $\sqrt[3]{8000}$.

  d $1728 = 27 \times 64$ Use this fact to work out $\sqrt[3]{1728}$.

Q6c hint

$\sqrt[3]{8000} = \sqrt[3]{8} \times \sqrt[3]{1000} = \square \times \square = \square$

Working with brackets

1 Work out these. The first one has been started for you.

a $(6 \times 3 - 10)^2$

$$6 \times 3 - 10 = \square$$
$$\square^2 = \square$$

b $(18 - 3 \times 5)^3$

c $8(10 - 4)$

d $(12 - 3)^2 - 11$

e $5 \times (\sqrt{9} + 7)$

f $7 \times (8 - \sqrt{25})^2$

Q1c hint

$8(10 - 4) = 8 \times (10 - 4)$
$= 8 \times \square$

Q1e hint

Work out the brackets first, then multiply by 5.

2 Work out these. The first one has been started for you.

a $\sqrt{23 + 26}$

$$\sqrt{23 + 26} = \sqrt{49} = \square$$

b $\sqrt{5^2 - 9}$

Q2b hint

Work out the calculation under the square root first.

3 Work out these.

a $\dfrac{32 - 2}{4 + 1} = \dfrac{\square}{\square}$

b $\dfrac{32 - 4^2}{4}$

c $\dfrac{6 + 39}{3^2}$

d $\dfrac{5^2 - 15}{\sqrt{4}}$

e $\dfrac{\sqrt[3]{64} + 46}{5^2}$

f $\dfrac{1 + \sqrt{81}}{\sqrt[3]{1000}}$

Q3a hint

Calculate the top and bottom of the fraction first.

4 Write down the number that you square for each calculation.

a 2×3^2

b $2^2 \times 3$

c $(2 \times 3)^2$

d $4^2 \times (5 - 2)$

e $4 \times (5 - 2)^2$

f $4 \times (5 - 2^2)$

Q4c hint

The whole bracket is squared, so $2 \times 3 = \square$

5 Match each calculation to the correct answer.

i $7^2 \times 2$ A   45

ii 7×2^2 B   75

iii $(7 + 2)^2$ C   98

iv $3^2 \times (1 + 4)$ D   15

v $3 \times (1^2 + 4)$ E   28

vi $3 \times (1 + 4)^2$ F   81

Enrichment

1 Here are some number cards.

-3   9   -4   6   -2   11

a Find two numbers that sum to 7.

b Find two other numbers that sum to 7.

c Find two numbers with a difference of 13.

d Find two other numbers with a difference of 13.

Q1 hint

Adding numbers gives the sum.

2 Reflect Write down five mathematical terms you have used in this lesson. Write next to them the meaning of the word and an example of when you have used this word.

Your first term might be:

Sum – this means adding together two or more values. The sum of −3 and 4 is 1.

Reflect

2 Extend

You will:
- Extend your understanding with problem-solving.

1 **Problem-solving** Eric is thinking of a number. It is smaller than 100.
It is divisible by 5 and 9.
What numbers could it be?

2 Write these numbers in ascending order.

2^3 3^3 4^2 4^3 5^2

3 **Reasoning** Which of these numbers do you think is bigger: 15^2 or 2^{15}?
Use your calculator to see if you are correct.

4 **Reasoning a** Copy and complete the Venn diagram for the
numbers between 1 and 20.
  b Bill completes the Venn diagram for all the numbers up to 100.
  Will any areas of the Venn diagram still be empty? Explain
  why.

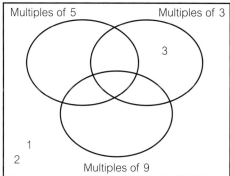

5 **Real / Problem-solving** At the end of each month a restaurant
owner shares the tips equally between the members of staff.
Any remainder is given to charity.
One month the tips are $856. There are 9 members of staff.
Will any money go to charity? Explain how you know.

6 **Real / Problem-solving** A class has fewer than 30 students.
The teacher is pleased because the students in her class can be
split into groups of 2, 3, and 4 without excluding any student. What
is the largest number of students that could be in her class?

7 **a** Write down all the factors of
    i 16   **ii** 40   **iii** 56
  b Write down the HCF of 16, 40 and 56.

8 **a** Write down the first ten multiples of
    i 3   **ii** 4   **iii** 6
  b Write down the LCM of 3, 4 and 6.

9 **Problem-solving** Sophie and Tina start swimming at the same time
from the same end of a swimming pool.
It takes Sophie 40 seconds to swim one length of the pool.
It takes Tina 30 seconds to swim one length of the pool.
After how many seconds will they meet for the first time at the same
end of the pool?

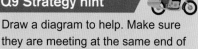

Q9 Strategy hint

Draw a diagram to help. Make sure
they are meeting at the same end of
the pool.

10 Two numbers have a difference of 10.
They are both between −20 and 0.
List all the possible pairs of numbers they could be.

11 Problem-solving Here are some number cards.

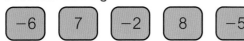

a i Which two cards could you use to make this calculation correct?

$$\boxed{} + \boxed{} = 2$$

   ii Which other two cards could you use to make the calculation correct?

b i Which two cards could you use to make this calculation correct?

$$\boxed{} - \boxed{} = -1$$

   ii Which other two cards could you use to make the calculation correct?

c Which cards could you use in this calculation to give you
   i the greatest possible answer
   ii the smallest possible answer?

$$\boxed{} - \boxed{} + \boxed{} =$$

12 Problem-solving / Reasoning The area of a square is $28\,cm^2$. Lamar says, 'I think the side length of the square is about 4.8 cm.' Without working out the side length, explain how you know there is a better estimate.

13 Problem-solving The area of a square is $70\,cm^2$. Estimate the perimeter of the square.

Q13 hint

The perimeter is the distance around the edge of the square.

14 Problem-solving Square A has a side length of 6.5 cm.
Square B has a perimeter of 25.6 cm.
Square C has an area of $47\,cm^2$.

a Which square has the smallest perimeter?
b Which square has the greatest area?

15 STEM Jenson works out the time it takes a car to cover different distances.
He uses the rule

$$\text{time} = \sqrt{\dfrac{2 \times \text{distance}}{\text{acceleration}}}$$

Time is measured in seconds. Distance is measured in metres. Acceleration is measured in metres per second per second.

a Work out the time taken when
   i distance = 50 and acceleration = 4
   ii distance = 400 and acceleration = 8
   iii distance = 90 and acceleration = 5

b Estimate the time taken when
   i distance = 120 and acceleration = 6
   ii distance = 300 and acceleration = 10

Q15a hint

$\text{time} = \sqrt{(2 \times 50) \div 4}$

16 Give both possible answers to each calculation.
The first one is done for you.

a $\sqrt{31 - 2 \times 3}$

$\qquad = \sqrt{31 - 6}$

$\qquad = \sqrt{25}$

$\qquad = 5 \text{ or } -5$

b $\sqrt{21 + 28}$

c $\sqrt{6 \times 5 - 14}$

d $\sqrt{7 \times 6 - 3 \times 11}$

17 Copy and complete.

a $-3 + \square = -8$

b $-4 - \square = 0$

c $-2 - \square = 2$

d $-3 + -3 + \square = -3$

e $-2 + \square + -2 = -8$

f $-9 + \square = -4 + -7$

18 a Copy and complete.

$2 + 2 + 2 = \square \times 2 = \square$

$1 + 1 + 1 = \square \times 1 = \square$

$0 + 0 + 0 = \square \times 0 = \square$

$-1 + -1 + -1 = \square \times -1 = -3$

$-2 + -2 + -2 = \square \times -2 = \square$

b Use the pattern in part **a** to write down the answer to

i 3×-3 **ii** 3×-4 **iii** 3×-5 **iv** 3×-6

c Copy and complete.

$3 \times 2 = \square$

$2 \times 2 = \square$

$1 \times 2 = \square$

$0 \times 2 = \square$

$-1 \times 2 = \square$

$-2 \times 2 = \square$

$-3 \times 2 = \square$

Discussion Try to explain what happens if you multiply a positive number by a negative number.

19 Write down the answer to

a -1×2 **b** -1×3 **c** -1×4 **d** -1×5

e -2×1 **f** -2×2 **g** -2×3 **h** -2×4

20 a Estimate the answer to each calculation.

i 12×2.8^2 **ii** $4.1^2 + 5.2 \times 9.8$ **iii** $8.2^2 - 5.1^2$

iv $\sqrt{18} \times 22$ **v** $6.7 \times 7.9 - \sqrt{50}$ **vi** $\dfrac{\sqrt{83}}{\sqrt{8}}$

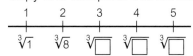

b Use a calculator to work out the accurate answers to the calculations in part **a**.
Were your estimates close to the accurate answers?

Q20a iv hint

Round 18 to the nearest square number, so it is easy to find the square root.

21 a Copy and complete this number line.

$$
\begin{array}{ccccc}
1 & 2 & 3 & 4 & 5 \\
\sqrt[3]{1} & \sqrt[3]{8} & \sqrt[3]{\square} & \sqrt[3]{\square} & \sqrt[3]{\square}
\end{array}
$$

b Use the number line to estimate a value for these cube roots.

i $\sqrt[3]{20}$ **ii** $\sqrt[3]{30}$ **iii** $\sqrt[3]{90}$

c Use a calculator to work out the accurate cube roots of the numbers in part **b**.
How close were your estimates to the accurate answers?

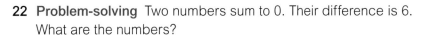

22 Problem-solving Two numbers sum to 0. Their difference is 6.
What are the numbers?

23 A square field has an area of $150\,m^2$.
Fencing costs \$55 per metre.
Estimate the cost of fencing the field. (Assume that the fencing will be around the whole perimeter.)

24 Here are four number cards.

$$\boxed{\sqrt{7^2 + 15}} \quad \boxed{20 - (4 + \sqrt[3]{64})} \quad \boxed{6 \times (\sqrt[3]{27} + 2^2)} \quad \boxed{\sqrt{6^2 - 36}}$$

a Work out the mean value of the number cards.

b Work out the range of the values of the number cards.

25 Problem-solving The sum of these two values is 8.

$$\boxed{\dfrac{32 + \square}{5^2}} \qquad \boxed{\dfrac{45 - \sqrt{81}}{2 \times 3}}$$

Work out the missing number.

Q25 hint

Work out the number on the right first.

26 Reasoning Decide whether the following statements are true or false. If false, give a **counter example**.

a The sum of two negative numbers is always negative.

b The sum of a negative and a positive number is always negative.

c The sum of two positive numbers is always positive.

d The difference between a negative and a positive number will always be greater than 1.

Q26a hint

A **counter example** is an example when the statement is not true.
For example, the statement 'The sum of two numbers is always positive' is false. A counter example is:
$-2 + 1 = -1$.

 27 STEM / Reasoning The energy of an object is related to its mass and velocity (speed).
Jenny is working out the energy of different fairground roller coaster cars.

She uses the rule $\quad \text{energy} = \dfrac{\text{mass} \times \text{velocity}^2}{2}$

a Work out the energy for each car.

Roller coaster car	A	B	C
Mass (kg)	450	625	450
Velocity (m/s)	20	38	40
Energy (joules)			

Q27a hint

$\text{energy} = \dfrac{450 \times 20^2}{2} = \square$

b Car C has the same mass as Car A. Its velocity is twice as fast. Does it have twice as much energy?

28 Reflect In these Extend lessons you used brackets for different calculations.
Which questions wouldn't have made sense without brackets?
Write a calculation that needs brackets for it to make sense.
Now write a calculation that *doesn't* need brackets.
Use a calculator and swap with a partner to make sure.

Reflect

Subject links: Science (Q27)

2 Unit test

1 Write down a number between 51 and 66 that is divisible by
   a 2   b 3   c 4   d 5   e 9   f 10

2 Look at this list of numbers.
   1   2   3   5   8   13
   Write down the numbers that are
   a cube numbers
   b prime numbers.

3 Work out the highest common factor of 12 and 16.

4 Work out the lowest common multiple of 12 and 15?

5 In the UK one year the lowest and highest recorded temperatures
   were −5 °C and 32 °C.
   Work out the difference between these temperatures.

6 Match each calculation with the correct answer.

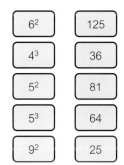

7 Work out
   a 9 + −5   b 8 − −12   c 9 + −12   d −9 + 2
   e −22 + −8   f −8 − 9   g −1 − −1

8 Work out an estimate for $\sqrt{8}$.

9 Work out
   a 6(3 + 4)

   b $(12 − 8)^2$

   c $\sqrt{90 − 26}$

   d $3^2 \times (\sqrt{25} + 1)$

   e $6^2 + (10 − 5)^2$

10 Write down two numbers whose square is 100.

11 Work out
   a 4×3^3 b $2 \times 2^2 \times 2^3$ c $\dfrac{10^3}{4}$ d $\dfrac{500}{5^3}$

12 Here are four calculation cards.

| **A** $2 \times 7^2 - 11$ | **B** $\dfrac{100}{\sqrt[3]{64}} + 3 \times 21$ | **C** $12 \times \sqrt[3]{27} + 50$ | **D** $3 \times 7 + 4^3$ |

Work out the value of the calculation on each card.

13 Write these numbers in order from smallest to largest.

$-12 \quad -9 \quad 15 \quad -2 \quad 0 \quad -8$

14 Work out the missing number in each calculation.

a $3 + \square = -2$ **b** $-5 - \square = -7$ **c** $-2 - \square = 9$

15 Work out an estimate for the answer to each calculation.

a $21 \times 39 + 19 \times 13$ **b** $89 - 7.8 \times 3.2$ **c** $48.6 + \dfrac{13}{4.3}$

16 $576 = 4 \times 9 \times 16$

Use this fact to work out $\sqrt{576}$.

17 Work out an estimate for $\sqrt{200}$.

18 $216 = 8 \times 27$

Use this fact to work out $\sqrt[3]{216}$.

19 Work out

a $\dfrac{4 + 6^2}{5}$ **b** $\dfrac{3^3 - 3}{2^2}$ **c** $\dfrac{\sqrt{64}}{3^2 - 1}$ **d** $\dfrac{\sqrt[3]{1000} + 40}{5^2}$

20 Work out

a $3^2 \times 4$ **b** 3×4^2 **c** $(3 \times 4)^2$ **d** $3^2 \times 4^2$

Challenge

21 Copy this secret code box.

		E											
1	15	25	13	24	16		56	12	19	24	15	15	14	16

Work out the answer to each calculation below.
Then use your answers to fill in the letters in the code box and find the secret message.
The first one is done for you.
$5 - -5 + 3 = 5 + 5 + 3 = 13$, so **E** = 13

E $5 - -5 + 3$	**D** $6 \times \sqrt{81} - 35$	**T** $5 \times \sqrt[3]{8} + 4$
A $6 \times 3 + 38$	**S** $5^2 - 3^2$	**P** $-3 - -7 - 3$
W $\dfrac{2 \times 5^3}{\sqrt{100}}$	**O** $\dfrac{\sqrt[3]{27} \times 10}{2}$	**N** $2 \times (9 - 3)$
R $(3^2 - 3)^2 - 3 \times 4$		

What is the secret message?

22 Write your own secret code questions and code box.

23 **Reflect** In this unit you have mostly done calculations involving:
Which type of calculation did you find easiest? What made it easy?

- negative numbers
- powers
- roots
- factors
- estimation.

Which type of calculation did you find hardest? What made it hard?
Write a hint, in your own words, for the type of calculation you found hardest.

Q23 hint

Look back through the unit to remind yourself of each type of calculation.

3.1 Simplifying algebraic expressions

You will learn to:
• Simplify expressions by collecting like terms.

Why learn this?
Algebra is a language that people in every country in the world can understand. It doesn't need to be translated into Japanese, Spanish or any other language.

Fluency
Write these additions as multiplications.
• 5 + 5 + 5
• 9 + 9 + 9 + 9 + 9
• 10 + 10
• 18 + 18 + 18 + 18 + 18

Explore
Why do we 'simplify' in algebra?

Exercise 3.1

1 Write using index notation.
   a $3 \times 3 \times 3 \times 3$　　　　**b** $2 \times 2 \times 2$
   c $5 \times 5 \times 5 \times 5 \times 5 \times 5$

> **Worked example**
>
> Simplify $x + x + x$
>
>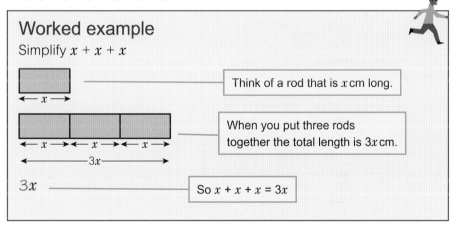
>
> Think of a rod that is x cm long.
>
> When you put three rods together the total length is $3x$ cm.
>
> $3x$ — So $x + x + x = 3x$

Key point

An **algebraic expression**, e.g. $3x + 2y$, contains numbers and letters.
Each part of an algebraic expression is called a **term**.

2 Simplify
   a $n + n$　　　　　　　**b** $y + y + y + y + y$
   c $2a + 3a$　　　　　　**d** $5b + 6b$
   e $5a - 3a$　　　　　　**f** $8b - 3b$
   g $7y + 2y - 3y$
   Discussion Why is $x + x + x + x$ the same as $4x$?

3 Simplify by collecting **like terms**.
   a $2x + 4x + 2 = 6x + \square$　　**b** $2b + 6c - 3c$
   c $6y - 2y + 8 - 3b$　　　　　**d** $4y - 2 + 3y$
   e $9x + 3 - 3y - 7x$　　　　　**f** $9a - 7b + 2a + 5$
   Discussion Are the two expressions $3x + 2y$ and $2y + 3x$ equivalent?

Key point

Like terms contain the same letter (or do not contain a letter).
You simplify an expression by collecting like terms.

Q3e hint

$9x - 7x = \square$

Topic links: Order of operations, Indices

Warm up

4 Copy and complete these addition pyramids.
Each brick is the sum of the two bricks below.

a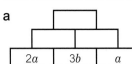

| 2a | 3b | a |

b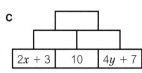

| 5x | 7 | −2x |

c

| 2x + 3 | 10 | 4y + 7 |

5 Simplify

a $b \times b$

b $t \times t \times t$

c $m \times m \times m \times m$

6 Simplify

a $2x^2 + 3x^2 = \square x^2$

b $4a + 2b^2 + 3b^2$

c $2b^2 + 3b + b^2$

d $5x + 2x^2 + 7x$

e $8x^4 - x^4$

f $12x^2 + 3x^3 - 2x^3$

7 Simplify

a $a \times b$

b $t \times t \times b$

c $p \times p \times p \times y \times y$

d $m \times 2$

e $x \times 5$

f $q \times 7 \times p$

Key point

$2 \times 2 \times 2 = 2^3$
In the same way, you can write
$b \times b \times b = b^3$

Key point

Write letters in alphabetical order.
Write numbers before letters.
$a \times 2 = 2 \times a = 2a$

Q6 hint

Like terms must have *exactly* the same letters and powers. For example, $2x^2$ and $3x^3$ are *not* like terms as the powers of x are different.

Q7a hint

$p \times q$ is written as pq

Worked example

Simplify

a $3b \times 2b$

$3b \times 2b = 3 \times b \times 2 \times b$
$\qquad = 3 \times 2 \times b \times b$ ——— The order of multiplication does not matter.
$\qquad = 6b^2$

b $\dfrac{8b}{4}$

$\dfrac{8b}{4} = 2b$ ——————— $\dfrac{8b}{4}$ means $8b \div 4$. Work out $8 \div 4$.

---

8 Simplify

a $2b \times 5b$

b $9a \times 3a$

c $3a \times 2a \times 3a$

d $\dfrac{12b}{4}$

e $\dfrac{9a}{2}$

f $\dfrac{36b}{12}$

9 Match the equivalent expressions.

$2x$ $\quad$ $4x - 3x$ $\quad$ $x \times x$ $\quad$ x $\quad$ $3x + 4x$

$x + x$ $\quad$ $4x^2$ $\quad$ $3x$ $\quad$ $2x \times 2x$ $\quad$ x^2

$x \times 2x$ $\quad$ $7x$ $\quad$ $\dfrac{9x}{3}$ $\quad$ $2x^2$

10 Copy and complete these multiplication pyramids.
Each brick is the product of the two bricks below.

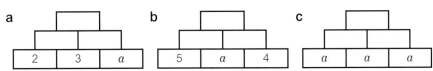

a | 2 | 3 | a
b | 5 | a | 4
c | a | a | a

Key point

The identity symbol ($\equiv$) shows that two expressions are *always* equivalent.
For example, $a + 2b \equiv 2b + a$.

11 In between which pairs of expressions can you write $\equiv$?
  a $a + b \ \square \ b + a$
  b $a - b \ \square \ b - a$
  c $ab \ \square \ ba$
  d $a \div b \ \square \ b \div a$

Q11 hint

Test with some numerical values for a and b.

Investigation   Problem-solving

1 This is an addition pyramid. Work out the missing values.

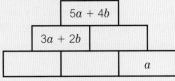

$5a + 4b$
$3a + 2b$ |
 | | a

2 How many different possibilities can you find for this addition pyramid?

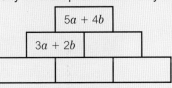

$5a + 4b$
$3a + 2b$ |
 | |

3 This is a multiplication pyramid. How many different possibilities can you find?

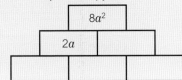

$8a^2$
$2a$ |
 | |

12 Explore Why do we 'simplify' in algebra?
Is it easier to explore this question now that you have completed the lesson?
What further information do you need to be able to answer this?

13 Reflect In algebra, letters are used to represent values we do not know. This lesson may be the first time you have done algebra.
Choose **A**, **B** or **C** to complete each statement.
In this lesson, I did...   **A** well   **B** OK   **C** not very well
So far, I think algebra is...   **A** easy   **B** OK   **C** difficult
When I think about the next lesson,
    I feel...   **A** confident **B** OK   **C** unsure
If you answered mostly **A**s and **B**s, did your experience surprise you? Why?
If you answered mostly **C**s, then look back at the questions you found most difficult. Ask a friend or your teacher to explain them to you. Then answer the statements above again.

Explore

Reflect

3.2 Writing algebraic expressions

Confidence

You will learn to:

* Write expressions using four operations.

Fluency

Work out

* 3^2
* 5^3
* 1^4

Why learn this?

Computers can work with algebraic expressions using a computer algebra system (CAS).

Explore

Think of a number. Double it. Add 10. Divide by 2. Subtract your original number. Try this with different numbers. What answer do you get? Why?

Exercise 3.2

Warm up

1 Simplify

a $2x + 3x - 5x$

b $3x^2 - 4x + 2x^2$

c $3x + 5 - 2x + 4$

2 Simplify

a $y \times y$

b $b \times b \times b$

c $4 \times 2n$

d $4b \times 2b$

e $\dfrac{16c}{4}$

3 John collects coins. He has b coins.

Write an expression for how many he has when there are

a 2 more

b 4 fewer

c 17 more

d 5 times as many

e half as many.

4 Haruto is m years old.

Write expressions for the ages of each of these people.

a Laila is 4 times as old as Haruto.

b Maggie is 5 years older than Haruto.

c Ami is 6 years younger than Haruto.

d Iman is half the age of Haruto.

e Rashid is 5 years older than twice Haruto's age.

f Ruth is 3 years younger than 5 times Haruto's age.

5 Write an algebraic expression for

a y more than x

b x multiplied by y

c y less than x

d x more than 2 times y

e 3 times y add 4 times x

f y multiplied by itself

g 4 times x multiplied by itself

h 7 less than y multiplied by itself

i x divided by y

j 2 more than 20 divided by x.

Q3a hint

Q3d hint

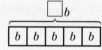

Q3e hint

Finding half is the same as dividing by 2.

Q5a hint

Try it with numbers. How would you write 5 more than 3?

Topic links: Order of operations, Graphs

6 t represents a number.
Write and simplify an expression for

   a 2 more than triple the number   **b** 5 less than double the number
   c 4 more than double the number   **d** the number added to itself
   e the number subtract 5   **f** the number multiplied by itself
   g the number divided by 3   **h** 3 divided by the number.

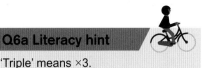

Q6a Literacy hint

'Triple' means ×3.

Worked example

Write an expression for each function machine.

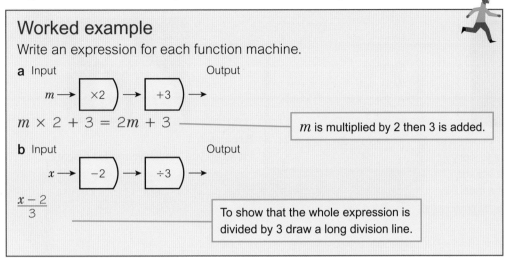

a Input   Output

$m \rightarrow \boxed{\times 2} \rightarrow \boxed{+3} \rightarrow$

$m \times 2 + 3 = 2m + 3$ ——— m is multiplied by 2 then 3 is added.

b Input   Output

$x \rightarrow \boxed{-2} \rightarrow \boxed{\div 3} \rightarrow$

$\dfrac{x-2}{3}$ ——— To show that the whole expression is divided by 3 draw a long division line.

7 Write an expression for the output of each function machine.

   a $\rightarrow \boxed{\times 3} \rightarrow \boxed{-17} \rightarrow$

   b $\rightarrow \boxed{\div 4} \rightarrow \boxed{+3} \rightarrow$

   c $\rightarrow \boxed{\times 5} \rightarrow \boxed{\times 5} \rightarrow$

   d $\rightarrow \boxed{+2} \rightarrow \boxed{\div 5} \rightarrow$

8 A rectangle has width b. The length is 5 more than the width.

b

   a Write an expression for the length.
   b Write and simplify an expression for the perimeter.
   c Calculate the perimeter of the rectangle when $b = 10$ cm.

9 Explore Think of a number. Double it. Add 10. Divide by 2. Subtract away your original number. Try this with different numbers. What answer do you get? Why?
Is it easier to explore this question now that you have completed the lesson?
What further information do you need to be able to answer this?

10 Reflect This lesson suggested bar modelling and function machines to help you with writing expressions. Did they help you? How?
Did you use any other methods? Explain the method(s) you used.

Explore

Reflect

3.3 STEM: Using formulae

Confidence

You will learn to:
* Substitute into formulae.

Why learn this?
You can substitute into formulae to work out all sorts of things – from the volume of the Earth to the cooking time of a meal.

Fluency
Work out
* $2 + 3 × 4$
* $\dfrac{4 + 5}{2}$
* $\dfrac{4 × (5 + 2)}{2}$

Explore
How can you predict your adult height?

Exercise 3.3

Warm up

1 A recipe gives this formula to work out how long it takes to cook a chicken:

  (50 × mass (in kg) + 40) minutes

  How long does it take to cook a 2 kg chicken?

2 **STEM** To calculate the maximum heart rate when exercising, use
  maximum heart rate = 220 – age in years.
  Work out the maximum heart rate for these ages.
  a 18   **b** 45   **c** 79

3 Work out the value of each expression when $a = 3$.
  a $2a$ **b** $a + 3$ **c** $a - 5$ **d** a^2 **e** $10 - a$

4 Given $x = 3$, $y = 5$, $z = 8$ work out the value of
  a xy **b** $xz + 5$ **c** $2(x + 1)$ **d** $\dfrac{z}{2}$ **e** $\dfrac{x + y}{2}$

Q3a hint

$2a = 2 × a = 2 × \square$

Q4a hint

$\square × \square$

Key point

A **formula** is a general rule for a relationship between quantities. You use a formula to work out an unknown quantity by substituting.

Worked example

The **formula** used to calculate speed is: speed = $\dfrac{\text{distance}}{\text{time}}$

Work out the speed of a cyclist who travels 1000 metres in 20 seconds.

$Speed = \dfrac{1000}{20}$ ⎯ Substitute the values into the formula. Write the units.

$= 50 \, m/s$ ⎯ m/s means metres per second.

5 **STEM** Use the formula speed = $\dfrac{\text{distance}}{\text{time}}$ to work out the speed of each of these cyclists in metres per second.
  a distance = 3000 m   time = 360 seconds
  b distance = 600 m   time = 50 seconds
  c distance = 10 000 m   time = 640 seconds

Topic links: Order of operations, Negative numbers   **Subject links:** PE (Q2), Science (Q5–9, Q11–12)

6 **STEM** In physics the formula $F = ma$ is used to calculate force, F,
where m = mass and a = acceleration.
Work out the value of the force (F) when
a $m = 2$, $a = 27$ **b** $m = 5$, $a = 32$ **c** $m = 25$, $a = 7$
Discussion When $F = 20$ and $a = 5$ could you work out the value of m?

7 **STEM** Weight (W) in newtons (N) is calculated using the formula
$W = mg$, where m = mass in kg and g = acceleration due to gravity in m/s^2.
a On Earth $g = 10$ m/s^2. Work out the weight, in newtons, of
   i a 5 kg dog
   ii a 70 kg man
   iii a 30 kg monkey.
b On the Moon $g = 1.6$ m/s^2.
   Work out the weight of the dog, the man and the monkey on the Moon.

8 **STEM** The formula to calculate pressure (P) in N/m^2 is $P = \dfrac{F}{A}$, where
F = force in N and A = area in m^2. Work out the pressure when
a $F = 20$, $A = 2$
b $F = 100$, $A = 25$

9 **STEM** An engineer uses the formula $V = IR$ to work out the voltage in a
circuit, where I is the current (in amps) and R is the resistance (in ohms).
Work out the voltage, V, of a circuit with
a current 4 amps and resistance 10 ohms
b current 3.1 amps and resistance 15 ohms
c current 7.2 amps and resistance 20 ohms.

10 The formula for the perimeter of a rectangle is $P = 2l + 2w$.
Work out the perimeter when
a $l = 12$ cm and $w = 2$ cm
b $l = 4$ m and $w = 5$ m
c $w = 10.5$ cm and $l = 6$ cm.

11 **STEM** To convert from °C (C) to kelvin (K) scientists use the
formula $K = C + 273$.
Convert these temperatures to kelvin.
a 100 °C   **b** −20 °C   **c** 0 °C   **d** −100 °C

12 **STEM** The formula for converting a temperature from Fahrenheit (F) to
Celsius (C) is $C = \dfrac{5(F - 32)}{9}$.
Convert these temperatures into °C.
a 41 °F   **b** 59 °F   **c** 77 °F   **d** 23 °F

13 **Explore** How can you predict your adult height?
Is it easier to explore this question now you have completed the lesson?
What further information do you need to be able to answer this?

14 **Reflect** Look back at the formula in Q6.
a Would it matter if this formula used the letters x and y instead of
m and a?
b Do the letters help you to understand a formula?

Q14 hint

If you used different letters would
your answers be different?

Explore

Reflect

3.4 Writing formulae

You will learn to:
- Write formulae from a description.

E3		fx	=B3+C3+D3		
	A	**B**	**C**	**D**	**E**
1	The Cupcake Shop - First Quarter Sales				
2		January	February	March	Total
3	Red velvet	£1,292	£1,156	£1,208	£3,656
4	Lemon drizzle	£2,047	£1,987	£1,999	£6,033
5	Vanilla	£1,795	£1,896	£1,689	£5,380
6	Fudge	£1,250	£1,346	£1,287	£3,883
7	Total revenues	£6,384	£6,385	£6,183	£18,952

Why learn this?
You can write formulae into a spreadsheet so that it automatically does all the calculations for you.

Fluency
Work out the mean of 6, 12, 12.

Explore
What is the formula to convert weeks into minutes?

Exercise 3.4

1 Write algebraic expressions for
  a 2 more than x
  b 5 less than y
  c the cost of x apples at 20p each.

2 When $x = 2$ and $y = 7$ work out the value of
  a xy
  b $2x + 4$
  c $9x - 2y$
  d $3y + 2x$

3 An online company charges $5 to rent a film and $10 to download a film. It uses the formula $C = 5r + 10d$.
  a What do you think r stands for?
  b What do you think d stands for?
  c How much would 3 rentals and 2 downloads cost?

4 Alika earns £9 per hour.
  a How much does she earn in 5 hours?
  b How much does she earn in 12 hours?
  c Write an expression for how much she earns in x hours.
  d Write a formula for her earnings, E, in x hours.
  Discussion What is the difference between an expression and a formula?

Q4 Literacy hint
To 'earn' money means to make money.

Q4d hint
E = your expression from part **c**.

Worked example
Storing furniture in a warehouse costs $12 per week.
Write a formula for the cost, C, of storing furniture for y weeks.

$12y$ ——— Write down the cost each week. Multiply the cost by the number of weeks.

$C = 12y$ ——— Write C = your expression.

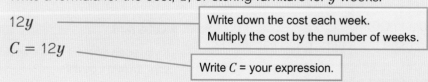

Literacy hint
'per week' means each week.

Topic links: Order of operations, Negative numbers

Subject links: Food technology (Q11)

5   Renting a go-cart costs £15 per hour.
    a Write an expression for the cost for x hours.
    b Write a formula, $C = \square$.

Q5a Strategy hint
Start by trying different numbers of hours to see the pattern.

6   The amount of bread a restaurant orders depends on the number of bookings each day. They order 10 more loaves of bread than they have bookings.
    Write a formula that connects the number of bookings, b, to the number of loaves of bread, L.

7   A library buys bookcases. Each bookcase has 6 shelves.
    Write a formula that connects the total number of shelves in the library, L, to the number of bookcases, B.

8   **Modelling**
    a Write an algebraic expression for finding the mean of three numbers x, y and z.
    b Write a formula for the mean of three numbers.
    c Use your formula to work out the mean when $x = 5$, $y = 22$ and $z = 12$.

Q8b hint
Write $m = \square$.

9   **Real** A mobile phone company charges £12.50 per month and £4 per gigabyte (GB) of data.
    a Work out the cost when
        i 10 GB are used
        ii no data is used.
    b Write a formula for the monthly cost, C, when n gigabytes of data are used.

10 A function machine multiplies each input by 5 and then adds 3.
    Work out the output when the input is
    a i 5
       ii −2
       iii −7
       iv x
    b Write a formula that connects the output, y, with the input, x.

Q10 hint
Draw the function machine.
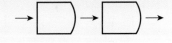

11 The cooking time for a piece of meat is 45 minutes per kg plus an extra 20 minutes.
    a Work out the cooking time for a 3 kg piece of meat.
    b Write a formula that connects the cooking time (in minutes), C, to the mass in kg, k.

12 **Explore** What is the formula to convert weeks into minutes?
    Is it easier to explore this question now that you have completed the lesson?
    What further information do you need to be able to answer this?

13 **Reflect** In this lesson you wrote your own formulae. In lesson 3.3 you were given formulae to work with. Which did you find more difficult? What made it more difficult?
    Are there particular kinds of questions you need more practice on? If so, what kinds?

3.5 Brackets and formulae

Confidence

You will learn to:
- Expand expressions involving brackets.

Why learn this?
Scientific formulae often contain brackets.

Fluency
Work out
- $5(2 + 3)$
- $2(10 - 4)$
- $4(3 - 6)$

Explore
How do you convert temperatures in degrees Celsius to degrees Fahrenheit?

Exercise 3.5

Warm up

1 Simplify
  a $3 \times y$ **b** $a \times 6$ **c** $p \times -3$ **d** $7 \times 2s$ **e** $9z \times 5$

2 Simplify
  a $b \times b$ **b** $m \times 2m$ **c** $a \times a \times a$ **d** $3b \times 2b$ **e** $6n \times 3n$

3 **a** Work out
  i $3(2 + 5)$ **ii** $3 \times 2 + 3 \times 5$
  What do you notice?
  b Work out
  i $4(6 - 1)$ **ii** $4 \times 6 + 4 \times (-1)$
  What do you notice?

Key point

Expand a bracket means multiply every number inside the bracket by the number or letter outside the bracket.

Worked example
Expand
a $2(x + 3)$

$2(x + 3) = 2 \times x + 2 \times 3$
$\qquad\quad\ = 2x + 6$

b $5(y - 2)$

$5(y - 2) = 5 \times y + 5 \times (-2)$
$\qquad\quad\ = 5y - 10$

4 Expand
  a $3(x + 4)$ **b** $2(n + 12)$
  c $3(p - 7)$ **d** $4(y - 5)$
  e $2(2 + r)$ **f** $5(8 - b)$
  g $8(2 - q)$ **h** $10(10 - a)$
  Discussion How could you check that your answers are correct?

Topic links: Order of operations, Negative numbers

5 Anne earns x pounds per hour. Jamil earns £3 more per hour than Anne. On Sunday he gets paid double.
Write an algebraic expression in terms of x for the amount Jamil earns per hour on Sunday.

Q5 hint

$2(\square + \square)$

6 The length of a rectangle is x cm.

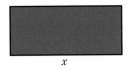

x

Its width is 5 cm less than its length.
a Write an expression for the width of the rectangle.
b Write and simplify an expression for the area of the rectangle.
c Copy and complete the formula for calculating the area, $A = \square$.
d Use the formula to work out the area of the rectangle when
   i $x = 10$
   ii $x = 12$

7 Ravi is x years old. Ana's age is the square of Ravi's.
Bryony is 5 years older than Ana.
a Write an expression for Ana's age.
b Write an expression for Bryony's age.
c Write and simplify an expression for the sum of all their ages.
d Ravi is 5 years old. What is the sum of their ages?
Discussion How did you answer part **d**? Is there more than one way?
Which is the quickest way?

8 Expand
  a $b(b + 4)$ **b** $y(y - 2)$
  c $t(10 + t)$ **d** $r(2 - r)$
  e $w(3w + 2)$ **f** $p(10 + 4p)$
  g $q(15 - 2q)$ **h** $2r(3r + 1)$
  i $8m(2m - 3)$ **j** $2b(20 - 4b)$

Q8a hint

$b \times b + b \times 4 = b^2 + \square$

9 **Explore** How do you convert temperatures in degrees Celsius to degrees Fahrenheit?
Is it easier to explore this question now that you have completed the lesson?
What further information do you need to be able to answer this?

10 **Reflect** Write a definition, in your own words, for
  • expand
  • simplify.
Compare your definitions with those written by others in your class.
Can you improve your definitions?

Q10 hint

Look back at questions where you were asked to 'expand' or 'simplify'. What did you do?

Explore

Reflect

3 Check up

Simplifying expressions

1 Simplify

  a $x^2 + 3x^2$ **b** $x + x^2 + x$ **c** $2 + x^2 + 2x^2 - 5$

2 Expand

  a $3(x + 4)$ **b** $2(a - w)$ **c** $5(11 - x)$

3 Simplify

  a $x + x$ **b** $4x + 7x$ **c** $10c - 5c$

  d $4t - t$ **e** $7x + 2b - 5x$

4 Simplify

  a $y \times y \times y$ **b** $x \times x$ **c** $3 \times t \times t$

  d $2 \times r \times r \times r \times 5$ **e** $5r \times r$ **f** $7t \times 2t$

  g $y \div 7$ **h** $\dfrac{12y}{6}$

5 Expand

  a $x(x + 3)$ **b** $b(b - 2)$ **c** $a(10 - a)$

  d $2x(3x + 1)$ **e** $4t(10 - 2t)$

Substitution

6 Area of rectangle = length × width

  Work out the area of a rectangle with width = 12 cm and length = 7 cm.

7 $T = 5B$ What is the value of T when $B = 12$?

8 Density = $\dfrac{\text{mass}}{\text{volume}}$, where mass is in kg, volume is in m³ and density is in kg/m³.

  Work out the density of a block with mass 20 kg and volume 4 m³.

9 The approximate perimeter, P, of a semicircle can be calculated using the formula $P = a + \dfrac{3a}{2}$

  Work out the approximate perimeter when $a = 4$ cm.

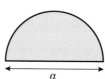

10 Use the formula $b = 10t - c$ to work out the value of b when

  a $t = 3, c = 5$

  b $t = 1, c = 7$

  c $t = 4, c = -2$

  d $t = 3, c = -4$

11 Work out the value of the expression $ab + 2c$ when $a = 2, b = 5, c = 9$.

12 What is the value of x^2 when $x = 7$?

Writing expressions and formulae

13 Mia has x stamps. Write expressions for the number of stamps each person has.

   a Carl has 7 fewer than Mia.

   b Onick has 12 times as many as Mia.

   c Mehmet has half as many as Mia.

14 Jack is paid $5 for each hour he babysits.
Write a formula that connects the total amount he is paid, T, and the number of hours he babysits, x.

15 Write an algebraic expression for

   a a more than b

   b 3 more than a, multiplied by b

   c a multiplied by itself

   d b divided by 5.

16 A class has 30 students. A teacher buys sweets to share between them.
Write a formula that connects the number of sweets each student receives, S, and the number of sweets the teacher buys, p.

17 A square has sides a cm long.
Write a formula for finding the area of the square, A, using the length of the side, a.

18 **How sure are you of your answers? Were you mostly**

   ☹ **Just guessing**   😐 **Feeling doubtful**   🙂 **Confident**

What next? Use your results to decide whether to strengthen or extend your learning.

Challenge

19 A pattern is made of squares and rectangles.

   Pattern 1   Pattern 2   Pattern 3

  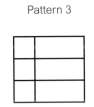

   Write and simplify an algebraic expression for the area of

   a Pattern 1   **b** Pattern 2   **c** Pattern 3

   d Pattern 10   **e** Pattern n.

20 Find a value of x so that

   a x^2 is equal to $2x$ **b** x^2 is equal to x^3.

21 $a + b = -2$ and $a - b = -6$.
a and b are whole numbers. What are the values of a and b?

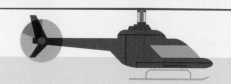

3 Strengthen

You will:

• Strengthen your understanding with practice.

Simplifying expressions

1 Copy and complete.

a $p + p + p = \square\, p$

b $m + m + m + m = \square m$

c $d + d$

d $t + t + t + t + t$

2 Simplify

a $2t + 3t$

b $5g + 7g$

c $10y - 3y$

d $5p - p$

e $10y + 2b + 3y$

f $6m + n + 5m$

g $4a + 3b - a$

h $3q + 2b - 3b$

i $4t + 7 - 2t$

j $4y + 8 - 2 + 3y$

3 Expand $3(2 + 4)$

> **Q3 hint**
>
> $3 \times (2 + 4)$
>
> | 2 | 4 | | 2 | 4 | | 2 | 4 |
> |---|---|---|---|---|---|---|---|
>
> $= 3 \times 2$ $+$ 3×4
>
> | 2 | 2 | 2 | | 4 | 4 | 4 |
> |---|---|---|---|---|---|---|

4 Copy and complete.

a $2(x + 3) = \square x + \square$

b $3(x + 4) = (x + 4) + (x + 4) + (x + 4) = \square + \square$

c $4(b + 2)$

d $5(t + 3) = \square \times t + \square \times 3 = \square t + \square$

e $3(6 + a)$

f $2(r - 3) = \square \times r + \square \times -3$

g $6(10 - b)$

> **Q1 hint**
>
> Draw bars to help.
>
> | p | p | p |
> |---|---|---|

> **Q2a hint**
>
>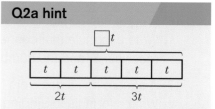

> **Q2e hint**
>
> Add the y terms first.
>
> | $10y$ | $3y$ |
> |---|---|
>
> $\square\, y$

> **Q2 i hint**
>
> Numbers, e.g. 7, can only be added to other numbers.

> **Q4a hint**
>
>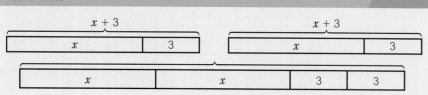

5 Write the missing numbers.

   a $6 \times 6 \times 6 = 6^{\square}$

   b $5 \times 5 \times 5 \times 5 = 5^{\square}$

   c $11 \times 11 = 11^{\square}$

6 Match each expression on the left-hand side to one on the right-hand side.

a $a \times a \times a$
b $a \times a$
c $a \times a \times a \times a \times a$
d $a \times a \times a \times a$
e $a \times a \times a \times a \times a \times a$

i a^4
ii a^6
iii a^2
iv a^3
v a^5

Q5 hint

How many times is a multiplied by itself?

7 Copy and complete.

   a $2w \times 3w =$

   b $4a \times 2a =$

   c $3b \times 5b =$

   d $8m \times 3m =$

   e $9n \times 11n =$

8 Simplify these. Which is the 'odd one out'?

   a $n \times n$

   b $n + n$

   c $2 \times n$

   d $n \times 2$

9 Copy and complete.

   a $m(m + 1) =$

   b $b(b + 2) =$

   c $d(3 + d) =$

   d $r(r - 1) =$

   e $m(m - 3) =$

   f $t(10 - t) =$

Q9a hint

Q9d hint

Draw the arrows.

10 a Complete the pattern.

     $t + t = 2t$

     $t^2 + t^2 = 2t^2$

     $t^3 + t^3 = 2t^3$

     $t^4 + t^4 = \square$

   b Simplify by collecting like terms.

     i $p^2 + p^2$

     ii $x^3 + x^3$

     iii $m^2 + m^2 + m^2$

     iv $2x^2 + 3x^2$

11 Simplify by collecting like terms.

   a $t^2 + t^2 + 3t = \square t^2 + \square$

   b $p^3 + p + p$

   c $3x + x^2 + 2x$

Q11 hint

You can only add terms with the same letters and powers.

Substitution

1 Molly earns £9 per hour. She uses this formula to work out her pay.
   Pay = 9 × number of hours
   Work out how much she is paid for 8 hours.

2 The formula to work out the distance a car travels is
   distance = speed × time
   A car travels at a speed of 50 km per hour for 2 hours.
   How far does it travel?

3 Work out the value of each expression when $m = 2$ and $n = 6$.
   a $m + 3$ **b** $n - 5$ **c** $m + n$
   d $4m$ **e** $3n$ **f** $\dfrac{n}{2}$
   g mn **h** $mn + 2$ **i** $\dfrac{n}{m}$

4 The formula for the area of a rectangle is $l \times w$ where l = length and w = width.
   Work out the area of a rectangle when
   a $l = 3, w = 5$
   b $l = 9, w = 7$
   c $l = 4, w = 4$
   d $l = 20, w = 1$

5 $P = 10(a + b)$
   Work out the value of P when
   a $a = 9, b = 3$
   b $a = 2, b = 5$
   c $a = 3, b = 12$

6 Use the formula $P = 10 + m$ to work out the value of P when
   a $m = -2$ **b** $m = -5$ **c** $m = -10$

7 Work out the value of n^2 when
   a $n = 5$ **b** $n = 1$ **c** $n = 7$

8 Copy and complete the calculations when $m = 2$.
   a $m^4 = \Box \times \Box \times \Box \times \Box = \Box$ **b** $m^2 + 1 = \Box \times \Box + 1 = \Box$
   c $m^2 - 2 = \Box \times \Box - 2 = \Box$ **d** $3m^2 = 3 \times \Box \times \Box = \Box$

Q1 hint

Pay = 9 × number of hours
                 ⏟
                 8

= 9 × 8 = $\Box$

Q3a hint

$\dfrac{m}{2} + 3$
$\dfrac{2}{2} + 3 = \Box$

Q3g hint

$mn = m \times n = \Box \times \Box$

Q4a hint

Area = $\underset{\smile}{l} \times \underset{\smile}{w}$
= 3 × 5
= $\Box$

Q5a hint

$P = 10(a + b)$
= 10(9 + 3)
= 10 × 12

Q6a hint

$P = 10 + -2$
= 10 − 2

Q7a hint

$5^2 = \Box$

Q8a hint

Remember to calculate powers first.

Writing expressions and formulae

1 Match each algebraic expression to its description.

a $x + 3$	**i** 3 less than x
b $x - 3$	**ii** x less than 3
c $3x$	**iii** 3 more than x
d $\dfrac{x}{3}$	**iv** one third of x
e $3 - x$	**v** 3 times x

2 To estimate the number of bulbs that will grow, S, Eddie divides the number planted, p, by 3.
Copy and complete the formula $S = \dfrac{\square}{\square}$

3 Write an expression for each function machine.
The first one has been done for you.

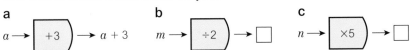

a
$a \longrightarrow \boxed{+3} \longrightarrow a + 3$

b
$m \longrightarrow \boxed{\div 2} \longrightarrow \square$

c
$n \longrightarrow \boxed{\times 5} \longrightarrow \square$

4 To convert a decimal, m, to a percentage, p, multiply by 100.
Choose the correct formula connecting m and p.

$$p = m + 100 \qquad p = 100m \qquad p = \frac{m}{100} \qquad p = 100 - m$$

> **Q4 hint**
>
> Draw a function machine.

5 Write a description for each expression.

a $x + y$ **b** xy **c** $x - y$ **d** $\dfrac{y}{x}$

e $y + x$ **f** $y - x$ **g** $\dfrac{y}{x}$ **h** yx

6 To convert from km, K, to miles, M, divide by 8 then multiply by 5.
Write the formula.

> **Q6 hint**
>
> Use these phrases: *more than, less than, multiplied by, divided by.*
> E.g. y more than ....

7 To find the mean, M, of two values, a and b, add them together and divide by 2.
  a Write an expression for a add b divided by 2.
  b Write a formula for finding the mean of a and b. $M = $ _____

8 I think of a number, add 3, and then divide by 8.
  a What would the result be if the original number was 21?
  b Copy and complete the function machine.

$x \longrightarrow \boxed{} \longrightarrow \boxed{} \longrightarrow y$

  c Which of these formulae describes the relationship between x and y?

$$y = \frac{x + 3}{8} \qquad y = 8(x + 3) \qquad y = \frac{x}{3} + 8 \qquad y = 3x + 8$$

Enrichment

1 a When $x = 1$ work out the value of
     i x^2 **ii** x^3 **iii** x^4 **iv** x^5
  b Predict the value of x^{119}.

2 Victoria says, '$x + 2 < x + 3$ for any value of x'.
Is she correct? Explain your answer.

3 Reflect Look back at the questions you answered in this section.
Which hints were most useful to you? What made them more useful?
Which hints were least useful to you? What made them less useful?
What do your answers tell you about how you learn maths best?

3 Extend

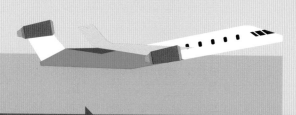

You will:
- Extend your understanding with problem-solving.

1 A square has sides of length x. Write and simplify an expression for
  a the perimeter   **b** the area.

2 A cube has edges of length 10 cm.

  a Work out the area of one of the square faces.
  b The cube is painted. Work out the total area that is painted.
  Another cube has edges of length x.
  c Write an algebraic expression for the area of one of the faces.
  d Write an algebraic expression for the total area of all the faces.

 3 **Finance** Company 1 uses the formula $C = 0.05M + 0.02T$ for calculating
  the cost of a mobile phone bill, where M = number of minutes of calls,
  T is the number of texts and C is in dollars.

  a Work out the cost of bills for each of these customers.
    Customer A: 10 minutes of calls, 1000 texts
    Customer B: 300 minutes of calls, 20 texts
    Customer C: 1000 minutes of calls

  b Company 2 uses the formula $C = 0.1M + 0.01T$.
    Work out the bill for each of the customers if they used this company.
  c Which company should each customer use?

4 **Problem-solving** Jasmin is working out coordinates using a rule.
  She takes the x-coordinate and puts it into the function machine to
  get a y-coordinate:

Q4 hint

Start with $x = 0$.

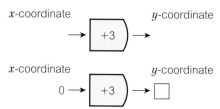

  Work out several pairs of coordinates and plot them on a coordinate
  grid. Join them with a line. What do you notice? Design your own
  function machine and generate coordinates. Plot them and join them
  with a line. What do you notice?

5 A triangle has one side of length n cm.
The second side is 5 less than double this length.
The third side is twice the length of the second side.
Write an expression for the perimeter of the triangle. Simplify your expression as much as possible.

Q5 hint

Sketch and label the triangle.

6 In the pyramid, each brick is the sum of the two bricks below.
Work out the missing expressions.

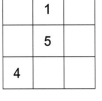

7 Your friend tells you this number trick: *Think of a number. Add 3. Multiply it by 2. Subtract double the number you first thought of. The number you have is 6.*
Explain the trick.

Q7 hint

Call the unknown number 'x' and construct an algebraic expression.

8 a Write the numbers 1–9 in the square (using each number only once) so that all the diagonals, rows and columns sum to 15.
Three numbers have been written for you.

b Write the algebraic expressions in the square so that all the rows, columns and diagonals sum to $3c$.

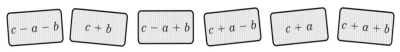

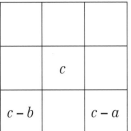

9 When $a = -2$ and $b = 4$ all but one of these expressions have the same value. Which is the 'odd one out'?

 $b - a$ $2b + a$ $b^2 - 2b + a$ $-a - b$ $a - b$

10 This is part of a spreadsheet a shop uses to calculate wages.

a What value will be calculated in cell D2?

b What expressions should be written in cells D3 and D4 to calculate the wages of Mr Gupta and Mrs Alam?

c The value in cell B4 is changed to £19. What value will show in cell D4?

d The expression in C5 calculates the mean number of hours worked.
What is this value?

e What does the expression in cell B5 calculate?

	A	B	C	D
1		Pay per hour	Number of hours	Pay
2	Mrs Badri	8	25	= B2*C2
3	Mr Gupta	7	17	
4	Mrs Alam	15	15	
5		= (B2+B3+B4)/3	= (C2+C3+C4)/3	
6				

Key point

In spreadsheets * is used instead of ×.

11 The length of a rectangle is 3 times the width. Write and simplify an expression for

    a the area

    b the perimeter.

Investigation

Problem-solving

This blue square has width a.

1 Write an expression for the area of the blue square.

This yellow square has sides twice as long.

2 Write and simplify an expression for the area of the yellow square.

3 How many blue squares will fit inside the yellow square?

Discussion When you double the length of the sides of a square what happens to the area?

Worked example

Draw a pair of number lines from 1 to 10.

Show the mapping: $x \rightarrow 2x + 3$

When $x = 0$, $2x + 3 = 0 + 3 = 3$

> Substitute each number on the top number line into the function $2x + 3$.

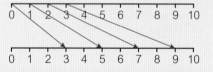

When $x = 1$, $2x + 3 = 2 + 3 = 5$

When $x = 2$, $2x + 3 = 4 + 3 = 7$

When $x = 3$, $2x + 3 = 6 + 3 = 9$

12 The function $x \rightarrow x + 2$ is shown on a **mapping diagram**.

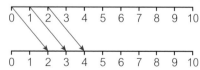

Copy and complete the mapping diagram.

Key point

A mapping diagram is a visual representation of a function.

13 Show each mapping on a pair of number lines from 0 to 10.

a $x \rightarrow x - 5$ **b** $x \rightarrow 3x - 3$ **c** $x \rightarrow \dfrac{2x + 4}{2}$

14 Show each mapping on a pair of number lines from –5 to 5.

a $x \rightarrow x + 2$ **b** $x \rightarrow 4 + x$ **c** $x \rightarrow 2 - x$

15 **a** Copy and complete the mapping diagram for $x \rightarrow \frac{1}{2}x$

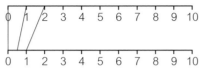

  b What value maps to 10?

16 The first of three **consecutive** whole numbers is x.

  a Write expressions for the next two numbers: x, $x + \square$, $x + \square$.

  b Write and simplify an expression for the sum of the three numbers.

17 Here is a function machine.

  a Write an expression for the function machine.

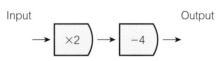

  b What is the value of the output when the input is

    i 5

    ii 1

    iii 0

  c What number, when you input it, will give the same output as the input?

18 Work out the missing values in this function machine.

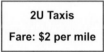

Is there more than one solution to this question?

19 Look at these advertisements.

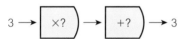

2U Taxis
Fare: $2 per mile

A 2 B Taxis
Fare: $4 per passenger + $1 per mile

  a Work out the cost of a 10-mile journey with 3 passengers with each company.

  b For each company write a formula for calculating the cost of a journey, T, with distance d and number of passengers p.

  c Which company is cheaper for 2 passengers to travel 15 miles?

  d A journey with 2U costs $40. What distance was the journey?

  e A journey for 2 passengers with A2B costs $40.
    What distance was the journey?

20 **Reflect** What kinds of jobs involve using formulae?
What careers are you interested in? Do you think you will need to use formulae in your job? How? What professionals are you likely to meet who might use formulae in their work?

3 Unit test

1 Simplify by collecting like terms.

   a $x + 2x$

   b $6x + 2y - 3x$

   c $10 + 12y + 7 - 14y$

2 To change between hours and minutes use the formula

   minutes = number of hours × 60

   Work out the number of minutes in 7 hours.

3 The formula for calculating the perimeter of a shape, P, is $P = 2a + 3b$.
   Work out the value of P when $a = 5$ and $b = 7$.

4 Use the formula $m = \dfrac{c}{100}$ for changing centimetres, c, to metres, m.
   Work out the value of m when $c = 325$.

5 Expand

   a $3(x + 4)$

   b $5(x - 7)$

   c $7(10 - x)$

6 Write an expression for

   a 2 less than y

   b 5 times m

   c y divided by 10

   d x more than y.

7 Angela is paid £10 more than Imogen.
   Write a formula connecting the amount Angela is paid, A, and the amount
   Imogen is paid, I.

8 Write an expression for

   a b multiplied by itself

   b double b

   c a divided by b.

9 Work out the value of each expression when $p = 3$ and $q = 6$.

   a $2(p + 3)$

   b $5(2p + q)$

10 When $a = 5$, $b = 11$ and $c = 9$ work out the value of
   a $4a + 2c$
   b $20 - 3a$
   c $10c - 2b + a$

11 Use the formula $D = \dfrac{n(n - 3)}{2}$ to work out the value of D when $n = 4$.

12 Use the formula $z = 2m - a$ to work out the value of z when
   a $m = 3$, $a = 5$
   b $m = 1$, $a = -7$

13 Simplify
   a $r \times r \times r \times r \times r$
   b $2 \times y \times 7 \times y \times y$
   c $3y \times y$
   d $3m \times 5m$
   e $18x \div 3$

14 Simplify by collecting like terms.
   a $3r^3 + 10r^3$
   b $12x + 3x^2 - 5x$

15 Expand
   a $x(x + 7)$
   b $r(r - 5)$
   c $2b(b + 5)$
   d $3b(2b - 4)$

16 Find the value of each expression when $b = 2$ and $m = 9$.
   a b^3
   b $b^2 - m$
   c $\dfrac{b + 2m}{2}$
   d $m^2 - b^2$
   e $3(m - b)$

Challenge

17 Are there any values of x that make these pairs of expressions equal?
   a $2x^2$ and $2x$
   b $6x - 3$ and $3x + 6$
   c $\dfrac{3x}{2}$ and $\dfrac{2x}{3}$
   d $2(3x + 5)$ and $2(3x - 5)$

18 **Reflect** Look back at the work you have done in this unit. Find a question
   that you could not answer immediately, but that you worked hard at, and then
   answered correctly.
   How do you feel when you find it difficult to answer a maths question?
   Write down the strategies you use to help you when you have difficulty.
   How do you feel when you eventually understand and get the correct answer?

Reflect

4.1 Working with fractions

You will learn to:
- Compare and simplify fractions.
- Write one number as a fraction of another.
- Work out simple fractions of amounts.

Why learn this?
You can compare fractions to find the best deals.

Fluency
What fraction of this rectangle is
- shaded
- unshaded?

Explore
What fraction of the stages in the Tour de France are mountain stages?

Confidence

Exercise 4.1

Warm up

1 Work out the highest common factor (HCF) of
 a 8 and 12 **b** 6 and 15
 c 7 and 35 **d** 24 and 40

2 Which fraction is larger in each pair?
 a $\frac{1}{2}$ or $\frac{1}{4}$ **b** $\frac{1}{5}$ or $\frac{1}{3}$
 c $\frac{1}{8}$ or $\frac{3}{8}$ **d** $\frac{5}{9}$ or $\frac{4}{9}$

3 Sort these fractions into pairs of **equivalent fractions**.
 $\frac{1}{4}$ $\frac{4}{5}$ $\frac{1}{2}$ $\frac{15}{20}$ $\frac{2}{8}$ $\frac{3}{4}$ $\frac{3}{6}$ $\frac{8}{10}$

4 Use the fraction wall to work out which is larger.
 Write < or > between each pair of fractions.
 a $\frac{2}{7} \square \frac{3}{8}$
 b $\frac{5}{6} \square \frac{3}{4}$
 c $\frac{1}{3} \square \frac{3}{7}$
 d $\frac{3}{5} \square \frac{1}{2}$

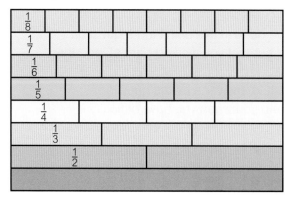

Key point

Equivalent fractions have the same value.

Q3 hint

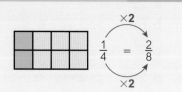

Q4 hint

> means 'is greater than' and < means 'is less than.'

Topic links: Pie charts, Area, Coordinates

5 Write these fractions in order of size. Start with the smallest.

$\frac{5}{8}$ $\frac{1}{2}$ $\frac{2}{5}$ $\frac{4}{7}$

6 **Problem-solving** Which is larger, $\frac{3}{4}$ or $\frac{7}{10}$?

7 **Problem-solving** Which is larger, $\frac{3}{4}$ or $\frac{4}{5}$?

8 Simplify

a $\frac{12}{20}$

b $\frac{9}{12}$

c $\frac{10}{15}$

d $\frac{5}{10}$

e $\frac{3}{9}$

f $\frac{14}{35}$

Q6 Strategy hint

Make two copies of this grid and shade in parts to compare. Use equivalent fractions to help you.

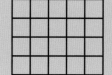

$\frac{3}{4} = \frac{\square}{20}$

$\frac{7}{10} = \frac{\square}{20}$

Key point

You can write a fraction in its **simplest form** by dividing the numerator and denominator by their highest common factor (HCF) to give an equivalent fraction.

Q8 Literacy hint

$5 \rightarrow$ __numerator__
$6 \rightarrow$ denominator

Q8a hint

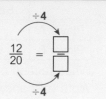

Discussion Is there more than one way to simplify $\frac{12}{20}$?

Investigation   Reasoning

a Copy and complete these equivalent fractions, and write each

fraction as a coordinate pair:

$\frac{1}{2}$, $\frac{2}{4}$, $\frac{3}{\square}$, $\frac{\square}{8}$, $\frac{5}{\square}$

(1, 2), (2, 4), (3, $\square$), ($\square$, 8), (5, $\square$)

b Copy the grid.

Plot all the coordinate pairs on the grid.
The first one has been done for you.

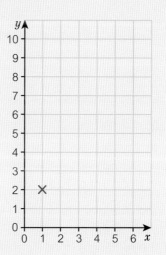

c Join together all the points you have plotted.
Discussion Why do you think all the points lie on a straight line?

d Go through parts **a** to **c** again, but this time with three fractions that are equivalent to $\frac{1}{3}$.

e **Discussion** Do think you will always have a straight line, whatever equivalent fractions you use?

9 A shop sells 18 rugby shirts. 9 of them are Harlequins shirts.
What fraction are Harlequins shirts?
Write your answer in its simplest form.

10 Out of the top 15 football clubs in Europe with the highest match attendance figures, 5 are British clubs.
What fraction of the top 15 clubs are British?
Write your answer in its simplest form.

Q9 hint

$\frac{\text{Harlequins shirts sold}}{\text{total shirts sold}}$

Simplify your fraction.

11 **STEM** The pie chart shows the composition of pink gold.
Write the fraction of pink gold that is
a gold
b copper
c silver.

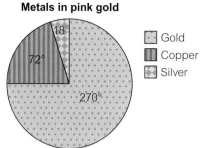

Metals in pink gold

Gold
Copper
Silver

Q11 hint

How many degrees are there altogether in a pie chart?
Simplify your answer.

12 **Real / Problem-solving** The table shows the number of games won by each player in each set of a match in a Wimbledon tournament.

	Set 1	Set 2	Set 3
Player A	4	3	2
Player B	6	6	6

What fraction of all the games in the match did Player B win?
Write your answer in its simplest form.

13 Work out

a $\frac{1}{2}$ of £40

b $\frac{1}{4}$ of 20 kg

c $\frac{1}{3}$ of 300 ml

d $\frac{1}{5}$ of 75 cm

Q13a hint

£40 ÷ 2 = …

14 Work out

a $\frac{3}{4}$ of £80

b $\frac{3}{5}$ of 35 m

c $\frac{2}{3}$ of 150 mm

d $\frac{4}{9}$ of 27 kg

Q14a hint

To work out $\frac{3}{4}$ of a number, first work out $\frac{1}{4}$, then multiply by 3.

15 Which is larger, $\frac{2}{3}$ of 18 m or $\frac{5}{6}$ of 24 m?

16 **Problem-solving** A rectangle is 12 cm long and 5 cm wide.
Ibrahim shades $\frac{7}{10}$ of the rectangle.
What area of the rectangle does Ibrahim shade?

17 **Explore** What fraction of the stages in the Tour de France are mountain stages?
Is it easier to explore this question now you have completed the lesson?
What further information do you need to be able to answer this?

18 **Reflect** After this lesson John says, 'Fractions are not really like whole numbers.'
Farooq says, 'Yes! Fractions can be written in many different ways.'
Look back at your work on fractions.
What do you think John means?
What do you think Farooq means?

Q18 hint

List all the ways you think fractions are not like whole numbers.
List all the different ways you can write fractions.

Explore

Reflect

4.2 Adding and subtracting fractions

You will learn to:
- Write an improper fraction as a mixed number.
- Add and subtract fractions.

Confidence

Why learn this?
Engineers add and subtract fractions when they calculate the size of bolts needed to join different pieces of metal.

Fluency
Sort these fractions into their equivalent pairs.
$\frac{5}{10}$ $\frac{2}{3}$ $\frac{16}{24}$ $\frac{1}{2}$

Explore
Can you add different unit fractions to get 1 whole?

Exercise 4.2

1 Write each fraction in its simplest form.
  a $\frac{4}{8}$
  b $\frac{3}{9}$
  c $\frac{6}{10}$
  d $\frac{12}{14}$

2 Work out the lowest common multiple (LCM) of
  a 2 and 3
  b 5 and 10
  c 6 and 8

3 Work out these divisions. Write each answer as a whole number and a remainder.
  a $8 \div 3$
  b $12 \div 5$
  c $18 \div 4$
  d $31 \div 2$

4 How many
  a quarters are in 1
  b fifths are in 1
  c thirds are in 1
  d tenths are in 1?

5 Which is larger, $1\frac{4}{5}$ or $\frac{11}{5}$?

6 Write these improper fractions as mixed numbers.
  a $\frac{7}{4}$
  b $\frac{12}{5}$
  c $\frac{31}{7}$
  d $\frac{23}{3}$

Key point

A **unit fraction** has numerator 1. For example, $\frac{1}{2}, \frac{1}{3}$ and $\frac{1}{4}$ are unit fractions.

Q3a hint

$10 \div 3 = 3$ remainder $\square$

Key point

A **mixed number** has a whole number part and a fraction part.
In an **improper fraction** the numerator is greater than the denominator.
A fraction greater than 1 can be written as a mixed number or an improper fraction.

Q6a hint

$7 \div 4 = 1$ remainder 3, so $\frac{7}{4} = 1\frac{\square}{4}$

Warm up

7 Work out

a $\frac{1}{3} + \frac{1}{3}$

b $\frac{3}{7} + \frac{3}{7}$

c $\frac{8}{11} - \frac{3}{11}$

d $1 - \frac{3}{5}$

8 Work out these. Give each answer in its simplest form.

a $\frac{2}{9} + \frac{1}{9}$

b $\frac{7}{12} - \frac{5}{12}$

9 **Problem-solving** Karl adds together two different fractions with the same denominator. He simplifies his answer and gets $\frac{2}{5}$.
Write down two fractions that Karl may have added.

Discussion What method did you use to solve this problem?

10 Work out these. Give each answer in its simplest form.

a $\frac{3}{10} + \frac{2}{5}$

b $\frac{11}{12} - \frac{3}{4}$

c $\frac{4}{9} + \frac{1}{3}$

d $\frac{7}{10} - \frac{1}{5}$

11 **Real** An engineer bolts together a piece of metal that has a thickness of $\frac{3}{8}$ inch and a piece of wood that has a thickness of $\frac{5}{16}$ of an inch.
What is the total thickness of the metal and wood when they are bolted together?

12 Ahmed has eaten $\frac{5}{12}$ of his pizza. Dom has eaten $\frac{5}{6}$ of his.
How much more has Dom eaten?

13 Work out these. Give your answers as mixed numbers.

a $\frac{5}{6} + \frac{2}{3}$

b $\frac{4}{9} + \frac{13}{18}$

c $\frac{3}{4} + \frac{11}{16}$

d $\frac{1}{3} + \frac{8}{9}$

Key point

When two fractions have the same denominator, add or subtract by adding or subtracting the numerators.

Q7a hint

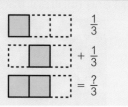

$$\frac{1}{3}$$
$$+ \frac{1}{3}$$
$$= \frac{?}{3}$$

Key point

When you add or subtract fractions with different denominators, first write them as equivalent fractions with the same denominator (**common denominator**).

Q10a hint

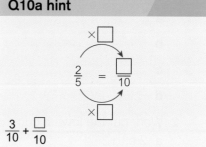

$$\frac{2}{5} = \frac{\square}{10}$$

$$\frac{3}{10} + \frac{\square}{10}$$

14 Problem-solving The diagram shows four fractions linked by lines.

$$\frac{3}{10} \quad \frac{13}{20}$$
$$\frac{22}{40} \quad \frac{2}{5}$$

   a Work out the total of any two linked fractions.
   b Which two fractions give the greatest total?
      Work out this total and write it as a mixed number in its simplest form.
   c Work out the difference between any two linked fractions.
   d Which two fractions give you the greatest difference?
      Work out this difference and write it in its simplest form.
   Discussion How did you work out your answers to parts **b** and **d**?

15 Work out these. Give each answer in its simplest form, and as a mixed number where necessary.
   a $\frac{1}{2} + \frac{2}{12} + \frac{1}{4}$
   b $\frac{3}{5} + \frac{3}{20} + \frac{1}{2}$
   c $\frac{5}{8} + \frac{7}{16} - \frac{1}{4}$
   d $\frac{26}{30} - \frac{2}{5} - \frac{4}{15}$

<table>
<tr><td>Q15a hint</td></tr>
<tr><td>$\frac{1}{2} + \frac{2}{3} + \frac{3}{4} + \frac{\square}{12} + \frac{\square}{12} + \frac{\square}{12}$</td></tr>
</table>

16 Answer these questions in fractions of an hour.
   a On Monday, Katherine spends $\frac{3}{4}$ of an hour on maths homework and $\frac{1}{2}$ an hour on French homework.
      How long does she spend doing homework on Monday?
   b On Wednesday, she spends $\frac{2}{3}$ of an hour on art homework and 15 minutes on creative writing.
      How long does she spend doing homework on Wednesday?

Investigation   **Problem-solving**

Two fractions add to $\frac{1}{4}$.
What could the fractions be?
Find at least four different pairs.

17 Explore Can you add different unit fractions to get 1 whole? Is it easier to explore this question now you have completed the lesson? What further information do you need to be able to answer this?

18 Reflect Look back at Q10.
What steps did you take to work out these calculations?
You might begin with 'Step 1: I looked at the denominators and…'.

Explore

Reflect

4.3 Fractions, decimals and percentages

Confidence

You will learn to:
- Work with equivalent fractions, decimals and percentages.
- Use division to write a fraction as a decimal.

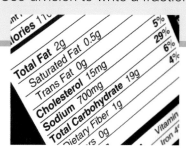

Why learn this?
Proportions can be given as fractions, decimals or percentages.

Fluency
Which of these are equivalent?

$\frac{1}{2}$ $\frac{1}{4}$ $\frac{3}{4}$ $\frac{1}{10}$

0.1   0.25   0.5   0.75

75%   10%   50%   25%

Explore
Which vegetables contain the greatest percentage of water?

Exercise 4.3

Warm up

1 Copy and complete.

   a $\frac{1}{5} = \frac{\square}{10}$ **b** $\frac{2}{5} = \frac{\square}{10}$ **c** $\frac{3}{5} = \frac{\square}{10}$

2 Work out
   a $8\overline{)7}$ **b** $20\overline{)9}$

3 What fraction of an hour is 25 minutes?

4 Copy and complete this table.

Fraction		$\frac{1}{5}$		$\frac{3}{10}$			$\frac{3}{5}$			$\frac{4}{5}$	
Decimal			0.25			0.5		0.7				0.9
Percentage	10%			40%					75%			

Q4 hint

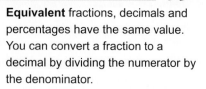

$$10\% = \frac{1}{10}$$
$$\times 2 \left(\right) \times 2$$
$$20\% = \frac{\square}{10}$$

5 Copy and complete this table.

Mixed number	$1\frac{3}{4}$					$1\frac{2}{5}$
Decimal		1.5			1.7	
Percentage			130%	120%		

Discussion What does it mean when people say 'house prices have increased by 200%'?

6 **Finance** A newspaper article states

> A business increased its profits by 250%.

   a Write 250% as a mixed number.
   b The business originally made a profit of £182 000.
      What is the increase in the profits in pounds?

7 Write these fractions as decimals.
   a $\frac{4}{5}$ **b** $\frac{3}{20}$ **c** $\frac{12}{16}$ **d** $\frac{15}{8}$ **e** $\frac{24}{60}$

Key point

Equivalent fractions, decimals and percentages have the same value. You can convert a fraction to a decimal by dividing the numerator by the denominator.

Key point

When a positive mixed number is greater than 1, its decimal equivalent is greater than 1, and its percentage equivalent is greater than 100%. For example, $1\frac{1}{4} = 1.25 = 125\%$

Topic links: Bar charts   **Subject links:** Science (Q9)

8 In a rugby match the Cardiff Blues won 13 out of the 20 line-outs.
   a What fraction of the line-outs did they win?
   b Write your answer to part **a** as a decimal.
   c What percentage of the line-outs did they win?

9 **STEM / Modelling** A new medicine was tested on 5 groups of people. The table shows the number of people in each group and the number of people successfully treated.

Group	A	B	C	D	E
Number in group	150	200	80	350	420
Number successfully treated	132	182	68	320	382

   a What fraction of each group was successfully treated?
   b Shaya says, 'There is about a 0.9 success rate for each group.'
      Do you agree with Shaya? Explain your answer.

10 **Problem-solving** The bar chart shows the number of slices of cake sold one day in a café. Steve thinks that approximately 45% of the slices of cake sold were carrot cake. Is Steve correct? Explain your answer.

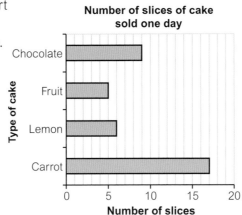

Number of slices of cake sold one day

Q10 Strategy hint
Work out the fraction of cake sold that was carrot cake. Then convert the fraction to a decimal, then a percentage.

11 Use the fact that $\frac{1}{4}$ = 0.25 to work out these fractions as decimals.
   a $\frac{1}{8}$
   b $\frac{1}{16}$
   c $\frac{1}{32}$

Q11 hint

$$\frac{1}{4} = 0.25$$
$$\div 2 \left(\right) \div 2$$
$$\frac{1}{8} = \square$$

12 Use the fact that $\frac{1}{100}$ = 0.01 to write these fractions as decimals.
   a $\frac{1}{200}$
   b $\frac{1}{400}$
   c $\frac{1}{50}$
   d $\frac{1}{25}$

Q12 hint

$$\frac{1}{100} = 0.01$$
$$\times 2 \left(\right) \times 2$$
$$\frac{1}{50} = \square$$

13 **Explore** Which vegetables contain the greatest percentage of water? Is it easier to explore this question now you have completed the lesson?
   What further information do you need to be able to answer this?

14 **Reflect** After this lesson Hillary says, 'Decimals are just another way of writing fractions.' Do you agree with Hillary? Explain.

Explore

Reflect

4.4 Multiplying by a fraction

You will learn to:
- Multiply a fraction by a whole number.
- Multiply a fraction by a fraction.

Why learn this?
Some medicine doses for children are fractions of adult doses. Doctors need to calculate with fractions to make sure they prescribe the right amount.

Fluency
What are the missing numbers?
- $4 \times 5 = 5 \times \square$
- $3 \times 8 = \square \times 3$

Explore
The half-life of a radioactive atom is the length of time it takes for half of the atoms to decay. If there are 100 radioactive atoms and the number halves every hour, how long until there are fewer than 2 atoms left?

Confidence

Warm up

Exercise 4.4

1 Work out

a $\frac{1}{4}$ of £120 **b** $\frac{1}{5}$ of 45 m

c $\frac{2}{3}$ of 18 cm **d** $\frac{5}{9}$ of 36 kg

2 Write each fraction in its simplest form.
$$\frac{4}{6}, \frac{12}{15}, \frac{16}{28}, \frac{35}{50}$$

Worked example

Work out $\frac{2}{3}$ of 12 m.

$\frac{1}{3}$ of 12 m = 12 ÷ 3 = 4 m

$\frac{2}{3}$ of 12 m = 2 × 4 = 8 m

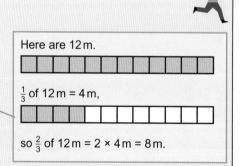

Here are 12 m.

$\frac{1}{3}$ of 12 m = 4 m,

so $\frac{2}{3}$ of 12 m = 2 × 4 m = 8 m.

Key point

When you work out a fraction of a quantity, you divide the quantity by the denominator, and then multiply by the numerator.

3 Work out

a $\frac{4}{5}$ of 30 **b** $\frac{2}{3}$ of 90 **c** $\frac{2}{7}$ of 42 **d** $\frac{3}{10}$ of 10

e $10 \times \frac{2}{5}$ **f** $45 \times \frac{1}{9}$ **g** $16 \times \frac{7}{8}$ **h** $22 \times \frac{4}{11}$

Discussion How are you using multiplying and dividing in these calculations? Does it make a difference if you use the operations the other way around?

Key point

In maths, $\frac{3}{4}$ of 100 is the same as $\frac{3}{4} \times 100$.

Q3e hint

$10 \times \frac{2}{5}$ is the same as $\frac{2}{5} \times 10$.

4 Work out the areas of these shapes. Simplify your answers.

a

$\frac{5}{6}$ m

4 m

b

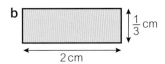

$\frac{1}{3}$ cm

2 cm

c

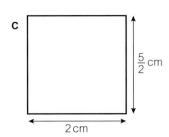

$\frac{5}{2}$ cm

2 cm

Worked example

Work out $\frac{3}{4} \times \frac{1}{2}$

$\frac{3}{4}$ of $\frac{1}{2}$

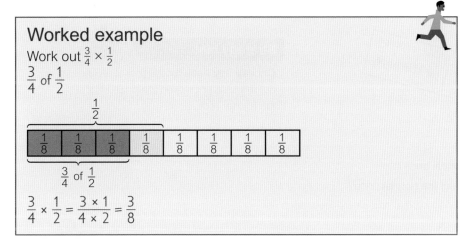

$$\frac{3}{4} \times \frac{1}{2} = \frac{3 \times 1}{4 \times 2} = \frac{3}{8}$$

Key point

To multiply two fractions, multiply their numerators and multiply their denominators.

5 Work out these multiplications. Use the fraction wall to check your answers.

1											
$\frac{1}{3}$				$\frac{1}{3}$				$\frac{1}{3}$			
$\frac{1}{6}$		$\frac{1}{6}$		$\frac{1}{6}$		$\frac{1}{6}$		$\frac{1}{6}$		$\frac{1}{6}$	
$\frac{1}{2}$						$\frac{1}{2}$					
$\frac{1}{12}$	$\frac{1}{12}$	$\frac{1}{12}$	$\frac{1}{12}$	$\frac{1}{12}$	$\frac{1}{12}$	$\frac{1}{12}$	$\frac{1}{12}$	$\frac{1}{12}$	$\frac{1}{12}$	$\frac{1}{12}$	$\frac{1}{12}$
$\frac{1}{4}$			$\frac{1}{4}$			$\frac{1}{4}$			$\frac{1}{4}$		
$\frac{1}{8}$		$\frac{1}{8}$		$\frac{1}{8}$		$\frac{1}{8}$		$\frac{1}{8}$		$\frac{1}{8}$	$\frac{1}{8}$

a $\frac{1}{2} \times \frac{1}{3}$

b $\frac{1}{4} \times \frac{2}{3}$

c $\frac{2}{5} \times \frac{1}{2}$

d $\frac{2}{3} \times \frac{2}{3}$

6 Work out the areas and perimeters of these squares.

a $\frac{1}{2}$ m

b $\frac{3}{4}$ cm

c $\frac{1}{4}$ m

7 In 2012, $\frac{1}{20}$ of a council's members were from minority ethnic groups.

Of these, $\frac{1}{3}$ were women.
What proportion of the council were minority ethnic women?

Investigation   **Problem-solving**

These are the tickets on a jacket that is reduced in price in a sale.

Sale Price! $\frac{1}{3}$ off normal price

Further reduction! $\frac{1}{4}$ off sale price

Strategy hint

Choose any price for the jacket. Work out the sale price then the price after the further reduction.

1 What is the total fraction off the normal price?

2 What is the final price as a fraction of the normal price?

3 Investigate other calculations involving normal and sale prices, such as $\frac{1}{2}$ off normal price then $\frac{3}{4}$ off sale price.
How can you work out the total fraction off for any pair of fractions?

---

8 Explore The half-life of a radioactive atom is the time it takes for half of the atoms to decay.
If there are 100 radioactive atoms and the number halves every hour, how long until there are fewer than 2 atoms left?
Is it easier to explore this question now you have completed the lesson?
What further information do you need to be able to answer this?

9 Reflect Write down two new things you have learned in this lesson.
Write down the questions that used these new things.
When you answered these questions, did you make any mistakes?
If so, check that you understand where you went wrong.

4.5 Working with mixed numbers

Confidence

You will learn to:
- Add and subtract mixed numbers.
- Multiply a mixed number by a fraction.

Why learn this?
Recipes often use mixed numbers when describing the volume of ingredients.

Fluency
Which of these calculations will give an answer larger than 1?
- $\frac{1}{2} + \frac{1}{3}$
- $\frac{1}{2} + \frac{1}{4}$
- $\frac{1}{2} + \frac{3}{4}$
- $\frac{1}{2} + \frac{2}{3}$

Explore
A recipe for 4 brownie cakes requires $1\frac{1}{2}$ tablespoons of sugar. How much sugar would be needed to make 10 brownies?

Exercise 4.5

1 Work out

   a $\frac{1}{3} + \frac{2}{5}$ **b** $\frac{7}{8} - \frac{5}{6}$ **c** $\frac{2}{3} \times \frac{3}{5}$

2 Write each improper fraction as a mixed number.

   a $\frac{5}{3}$

   b $\frac{7}{2}$

   c $\frac{9}{5}$

   d $\frac{16}{7}$

3 Write these improper fractions as decimals.

   a $\frac{13}{4} = 3.\square\square$

   b $\frac{11}{5}$

   c $\frac{36}{10}$

> **Q3 hint**
> Write as a mixed number first. Then write the fraction part as a decimal.

4 Work out these additions. Write your answer in its simplest form.

   a $2\frac{3}{4} + 1\frac{1}{8} = 3 + \frac{3}{4} + \frac{1}{8} = 3 + \frac{\square}{8} + \frac{1}{8}$

   b $11\frac{3}{5} + 9\frac{2}{15}$

   c $3\frac{7}{10} + 2\frac{3}{5} = 5 + \frac{7}{10} + \frac{3}{5} = \square$

   d $1\frac{2}{3} + 3\frac{5}{6}$

   e $3\frac{3}{6} + 2\frac{2}{3}$

   f $4\frac{3}{4} + 7\frac{7}{16}$

> **Key point**
> When you add mixed numbers, add the whole numbers first, then add the fraction parts.

> **Q4c hint**
> $\frac{7}{10} + \frac{6}{10} = \frac{\square}{10}$

Warm up

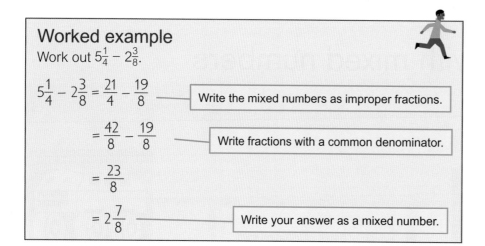

Worked example

Work out $5\frac{1}{4} - 2\frac{3}{8}$.

$$5\frac{1}{4} - 2\frac{3}{8} = \frac{21}{4} - \frac{19}{8}$$ — Write the mixed numbers as improper fractions.

$$= \frac{42}{8} - \frac{19}{8}$$ — Write fractions with a common denominator.

$$= \frac{23}{8}$$

$$= 2\frac{7}{8}$$ — Write your answer as a mixed number.

Discussion Why didn't the worked example subtract the whole numbers first, then the fraction parts?

5 Work out these subtractions. Write each answer in its simplest form.

a $4\frac{2}{3} - 2\frac{1}{6}$ **b** $5\frac{6}{10} - 3\frac{1}{2}$ **c** $7\frac{15}{24} - 4\frac{5}{12}$ **d** $3\frac{1}{3} - 1\frac{3}{6}$

e $5\frac{1}{4} - 3\frac{5}{8}$ **f** $10\frac{2}{5} - 7\frac{10}{15}$ **g** $9\frac{8}{28} - 6\frac{3}{4}$

6 Here are some mixed number cards.

$6\frac{5}{7}$ $8\frac{7}{12}$ $4\frac{9}{13}$ $3\frac{5}{6}$ $8\frac{1}{2}$

Work out the range.

7 Work out these. The first one has been started for you.
Write each answer in its simplest form.

a $3\frac{1}{2} \times 5 = \frac{7}{2} \times 5 = \frac{7 \times 5}{2} = \square\frac{\square}{2}$

b $8 \times 3\frac{5}{12}$

c $2\frac{1}{4} \times \frac{2}{3}$

d $\frac{4}{7} \times 2\frac{4}{5}$

> **Key point**
>
> When you multiply a mixed number by a fraction, start by writing the mixed number as an improper fraction.

8 **Problem-solving** Work out the area of the brown section of this rectangle.

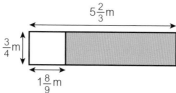

$5\frac{2}{3}$ m

$\frac{3}{4}$ m

$1\frac{8}{9}$ m

9 **Explore** A recipe for 4 brownies requires $1\frac{1}{2}$ tablespoons of sugar. How much sugar would be needed to make 10 brownies? Is it easier to explore this question now you have completed the lesson? What further information do you need to be able to answer this?

10 **Reflect** What is the same when you calculate with fractions or with mixed numbers?
What is different?

ActiveLearn Homework, Year 7, Unit 4   **Topic links:** Area

4 Check up

Equivalence

1 Which is larger, $\frac{5}{8}$ or $\frac{7}{10}$?

2 Write each fraction in its simplest form.

  a $\frac{6}{12}$ **b** $\frac{16}{24}$

3 A shop sells 30 pairs of flip-flops (plastic beach shoes) in one day.
  10 pairs are men's flip-flops.
  What fraction of the flip-flops sold are men's?
  Write your answer in its simplest form.

4 Work out these. Give each answer in its simplest form.

  a $\frac{1}{6} + \frac{2}{3}$ **b** $\frac{1}{3} + \frac{2}{9}$

  c $\frac{4}{5} - \frac{3}{10}$ **d** $\frac{11}{15} - \frac{2}{3}$

5 Copy and complete this table.

Fraction		$\frac{2}{5}$		$\frac{7}{10}$			$3\frac{1}{5}$
Decimal			0.5			2.75	
Percentage	25%			150%			

6 The table shows some students' favourite sport.

Favourite sport	Football	Tennis	Athletics	Rugby	Hockey
Number of students	32	12	5	14	17

  What fraction of the students chose football as their favourite sport?
  Write your answer in its simplest form.

7 Write these fractions as decimals.

  a $\frac{7}{8}$ **b** $\frac{22}{5}$

Multiplying fractions

8 Work out
  a $\frac{1}{4}$ of £20   **b** $\frac{2}{5}$ of 25 kg

9 Work out $21 \times \frac{6}{7}$.

10 Mr Jones orders $\frac{4}{5}$ of a lorry load of gravel (small stones).
  The lorry holds 20 tonnes of gravel when full.
  How much does Mr Jones order?
  Write your answer as a mixed number in its simplest form.

11 Calculate the area of the square.

$\frac{4}{5}$ cm

12 $\frac{1}{5}$ of the students in a class have green eyes.

$\frac{1}{2}$ of the students with green eyes are boys.

What fraction of the class are boys with green eyes?

13 Work out $\frac{2}{3} \times \frac{9}{10}$

14 A recipe for soup requires $\frac{2}{3}$ of a litre of water per person.
How much water is needed to make soup for 9 people?

Working with mixed numbers

15 Work out these additions. Write your answers in their simplest form.

    a $3\frac{2}{3} + 6\frac{1}{6}$ **b** $4\frac{5}{6} - 3\frac{1}{3}$

16 Work out $9 \times 3\frac{1}{5}$

17 A rectangle is $5\frac{2}{3}$ cm long and $\frac{2}{3}$ cm wide.
Work out

    a the perimeter

    b the area of the rectangle.

18 **How sure are you of your answers? Were you mostly**

  😞 **Just guessing**   😐 **Feeling doubtful**   🙂 **Confident**

What next? Use your results to decide whether to strengthen or extend your learning.

Challenge

19 Here are some fraction cards and money cards.

Aleesha arranges the cards like this:

Which cards does she use to get

    a the largest possible answer

    b the smallest possible answer?

$$\boxed{\tfrac{?}{?}} \text{ of } \boxed{\$\square} + \boxed{\tfrac{?}{?}} \text{ of } \boxed{\$\square} =$$

20 In this addition pyramid each number is made by adding the two numbers below it. Work out the missing numbers.

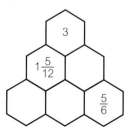

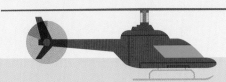

4 Strengthen

You will:
* Strengthen your understanding with practice.

Equivalence

1 Write each fraction in its simplest form.
The first one has been started for you.

a $\frac{2}{4} = \frac{\square}{\square}$

b $\frac{12}{16}$

c $\frac{25}{30} = \frac{?}{?}$

d $\frac{15}{40}$

e $\frac{24}{33}$

> **Q1b hint**
>
> Start by dividing both numbers by 2, then check to see if you can divide again.

2 Out of a group of 32 students, 12 are girls.
Complete the workings to show the fraction of the students who are girls.

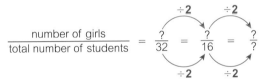

$$\frac{\text{number of girls}}{\text{total number of students}} = \frac{?}{32} = \frac{?}{16} = \frac{?}{?}$$

3 There are 15 dogs in a dog training class. 5 of them are collies.
What fraction of the dogs are
  a collies
  b not collies?
Give each answer in its simplest form.

> **Q3a hint**
>
> $\frac{\text{number of collies}}{\text{total number of dogs}}$

4 The table shows favourite ice cream flavours.

Favourite flavour	Vanilla	Chocolate	Caramel	Strawberry	Other
Number of students	24	8	12	16	4

  a Work out the total number of students.

  b What fraction of the students chose these flavours as their favourite?
    i chocolate
    ii vanilla
Write each answer in its simplest form.

5 Copy and complete these equivalent fractions, decimals and percentages.

a $\times 3 \Big(\begin{array}{l} \frac{1}{4} = 0.25 = 25\% \\ \frac{3}{4} = \square = \square\% \end{array} \Big) \times 3$

b $\times 2 \Big(\begin{array}{l} \frac{1}{5} = 0.2 = 20\% \\ \frac{2}{5} = 0.4 = \square\% \end{array} \Big) \times 2$

$\frac{3}{5} = 0.6 = \square\%$

$\frac{4}{5} = \square = \square\%$

c $\frac{1}{10} = 0.1 = 10\%$ $\frac{2}{10} = 0.2 = \square\%$ $\frac{3}{10} = 0.3 = \square\%$

$\frac{4}{10} = \square = \square\%$ $\frac{5}{10} = \square = \square\%$ $\frac{6}{10} = \square = \square\%$

$\frac{7}{10} = \square = \square\%$ $\frac{8}{10} = \square = \square\%$ $\frac{9}{10} = \square = \square\%$

6 Use your answers to Q5 to complete this table.

Fraction	$1\frac{1}{2}$	$1\frac{2}{5}$			
Decimal			2.5	2.6	
Percentage					310%

Q6 hint

$1\frac{1}{4} = 1.\square\,\square$

7 Write these fractions as decimals.
The first one has been started for you.

a $\frac{1}{8} = 1 \div 8$

$1 \div 8 = 8 \overline{)1 . {}^1 0\ {}^2 0\ 0}$ $\begin{array}{c} 0 . 1\ \square\ \square \end{array}$

b $\frac{11}{8}$

c $\frac{9}{4}$

d $\frac{7}{20}$

Multiplying fractions

1 Work out

a $\frac{1}{3}$ of 15

b $\frac{2}{3}$ of 15

2 Work out

a $\frac{1}{5}$ of 20

b $\frac{2}{5}$ of 20

c $\frac{3}{5}$ of 20

d $\frac{4}{5}$ of 20

3 Work out

a $\frac{2}{3}$ of £18

b $\frac{3}{5}$ of 35 kg

c $\frac{5}{7}$ of 21 km

Q1 hint

£15

£5   £5   £5

Q3a hint

£18

$\frac{1}{3} = £6$ $\frac{1}{3} = £6$ $\frac{1}{3} = £6$

$\frac{2}{3}$

4 Work out

   a $\frac{2}{3} \times 39$ **b** $28 \times \frac{3}{7}$ **c** $32 \times \frac{5}{8}$

Q4a hint

$\frac{2}{3} \times 39 = \frac{2}{3}$ of 39

5 Here is a bar.

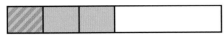

   $\frac{1}{2}$ of the bar is shaded pink.

   $\frac{1}{3}$ of the pink section is striped.

   a What fraction of the bar is pink **and** striped?

   b Complete $\frac{1}{3} \times \frac{1}{2} = \frac{\square}{\square}$

6 a Copy this bar.

   b Shade $\frac{1}{2}$ of the bar green.

   c Add stripes to $\frac{1}{4}$ of $\frac{1}{2}$ of the bar.

   d Complete $\frac{1}{4} \times \frac{1}{2} = \frac{\square}{\square}$

7 Use the bar models to help work out these multiplications.

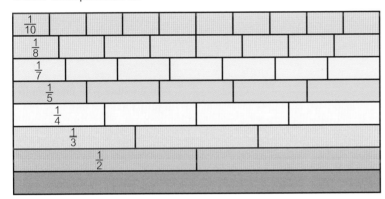

   a $\frac{1}{2} \times \frac{2}{3}$

   b $\frac{1}{2} \times \frac{1}{4}$

   c $\frac{1}{3} \times \frac{2}{5}$

   d $\frac{3}{5} \times \frac{1}{4}$

8 Work out

   a $\frac{1}{7} \times \frac{1}{2} = \frac{1 \times 1}{7 \times 2} = \frac{\square}{\square}$

   b $\frac{3}{5} \times \frac{2}{7} = \frac{\square \times \square}{\square \times \square} = \frac{\square}{\square}$

   c $\frac{3}{4} \times \frac{2}{5}$

   d $\frac{4}{5} \times \frac{5}{12}$

Q8 hint

Simplify your answers.

Working with mixed numbers

1 Write these mixed numbers as improper fractions.

   a $2\frac{1}{4}$ **b** $3\frac{1}{2}$ **c** $5\frac{2}{3}$

     $2\frac{3}{10}$ **e** $2\frac{5}{6}$ **f** $10\frac{3}{5}$

2 Write these improper fractions as whole numbers or mixed numbers.

   a $\frac{15}{3}$ **b** $\frac{12}{4}$ **c** $\frac{13}{4}$

   d $\frac{20}{6}$ **e** $\frac{10}{3}$ **f** $\frac{16}{7}$

3 Work out

   a $3\frac{1}{3} + 5\frac{5}{6} = \frac{\square}{3} + \frac{\square}{6} = \frac{\square}{6} + \frac{\square}{6} =$

   b $1\frac{3}{10} + 7\frac{4}{5}$ **c** $6\frac{1}{6} + 3\frac{13}{18}$ **d** $1\frac{3}{8} + 2\frac{5}{24}$

4 Work out

   a $4\frac{2}{3} - 1\frac{2}{9} = \frac{\square}{3} - \frac{\square}{9}$

   b $9\frac{5}{6} - 9\frac{1}{3}$ **c** $3\frac{3}{10} - 2\frac{4}{5}$ **d** $3\frac{3}{4} - 2\frac{1}{12}$

5 Work out

   a 2×3 **b** $2 \times \frac{1}{4}$ **c** $2 \times 3\frac{1}{4}$

6 Work out

   a $8 \times 2\frac{1}{5}$ **b** $6\frac{2}{3} \times 4$

Enrichment

1 Here are four fraction cards.

   a Which two fractions sum to $1\frac{1}{2}$?

   b Which two fractions will give the greatest total? What is that total?

   c Which two fractions will give the greatest difference? What is that difference?

2 Reflect: Look back at any questions you got wrong in the Check up. Were they mostly questions about
- equivalence
- multiplying fractions
- working with mixed numbers?

Now look back at the Strengthen questions you answered.
Write down one thing you now understand better.
Is there anything you still need help with? Ask a friend or your teacher to help you with it.

Q1a hint

How many quarters are there?

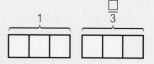

Q2a hint

How many wholes can you make from 5 thirds?

Q3c hint

Convert to improper fractions first. Simplify your answer.

Q4a hint

Convert to improper fractions first.

Q6c hint

Add together your answers to parts **a** and **b**.

Q1 hint

Adding gives the sum. Subtracting gives the difference.

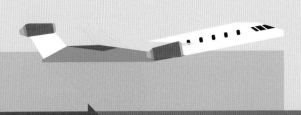

4 Extend

You will:
- Extend your understanding with problem-solving.

1 **Problem-solving / Reasoning** Here are six fractions.

$$\frac{15}{20} \quad \frac{30}{36} \quad \frac{19}{38} \quad \frac{28}{49} \quad \frac{34}{51} \quad \frac{36}{45}$$

Which fraction is the odd one out? Explain your answer.

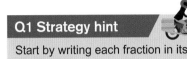

> **Q1 Strategy hint**
> Start by writing each fraction in its simplest form.

2 **Real** The recipe for a loaf of bread uses 150 g of rye flour, 150 g of barley flour and 100 g of rice flour.
  a What is the total mass of flour in the loaf?
  b What fraction of the flour used in the loaf is rice flour?
    Give your answer in its simplest form.

3 **Real / Problem-solving** The bar chart shows the composition of a piece of Cheddar cheese. The total mass of the piece of cheese is 120 g.

Composition of a 120 g piece of Cheddar cheese

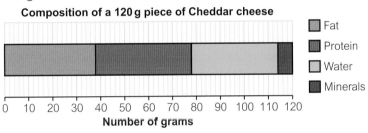

Fat
Protein
Water
Minerals

What fraction of the piece of cheese is protein?
Give your answer in its simplest form.

4 Copy and complete these fraction pyramids.
Each brick is the sum of the two bricks below it.

a

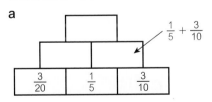

$\frac{1}{5} + \frac{3}{10}$

$\frac{3}{20}$ $\frac{1}{5}$ $\frac{3}{10}$

b

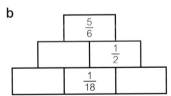

$\frac{5}{6}$

$\frac{1}{2}$

$\frac{1}{18}$

5 Here is a set of dominoes.

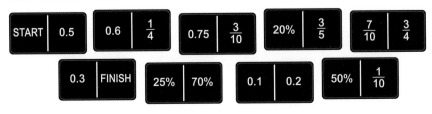

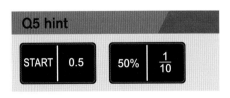

> **Q5 hint**
> | START | 0.5 | | 50% | $\frac{1}{10}$ |

Work out how to link the dominoes together. One domino can only touch another domino when they have an equivalent fraction, decimal or percentage.

6 STEM / Problem-solving The pie chart shows the composition of a fertiliser.

Composition of fertiliser

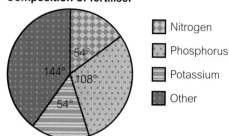

- Nitrogen
- Phosphorus
- Potassium
- Other

Work out the amount of nitrogen and the amount of phosphorus in 40 tonnes of fertiliser.

Q6 Strategy hint

Work out the fractions of fertiliser that are nitrogen and phosphorus first.

7 The rectangle contains four fractions and the oval contains four numbers.

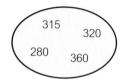

$\frac{5}{8}$ $\frac{3}{5}$ $\frac{7}{9}$ $\frac{4}{7}$

315   320   280   360

a Choose a fraction from the rectangle and multiply it by a number from the circle.

b Which fraction and number, when you multiply them together, will give you

  i the largest answer possible

  ii the smallest answer possible?

Q7a hint

$320 \times \frac{7}{9} = \frac{2240}{9}$

Write the improper fraction as a mixed number.

8 Reasoning

a Ali says, 'When you add two positive fractions, the answer is always bigger than the individual fractions.'

  Is Ali correct? Explain why.

b George says, 'When you subtract two positive fractions, the answer is always smaller than the individual fractions.'

  Is George correct? Explain why.

9 Reasoning Eleri writes the fraction $\frac{15}{16}$ as a decimal.

This is what she writes:

$$15\overline{)16\,.\,^{1}0\,^{10}0\,^{10}0\,^{10}0}\quad \begin{array}{c}1\,.\,0\;\,6\;\,6\;\,6\,\ldots\end{array}\quad \text{so } \frac{15}{16} = 1.0666\ldots$$

a Explain the mistake that Eleri has made.

b Work out the correct decimal equivalent of $\frac{15}{16}$.

10 Copy and complete to work out

a $1\frac{1}{2} + 2\frac{2}{3} + 3\frac{5}{6} = \frac{\square}{2} + \frac{\square}{3} + \frac{\square}{6} + = \frac{\square}{12} + \frac{\square}{12} + \frac{\square}{12} =$

b $7\frac{3}{4} + 5\frac{2}{9} - 4\frac{11}{12} = \frac{\square}{4} + \frac{\square}{9} - \frac{\square}{12} + = \frac{\square}{36} + \frac{\square}{36} - \frac{\square}{36} =$

Q10 hint

Simplify your answers.

11 Work out the perimeter of each shape.

a

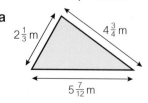

$2\frac{1}{3}$ m $4\frac{3}{4}$ m $5\frac{7}{12}$ m

b

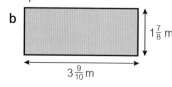

$1\frac{7}{8}$ m $3\frac{9}{10}$ m

12 STEM The Millennium Stadium in Cardiff is made from 4000 tonnes of concrete, 12 000 tonnes of structural steel and 40 000 tonnes of steel reinforcement.
What fraction of the stadium is made from
a concrete
b steel reinforcement?
Give each fraction in its simplest form.

13 STEM By volume, dry air contains approximately 78% nitrogen, 21% oxygen and the remainder is other gases and water vapour.
What fraction of dry air is
a nitrogen
b oxygen
c other gases and water vapour?
Give each fraction in its simplest form.

Q13a hint

$78\% = \dfrac{\square}{100}$

14 What fraction of 1 hour is
a 30 minutes
b 15 minutes
c 45 minutes
d 10 minutes
e 5 minutes
f 1 minute?
Give each fraction in its simplest form.

15 Ellie exercises for 45 minutes every day.
How many hours in total does she exercise in March?

16 You can work out the distance, in miles, a car travels using the formula
    distance = average speed × time
Work out the distance a car travels when
a average speed = 60 miles per hour and time = 1 hour 30 minutes
b average speed = 50 miles per hour and time = 2 hours 45 minutes
c average speed = 48 miles per hour and time = 4 hours 10 minutes
d average speed = 62 miles per hour and time = 3 hours 24 minutes

Q16 hint

Enter the time as a mixed number on your calculator

17 Reasoning
a Work out
    i $\frac{1}{2}$ of $30 and then $\frac{1}{3}$ of the answer
    ii $\frac{1}{3}$ of $30 and then $\frac{1}{2}$ of the answer.

Q17a hint

$\frac{1}{2}$ of $30 = $\square$, $\frac{1}{3}$ of $\square$ = $\square$

    iii What do you notice about your answers to parts i and ii?
        What is the overall fraction of $30 that you have found?
        How can you combine $\frac{1}{2}$ and $\frac{1}{3}$ to give you this overall fraction?
b Work out
    i $\frac{3}{4}$ of $80 and then $\frac{2}{5}$ of the answer
    ii $\frac{2}{5}$ of $80 and then $\frac{3}{4}$ of the answer.

    iii What is the overall fraction of $80 that you have found?
        How can you combine $\frac{2}{5}$ and $\frac{3}{4}$ to give you this overall fraction?
c Will your method for **a iii** and **b iii** work for any fraction of an amount followed by a fraction of an amount?

18 Sort these cards into groups that give the same answer.

$9\frac{13}{30} - 6\frac{9}{10}$ $4\frac{2}{5} - 2\frac{1}{4}$ $5\frac{17}{20} - 3\frac{7}{10}$ $5\frac{19}{36} - 3\frac{7}{9}$ $8\frac{2}{3} - 6\frac{2}{15}$ $7\frac{2}{3} - 5\frac{11}{12}$

19 Problem-solving Copy and complete this calculation.

$$\square\tfrac{\square}{\square} - \square\tfrac{\square}{\square} = 4\tfrac{1}{5}$$

20 Reasoning Hassan says, 'When you multiply a positive number by a fraction less than 1, your answer will always be smaller than the number you started with.'
Is Hassan correct? Explain why.

21 Finance / Problem-solving Martha spends $\frac{1}{4}$ of her pocket money on food.
She spends $\frac{3}{5}$ of what is left on clothes. She saves the rest.
What fraction of her money does she save?

22 a i Copy and complete.

$100 \div 4 = 25$

$100 \div 2 = 50$

$100 \div 1 = 100$

$100 \div \frac{1}{2} = 200$

$100 \div \frac{1}{4} = \frac{\square}{\square}$

$100 \div \frac{1}{8} = \frac{\square}{\square}$

ii Describe any pattern you notice.

b i Copy and complete.

$1 \div \frac{1}{2} = 2$

$2 \div \frac{1}{2} = 4$

$3 \div \frac{1}{2} = \square$

$4 \div \frac{1}{2} = \square$

$5 \div \frac{1}{2} = \square$

ii Describe any pattern you notice.

> **Q22b i hint**
>
> $1 \div \frac{1}{2}$ can be read as 'How many $\frac{1}{2}$ s are there in 1?'

Investigation

Reasoning

1 Work out $1 + \frac{1}{2}$ **2** Work out $1 + \frac{1}{2} + \frac{1}{3}$ **3** Work out $1 + \frac{1}{2} + \frac{1}{3} + \frac{1}{4}$

4 Look at this sum of fractions: $\frac{1}{1} + \frac{1}{2} + \frac{1}{3} + \frac{1}{4} + \frac{1}{5} + \frac{1}{6} + \frac{1}{7} + \frac{1}{8} + \dots + \frac{1}{x}$

    a Explain what happens to the sum of the series as x gets bigger and bigger.
    b How many fractions must be added to get a sum greater than 3?
    c Will the sum ever be greater than 4? Explain your answer.

---

23 Reflect The word 'fraction' is used in lots of ways. For example,
- In everyday English, a fraction means 'a small amount'. For example, when hanging a picture 'move it up a fraction', or you might ask someone to 'budge up a fraction' so you can sit beside them.
- In chemistry, the fractionating process separates a mixture into its components.

Write a definition, in your own words, of 'fraction' in mathematics.
What do you think 'fractional ownership' means? When might it be a good idea?

Topic links: Bar charts, Pie charts, Rounding, Perimeter, Mean

Reflect

4 Unit test

1 Write each fraction in its simplest form.

$\frac{6}{9}$ $\frac{7}{14}$ $\frac{9}{12}$ $\frac{25}{30}$ $\frac{24}{40}$

2 There are 40 chocolates in a box. 15 of the chocolates contain nuts.
What fraction of the chocolates contain nuts?
Write down your answer in its simplest form.

3 Write these amounts in order of size, starting with the smallest.

$\frac{1}{5}$ of 100 $\frac{2}{3}$ of 36 $\frac{6}{7}$ of 21

4 A chef uses $\frac{3}{5}$ of a 750 ml container of cooking oil.
How much cooking oil does the chef use?
Write your answer as a mixed number in its simplest form.

5 Work out these. Write each answer in its simplest form.

a $\frac{1}{8} + \frac{3}{4}$ **b** $\frac{1}{3} + \frac{5}{12}$ **c** $\frac{21}{25} - \frac{1}{5}$ **d** $\frac{9}{10} - \frac{2}{5}$

6 Write $\frac{27}{4}$ as a mixed number.

7 Write $6\frac{7}{10}$ as an improper fraction.

8 Work out

a $\frac{4}{9} \times 27$ **b** $36 \times \frac{5}{12}$

9 Copy and complete this table.

Fraction		$\frac{4}{5}$		$\frac{3}{10}$			$6\frac{2}{5}$
Decimal			0.75			4.7	
Percentage	50%			125%			

10 Write $\frac{17}{5}$ as a decimal.

11 Work out these. Write each answer in its simplest form.

a $5\frac{3}{4} + 2\frac{5}{8}$ **b** $1\frac{2}{15} + 1\frac{2}{3}$ **c** $8\frac{8}{9} - 4\frac{1}{3}$ **d** $3\frac{9}{14} - 3\frac{1}{2}$

12 The table shows the amounts of money raised for charity by a scout group.

Event	Cake sale	Concert	Sponsored swim	Quiz night
Amount	£75	£165	£250	£160

What fraction of the money was raised at the sponsored swim?
Write your answer in its simplest form.

13 A piece of paper is $\frac{1}{10}$ of a mm thick. A ream (packet) of paper contains 500 sheets.
Work out the thickness (in cm) of a ream of paper.

14 In a triathlon competition a competitor must
  run 10 km
  swim 1500 m
  cycle 40 km.
Work out the fraction of the total distance spent swimming.

15 $\frac{2}{3}$ of the students in a class have a mobile phone.

$\frac{2}{5}$ of the students who have a mobile phone have a tablet.

Work out the fraction of the class who have a tablet.

16 Work out $5\frac{2}{15} + 6\frac{1}{5} - 3\frac{2}{3}$
Write your answer in its simplest form.

17 Work out these multiplications.

a $\frac{5}{8} \times \frac{4}{7}$

b $\frac{2}{5} \times \frac{3}{8}$

18 Work out $5 \times 2\frac{2}{3}$

Challenge

19 This rectangle has a perimeter of $10\frac{5}{6}$ cm.
Work out the area of the rectangle.
Give your answer as a fraction in its simplest form.

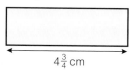
$4\frac{3}{4}$ cm

20 Work out the missing values in each calculation.

a $1\frac{3}{10} + \square\frac{\square}{4} = 6\frac{1}{20}$

b $\frac{5}{9} \times \frac{\square}{15} = \frac{7}{27}$

c $3\frac{1}{5} - \frac{\square}{\square} = 2\frac{9}{20}$

21 **Reflect** In this unit, did you work
  • slowly
  • average speed
  • quickly?
Did you find the work easy, OK or hard?
How did that affect how fast you worked?
Is it always good to work quickly? Explain.
Is it always bad to work slowly? Explain.

5.1 Working with angles

You will learn to:
- Use a protractor to measure and draw angles.
- Solve problems involving angles.
- Work out unknown angles when two or more lines cross at a point.

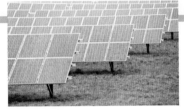

Why learn this?
Solar panels must be set at a specific angle to collect the most energy from the Sun.

Fluency
Which of these angles is acute? obtuse? reflex?
- 137°
- 88°
- 291°

What do angles on a straight line add up to? What is
- 180 – 110
- 360 – 250?

Explore
At what angle from the horizontal should a solar panel be set to collect the most energy?

Exercise 5.1

1 Write down the size of each angle.

a

b

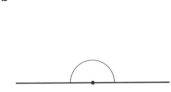

2 Sketch an angle that is
  a acute
  b obtuse
  c reflex.

3 What is the size of each angle marked with a letter?

Q3 hint

Read up from 0 on the correct scale.

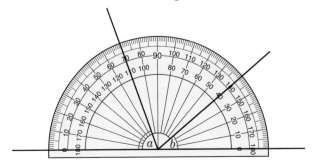

4 Look at each angle.

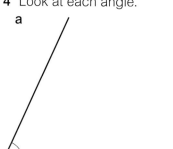
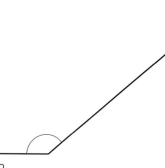

a   b

  i Is the angle acute, obtuse or reflex?
  ii Estimate the size of the angle.
  iii Measure the angle to the nearest degree.

5 Isabel needs to measure these angles to the nearest degree.

a   b

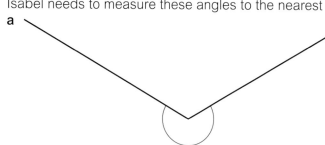
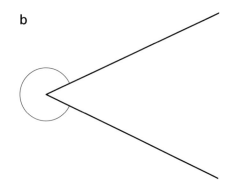

Copy and complete Isabel's work.

a smaller angle = 120°, so marked angle = 360° − 120° = ☐
b smaller angle = ☐, so marked angle = ☐

Discussion Why do you subtract the smaller angle from 360°?

6 Use a protractor to draw these angles.
The first one has been started for you.
 a 60°
 b 75°
 c 100°
 d 145°

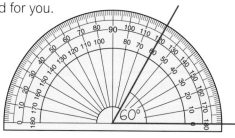

7 **Reasoning** Ismail says that to draw a 220° angle you begin by
drawing a 140° angle.
 a Explain why Ismail is correct.
 b Draw and label an angle of 220°.

8 **Real / STEM** A study looked at the best position
for sitting at a desk. One seating position is shown.
 a Draw angles to show 90° and 135° seating positions.
 b Which seating position do you think is best? Explain.

less than 70°

9 **Real** Safety regulations state that ladders should be placed at 75°
from the horizontal. Draw a diagram to show this angle accurately.

Q4 hint

Place the cross of the protractor on
the point of the angle. Line up the
zero line with one line of the angle.
Read up from 0 on the correct scale.

10 a Draw two lines crossing like the ones shown here.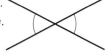

b Measure one acute angle and the angle opposite. What do you notice?

c Measure the other two **vertically opposite** angles. What do you notice?

d Repeat for another two sets of crossing lines.

e Copy and complete this rule.
Vertically opposite angles are _____

Discussion Do everybody's angles fit the rule?
Is this enough evidence to show that the rule is true?

11 Reasoning Work out the angles marked with letters. Give your reasons.

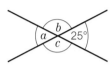

Worked example

Work out the angles marked with letters. Give a reason for each answer.

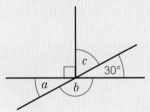

You need to write a reason.

$a = 30°$ (vertically opposite angles are equal)
$b = 180° - 30° = 150°$ (angles on a straight line add up to 180°)
$c = 360° - 90° - 30° - 150° - 30° = 60°$
(angles at a point add up to 360°)

---

12 Reasoning Work out the angles marked with letters. Give reasons for your answers.

a

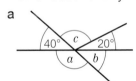

b

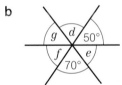

c

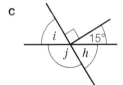

13 Explore At what angle from the horizontal should a solar panel be set to collect the most energy?
Look back at the maths you have learned in this lesson.
How can you use it to answer this question?

14 Reflect Look back at Q4.
First you estimated the size of the angles, and then you measured them accurately.
Why is estimating first a good strategy?
Write other maths topics where you have used this strategy.
Why is it a good strategy for other maths topics?
Can you use this strategy in other subjects too? Explain.

Explore

Reflect

5.2 Triangles

You will learn to:

- Describe the line and rotational symmetry of triangles.
- Use properties of a triangle to work out unknown angles.
- Understand how to prove that a result is true.
- Use the properties of isosceles and equilateral triangles to solve problems.

Confidence

Why learn this?
The isosceles shape of a step ladder makes it strong and stable.

Fluency
Work out

- 180° − 40° − 40°
- 180° − 35° − 110°
- 55° + □ = 180°

What is the missing angle?

Explore
What is the angle at the top of a folding ladder?

Exercise 5.2

Warm up

1 **a** For each triangle say whether it is equilateral, isosceles or scalene.
   b Which angles are equal?

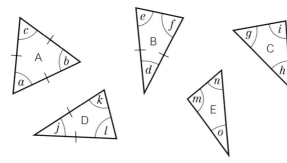

Key point

A **line of symmetry** divides a shape into two halves that fit exactly on top of each other.
The **order of rotational symmetry** of a shape is the number of times it exactly fits on top of itself when rotated a full turn.

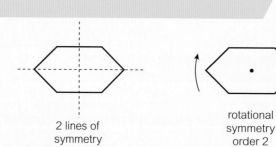

2 lines of symmetry

rotational symmetry order 2

2 Copy and complete this table showing the number of lines of symmetry and order of rotational symmetry of triangles.

Triangle	Equilateral	Isosceles	Scalene
number of lines of symmetry			
order of rotational symmetry			

3 Reasoning Work out the unknown angle in each triangle.
Give a reason for each answer.

a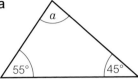

b

c

Q3a hint

$a = \square$
Angles in a triangle add up to $\square°$

4 Reasoning Work out the angles marked with letters.
Give a reason for each step.

a

b

c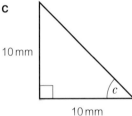

d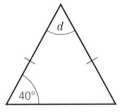

Q4 Strategy hint

Explain how you know each triangle is isosceles.
Next, identify the two equal base angles.

5 Problem-solving One angle of an isosceles triangle is 100°.
What are the other two?

6 Work out the angles marked by letters.
Give a reason for each answer.

a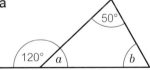

b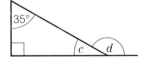

Key point

An **interior angle** is inside a shape.
An **exterior angle** is outside the shape on a straight line with the interior angle.

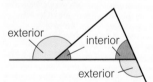

c

7 a Copy and complete the table for triangles **a**, **b** and **c** in Q6.

	a	b	c
exterior angle	120°		
sum of opposite interior angles	50° + □ = □		

Q7a hint

b What do you notice about the **exterior angle** and opposite **interior angles**?

8 **Reasoning** Prove that an exterior angle of a triangle is equal to the sum of the opposite interior angles.

The exterior angle e is opposite the two interior angles b and c.
You must prove that $e = b + c$.
Copy and complete this proof.
$e + a = □°$ because they lie on a _____
$b + c + a = □°$ because the angles in a triangle sum to $□°$.
This proves that $e = b + c$.
Discussion Why does the last statement follow from the other two statements?

Key point

Showing that a rule works for a few values is not enough. You need to **prove** it works for *all* values. A **proof** uses logical reasoning to show a rule is true.

9 **Reasoning a** What are the interior angles of an equilateral triangle? Give a reason for your answer.
   b What is the exterior angle of an equilateral triangle? Give a reason for your answer.

Q9 Strategy hint

Draw a diagram.

10 **Reasoning** Work out the angles marked with letters. Give a reason for each step.

a
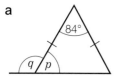

b
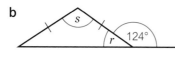

c
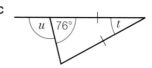

11 **Problem-solving / Reasoning** The diagram shows the front of a tent.

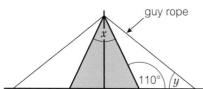

Q11 Strategy hint

Sketch a diagram. Write on the diagram each angle you work out.

Two equal guy ropes hold up the central pole.
a Work out angle x.
b The angle between the two guy ropes is 100°. Work out angle y.
c Work out the angle the guy rope makes with the side of the tent.

12 **Explore** What is the angle at the top of a folding ladder? Is it easier to explore this question now you have completed the lesson? What further information do you need to answer this?

13 **Reflect** After this lesson Safia says, 'I measured all the angles in three different triangles and they all add up 180°.'
Do you think Safia's statement proves that the angles in all triangles add up to 180°?

Explore

Reflect

5.3 Quadrilaterals

You will learn to:
- Describe the line and rotational symmetry and the properties of quadrilaterals.
- Understand how to prove that angles of a quadrilateral add up to 360°.
- Solve problems involving quadrilaterals.

Why learn this?
Quadrilaterals will help you draw 3D shapes.

Fluency
- What is the sum of angles in a triangle? Or in a quadrilateral?
- How many sides does a quadrilateral have?

Explore
What is the quickest way to draw a kite? Or a rhombus?

Exercise 5.3

1 How many lines of symmetry does each shape have?

a   b   c   d

2 Use a protractor. Which lines cross at a right angle?

a   b   c   d

3 Copy and complete this table showing the number of lines of symmetry and the order of rotational symmetry of these quadrilaterals.

Quadrilateral	Square 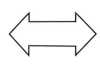	Rectangle	Parallelogram	Rhombus	Kite	Arrowhead	Trapezium	Isosceles trapezium
number of lines of symmetry								
order of rotational symmetry								

4 Sketch each shape in Q3.
- Mark equal sides with dashes. Use double dashes for a second pair of equal sides.
- Mark equal angles with arcs. Use double arcs for a second pair of equal angles.
- Mark right angles.
- Mark parallel sides with arrows. Use double arrows for a second pair of parallel sides.

The arrowhead has been done for you.

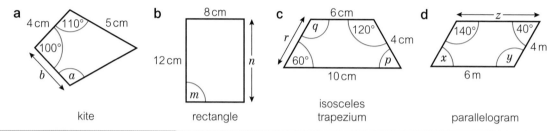

Arrowhead

line of symmetry means sides and angles are equal.

Discussion What can you say about opposite angles in a parallelogram? Is this the same for a rhombus?

Q4 hint

Use line and rotational symmetry to find equal sides and angles.

5 Work out the angles and sides marked with letters.

a 4 cm, 110°, 5 cm, 100°, b, a — kite

b 8 cm, 12 cm, n, m — rectangle

c 6 cm, q, 120°, r, 4 cm, 60°, 10 cm, p — isosceles trapezium

d z, 140°, 40°, x, y, 4 m, 6 m — parallelogram

Investigation

Reasoning

Sketch these quadrilaterals: square, rectangle, parallelogram, rhombus and kite.
1 Draw the **diagonals**.
2 Use line and rotational symmetry to find equal lengths and angles. Mark them on your diagram.
3 Do any of the diagonals **bisect** each other?
4 Copy and complete this table to show the properties of the quadrilaterals.

Quadrilateral	Diagonals bisect each other	Diagonals bisect the interior angles	Diagonals cross at right angles

6 Work out the angles and sides marked with letters.

a f, e — square

b 8 cm, 5 cm, p, q, 12 cm — parallelogram

c x, y, 80° — rhombus

Literacy hint

A **diagonal** is a straight line joining two opposite corners (**vertices**) of a shape.
Bisect means to cut in half.

Q6 hint

Use the table in the investigation.

7 Reasoning A square is a special type of rectangle.
  a Copy and complete this sentence.
    A rectangle is a special type of _____
  b Write two more sentences like this about different shapes.

8 Problem-solving
  a What shape am I?
    i I have two pairs of equal angles and two pairs of parallel sides.
    ii My diagonals cross at right angles and I have two pairs of equal sides.
    iii My opposite sides are parallel and my diagonals divide me into four identical triangles.
    iv I have two pairs of equal sides and one line of symmetry.
  b Write your own description of a shape for your classmates to work out.

Topic links: Algebra

9 Reasoning Prove that the angles of a quadrilateral add up to 360°.
Prove that $a + b + c + d = 360°$.
Copy and complete this proof. Give a reason for each statement.
$p + r + c = \square°$ because the angles in a triangle sum to $\square°$.
$q + s + d = \square°$ because the angles in a triangle sum to $\square°$.
$p + q + r + s + c + d = \square° + \square° = \square°$
$a + b + c + d = 360°$ because $a = p + q$ and $b = r + s$
This proves that the angles in a quadrilateral sum to $\square°$.

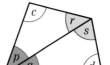

10 a Work out $\angle BCD$.

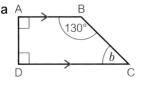

b Work out $\angle JML$.

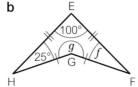

11 Reasoning For each shape

a
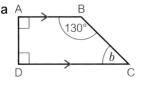

b
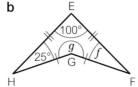

c
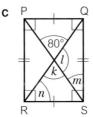

d
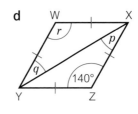

  i name the shape
  ii work out the angles marked with letters. Give a reason for each answer. The first one has been started for you.

12 Work out the angles marked with letters. Give reasons for each answer.

a
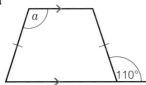

b
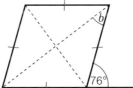

c
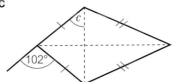

13 Explore What is the quickest way to draw a kite? a rhombus?
Is it easier to explore this question now you have completed the lesson?
What further information do you need to be able to answer this?

14 Reflect Frankie says that to identify a shape, he begins by asking himself:
• Are its sides straight?
• Are any sides equal lengths?
• Are the equal sides next to each other, or opposite?
Write down all the questions you ask yourself to identify a shape.
Test your questions on some quadrilaterals. Can you improve your questions?
Compare your questions with other people's. Can you improve your questions any more?

5.4 Construction

You will learn to:
* Draw triangles accurately using a ruler and a protractor.
* Draw diagrams to scale.

Confidence

Why learn this?
Mapmakers and surveyors use accurate scale drawings to work out positions of objects.

Fluency
What can you say about the sides and symmetries of
* an equilateral triangle
* an isosceles triangle?

Explore
How is triangulation used to make maps?

Exercise 5.4

Warm up

1 Draw each of these lines accurately.
  a 7 cm
  b 8.2 cm
  c 46 mm

2 On a **scale drawing** 1 cm represents 1 m.
  Use a ruler to draw a line to represent 4 m.

3 Draw these angles accurately.

  a
  27°

  b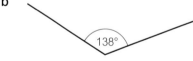
  138°

> **Key point**
>
> A **scale** of 1 cm to 1 m means that 1 cm on the **scale drawing** represents 1 m in real life.

4 For each triangle
   i use a ruler and protractor to draw the triangle accurately
   ii measure the length of side BC and write it on your diagram
   iii measure angles ABC and BCA and write them on your diagram.

  a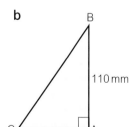
  B
  8 cm
  A 50° C
  10 cm

  b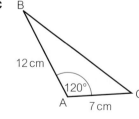
  B
  110 mm
  C 80 mm A

  c B
  12 cm
  120°
  A 7 cm C

> **Strategy hint**
>
>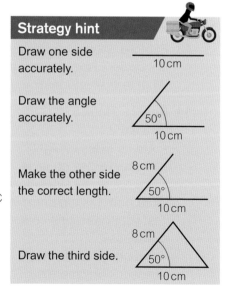
>
> Draw one side accurately.
> 10 cm
>
> Draw the angle accurately.
> 50°
> 10 cm
>
> Make the other side the correct length.
> 8 cm
> 50°
> 10 cm
>
> Draw the third side.
> 8 cm
> 50°
> 10 cm

5 Triangle PQR is a right-angled triangle with PQ = 3 cm, QR = 7 cm and ∠PQR = 90°.
   a Draw a sketch of this triangle.
   b Make an accurate drawing of the triangle.

6 a Draw accurately an isosceles triangle DEF with DE = DF = 12 cm and angle EDF = 32°.
   b Measure and write the length of EF.

Q6 hint

Sketch the triangle first.

7 **Reasoning** The diagram shows a water ski jump.

2.5 m

7 m

   a Make an accurate scale drawing of the water ski jump. Use a scale of 1 cm to 1 m.
   b Measure the marked angle the jump makes with the horizontal.
   c **i** Measure the sloping length of the scale drawing.
      ii Work out the sloping length of the actual jump.

Q7a hint

Scale drawing   Real life

×☐   1 cm   is   1 m   ×☐
         is   7 m

8 For each triangle
   i use a ruler and protractor to draw the triangle accurately
   ii measure the missing sides and write them on your diagram
   iii measure the missing angle and write it on your diagram.

Q8a hint

Draw lines at 40° and 70° to AC.
Point B is where the two lines cross.

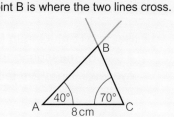

A   40°   70°   C
        8 cm

a

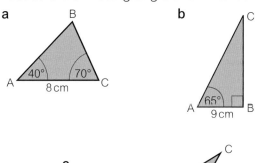

B

A   40°   70°   C
      8 cm

b

C

A   65°   ⌐   B
      9 cm

c

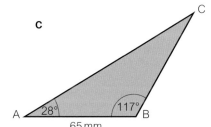

C

A   28°   117°   B
        65 mm

9 Triangle ABC is a right-angled triangle with AB = 55 mm, ∠BAC = 70° and ∠ABC = 70°.
   a Draw a sketch of this triangle.
   b Make an accurate drawing of the triangle.
   c What type of triangle have you drawn?

10 STEM / Problem-solving This is a common roof truss.

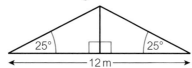

a Make an accurate drawing of the truss.
Use 1 cm to represent 1 m in real life.
b Ray needs a truss with a height of 4 m.
Is this truss big enough? Explain your answer.

Q10b Strategy hint

Measure the central height of the truss. Work to the nearest metre.

11 Problem-solving Use a ruler and protractor to draw each quadrilateral accurately.

a
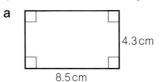
4.3 cm
8.5 cm

b
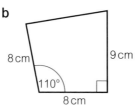
8 cm   9 cm
110°
8 cm

c
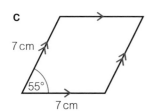
7 cm
55°
7 cm

d
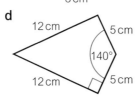
12 cm   5 cm
140°
12 cm   5 cm

Q11c, d Strategy hint

Sketch the quadrilateral first.
Use your knowledge of quadrilaterals to label the angles and sides on your sketch.

12 Real / STEM Gareth uses a **clinometer** to work out the height of a tree by measuring the angle between the top of the tree and his eye level. He is 2 m tall.

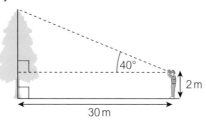
40°
2 m
30 m

Make a scale drawing of the right-angled triangle and work out the height of the tree. Use a scale of 1 cm to 2 m.

Q12 Literacy hint

A **clinometer** is a tool used to measure the angle from the horizontal in a right-angled triangle.

Q12 hint

Don't forget to add Gareth's height to the height of the triangle.

13 Explore How is triangulation used to make maps?
Is it easier to explore this question now you have completed the lesson?
What further information do you need to be able to answer this?

14 Reflect Rhianne says, 'You can draw a triangle with any length sides, as long as they aren't negative.'
Give an example to show that Rhianne is wrong.

Explore

Reflect

5 Check up

Working with angles

1 a What type of angle is shown?

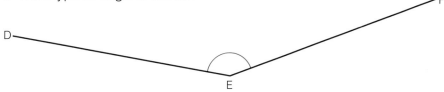

b Use a protractor to measure the angle to the nearest degree.

2 The diagram shows an angle.
Kevin measures the angle.
He says, 'The angle is 120°.'
Is he correct? Explain your answer.

3 Use a protractor to draw an angle of 115°.

4 Work out the angles marked with letters. Give reasons for your working.

a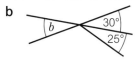

b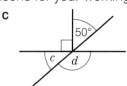

c

Triangles and quadrilaterals

5 Work out the angles marked with letters. Give a reason for each answer.

a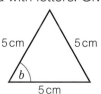

b

6 Work out the angles marked with letters. Give a reason for each answer.

a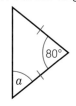

b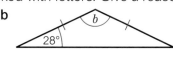

7 The diagram shows a flag on a pole. Work out angle x.
Give a reason for your answer.

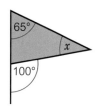

8 The diagram shows an isosceles trapezium.
  a Copy the diagram.
    Draw on any lines of symmetry.
  b Mark the equal sides, equal angles and parallel lines.
  c What is the order of rotational symmetry of an isosceles trapezium?

9 Name the two quadrilaterals whose diagonals bisect each other at right angles.

10 Work out the angles marked with letters.
  Give reasons for your working.

  a 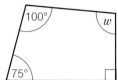   **b**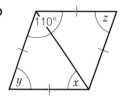

Accurate drawings

11 **a** Make an accurate drawing of this triangle.
  b Measure angle ACB.
  c What type of triangle have you drawn?

12 **Real** The diagram shows a wheelchair ramp.

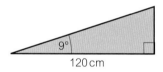

  a Make an accurate scale drawing of the ramp.
    Use a scale of 1 cm to 10 cm.
  b Measure the sloping length of the scale drawing.
  c Work out the sloping length of the actual ramp.

13 **How sure are you of your answers? Were you mostly**
  😟 **Just guessing**   😐 **Feeling doubtful**   🙂 **Confident**
  What next? Use your results to decide whether to strengthen or extend your learning.

Challenge

14 The diagram shows hexagons drawn on squared paper.

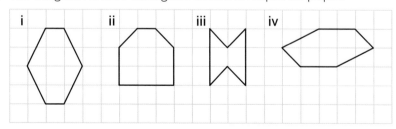

  a Describe the line symmetry of each hexagon.
  b Describe the rotational symmetry of each hexagon.
  c Draw a different hexagon with no symmetry.
  d Draw three pentagons with different line and rotational symmetry.
  e Draw four octagons with different line and rotational symmetry.

Q14a and b hint

☐ lines of symmetry
rotational symmetry order ☐

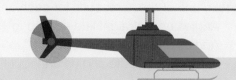

5 Strengthen

You will:
• Strengthen your understanding with practice.

Working with angles

1 Read the size of each angle from the protractor.

a

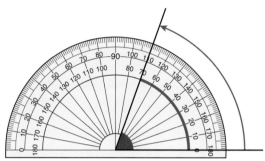

b

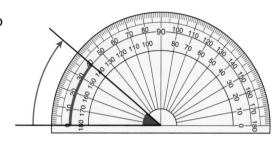

2 Mehdi uses a protractor to measure angle ABC.
He says, 'Angle ABC is 40°.'
Without using a protractor, can you say
whether or not he is correct?
Give a reason for your answer.

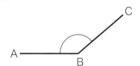

> **Q2 hint**
>
> What type of angle is angle ABC?

3 Use a protractor to measure these angles.

a   b

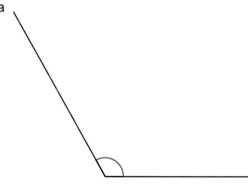

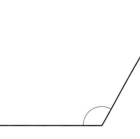

> **Q3 hint**
>
> Place the cross of the protractor on
> the point of the angle.
> Line up the zero line with one line of
> the angle.

4 Work out the angles marked with letters.

a   b

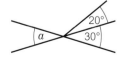

> **Q4 hint**
>
> Which two lines are crossing in an X
> shape?
>
>

5 Work out the angles marked with letters.
Choose one of these reasons for each answer:
- Angles on a straight line add up to 180°.
- Angles at a point add up to 360°.
- Vertically opposite angles are equal.

Q5 hint

You don't have to work out the angles in alphabetical order.

a   **b** 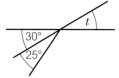 **c** 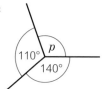 **d**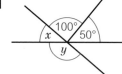

Triangles and quadrilaterals

1 Work out the angles marked with letters.
Give a reason for each answer.

Q1a hint

The angles in a triangle add up to 180°. Start with 180° and subtract the other angles.
$x = 180 - 80 - \square = \square°$
(angle sum of a triangle)

a 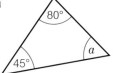 **b** 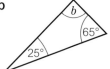 **c**

2 Work out angle x for each quadrilateral.

Q2a hint

Start with
$x = 360 - 110 - \square - \square = \square°$
(angle sum of a quadrilateral)

a 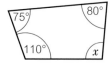 **b** 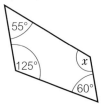 **c**

3 All of these triangles are isosceles. Work out the angles marked with letters. Give a reason for each answer.

Q3 hint

The two angles at the base of the equal sides of an isosceles triangle are equal.

a 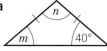 **b**   **c**

d   **e**

4 a Which is the exterior angle, x or y?
b Work out the size of angle x.
Give reasons for your working.
c Work out the size of angle y.
Give reasons for your working.

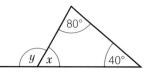

5 Work out the angles marked with letters.

Q5 hint

Follow the method in Q4.

a 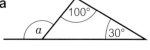 **b**   **c**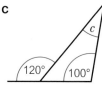

6 Copy these quadrilaterals.

  a Draw the lines of symmetry using dashed lines.

square   rectangle   parallelogram   rhombus   kite   trapezium   isosceles trapezium   arrowhead

  b Which quadrilaterals have rotational symmetry of
    i order 2   **ii** order 1?

7 The dashed lines are lines of symmetry. Use the symmetry of each shape to find equal angles. Work out the angles marked with letters.

  a 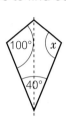   **b** 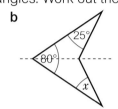   **c**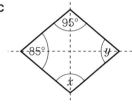

8 a Work out the angles marked with letters.
  b Copy and complete this sentence.
    Opposite angles of a parallelogram are _____

9 Look at each quadrilateral.

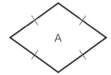   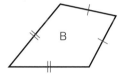

  a What type of quadrilateral is it?
  b Sketch each quadrilateral and mark equal angles using arcs.
    Use double arcs for a second pair of equal angles.

10 Work out the angles marked with letters.
    $a = \Box°$ (opposite angles of a parallelogram)
    $b = \Box°$ (angles on a straight line)
    $c = \Box°$ (angle sum of a triangle)

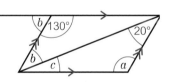

Accurate drawings

1 a Use a ruler and protractor to draw this angle.
  b Join points B and C to make a triangle.

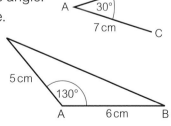

2 a Use a ruler to draw a line of length 6 cm. Label it AB.
  b Use a protractor to draw an angle of 130° at point A.
  c Draw in the other lines needed to complete this triangle accurately.

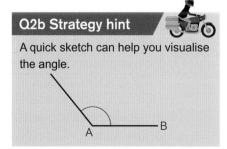

3 Use a ruler and protractor to draw each triangle accurately.

  a 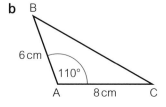   **b** 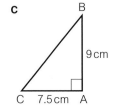   **c**

Q6 hint

Use a mirror to check for line symmetry.
Use tracing paper to check for rotational symmetry.

Q7 hint

Look at Q6 to work out what shapes they are first.

Q8 hint

Does the parallelogram have rotational symmetry?
Which angles must be equal?

Q9b hint

Draw lines of symmetry to find the equal angles.

Q2b Strategy hint

A quick sketch can help you visualise the angle.

Q3 Strategy hint

Draw the angle first.

4 Use a ruler and protractor to draw each triangle accurately.

a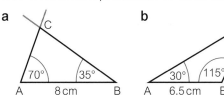

b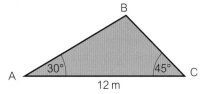

c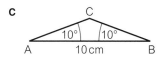

5 The diagram shows a sketch of a roof.

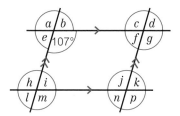

Make an accurate scale drawing of the roof. Use a scale of 1 cm to represent 1 m.

a Copy and complete.

b Follow the steps to draw the roof accurately.

   i Draw a line ___ cm long

   ii Measure an angle 30° at the left edge of the line.

   iii Measure an angle 45° at the right end of the line.

   iv Extend each line until they cross.

Enrichment

1 The diagram shows a parallelogram with all the sides extended.

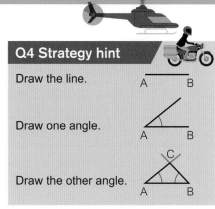

a Use your knowledge of angles on a straight line, vertical angles and angles around a point to find all the missing angles.

b Make a copy of the diagram and colour all the angles the same size in the same colour.

c Describe any patterns you notice.

2 **Reflect** These Strengthen lessons cover the topics:
- working with angles
- triangles and quadrilaterals
- accurate drawings.

Which topic did you find easiest?

Write down one thing about this topic you fully understand and you are sure about.

Which topic did you find hardest?

Write down one thing about this topic you still do not understand, or you are not sure about.

Q4 Strategy hint

Draw the line. A ——— B

Draw one angle. A ◿ B

Draw the other angle. A ◿ B (C)

Q5 hint

Scale drawing		Real life
×☐ ⤸	1 cm is	1 m ⤸ ×☐
	is	12 m

Q2 hint

Show what you have written down to a friend or your teacher. Ask them to help you with the topic you are not sure about.

5 Extend

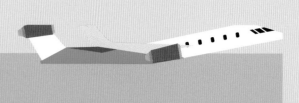

You will:
- Extend your understanding with problem-solving.

1 **Problem-solving** This pattern is a combination of three identical red rhombus tiles and three identical blue rhombus tiles.

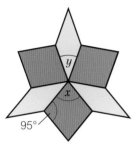

   a Work out angle x.
   b Work out angle y. Show your working.

2 **Problem-solving / Reasoning**
   a Measure angles to decide which triangles in the diagram are isosceles, which triangles are scalene and which are right-angled.
   b What shape is
      i EGCF
      ii ABCD?

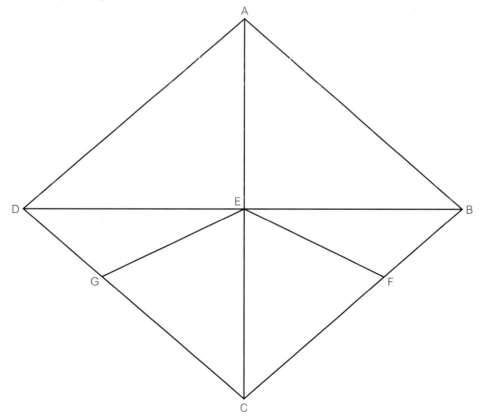

3 Reasoning Work out all of the angles.
Give reasons for your answer.

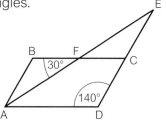

a ABCD is a parallelogram.
AFE is a straight line.
Angle BFA = 30°
Angle CDA = 140°

b ABCD is a kite. ABE and DCE
are both straight lines.
Angle BCE = 85°
Angle ADC = 65°

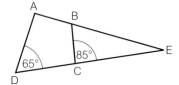

4 Reasoning The diagram shows four identical quadrilaterals.

a Write down the angle sum of the quadrilateral.
$$a + \Box + \Box + \Box = \Box°$$

b Use your answer to part **a** to explain why the quadrilaterals
fit exactly together at the point marked with a red dot.

5 Problem-solving a Draw two identical equilateral triangles joined
together along one of their sides. What shape have you made?

b Repeat part **a** for two identical

  i isosceles triangles   **ii** right-angled triangles.

Discussion How many different quadrilaterals can you make in
part **b**?

6 Work out the angles marked with letters. Give a reason for each step
in your answer.

a

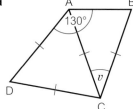

b

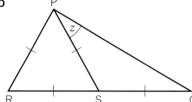

7 Work out angle x. Give a reason for each step in your answer.

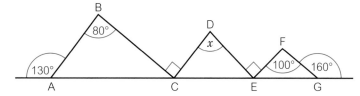

8 Problem-solving Work out the angle between the hands of
a clock at

  a 5 o'clock   **b** 7 o'clock   **c** half past 8   **d** half past 4.

9 Work out the size of
each unknown angle.

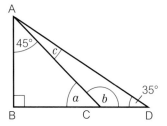

10 Work out the size of angle x in each diagram.

a   b 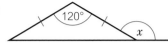   c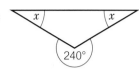

d 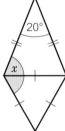   e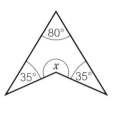

Discussion Why can a triangle never have a reflex angle but a quadrilateral can?

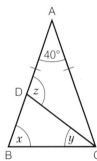

11 Problem-solving In triangle ABC, AB = AC and angle CAB = 40°.
Line DC bisects angle ACB.
Work out the sizes of angles x, y and z.

12 Decide whether each of these statements is always true, sometimes true or never true.
a A rhombus is a parallelogram.
b A parallelogram is a square.
c A kite is a rectangle.
d A rectangle is a rhombus.
e A square is a rectangle.

13 The diagram shows a person walking a tightrope.
The two poles are 16 m apart.
The two halves of the tightrope make an angle of 10° to the horizontal.

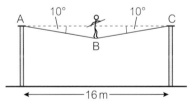

a Make a scale drawing of the triangle ABC using a ruler and protractor. Use a scale of 1 cm to 2 m.
b How long is the tightrope ABC?

14 For each triangle

a 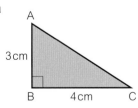   b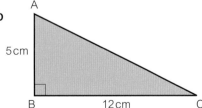

  i draw the triangle accurately using a ruler and a protractor
  ii measure the length of side AC
  iii work out AB² + BC² and then AC²
  iv write down anything you notice.

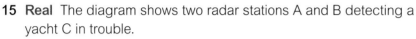

Investigation

Problem-solving / Reasoning

Make a large copy of this table.

1 Write each of these quadrilaterals in the correct position in the table:
rectangle, rhombus, kite, parallelogram, arrowhead, trapezium

Hint

Think carefully about the definitions of each shape.

		Number of pairs of parallel sides		
		0	1	2
Number of pairs of equal sides	0			
	1			
	2			

2 One of the shapes can fit in more than one box. Which shape is this?

3 Draw a quadrilateral to fit in each empty box. Use markings to show which sides are parallel and which are equal.

15 **Real** The diagram shows two radar stations A and B detecting a yacht C in trouble.
The radar stations are 40 km apart.

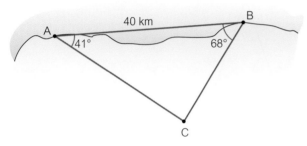

a Make an accurate scale drawing using a scale of 1 cm to 5 km.

b Work out the real distances AC and BC.

c A lifeboat travels from each radar station at a speed of 25 km/h.
Use the formula time = $\dfrac{\text{distance}}{\text{speed}}$ to work out how long it takes each lifeboat to reach the yacht at C.

Q15b hint

Start by using your scale drawing to measure the distance of the yacht from each radar station.

16 **Reflect** Look back at the questions you answered in these Extend lessons.
Find a question that you could not answer straightaway, or that you really had to think about.
While you worked on this question:
• What were you thinking about?
• How did you feel?
• Did you keep trying until you had an answer? Did you give up before reaching an answer, and move on to the next question?
• Did you think you would get the answer correct or incorrect?
Write down any strategies you could use to help you stay calm when answering tricky maths questions. Compare your strategies with others.

Reflect

5 Unit test

1 Draw and label an angle of 310°.

2 Work out the sizes of the angles marked with letters.
   Give a reason for each answer.

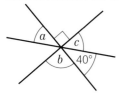

3 Work out the size of angle x.

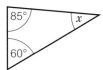

4 For each diagram, work out the value of x.

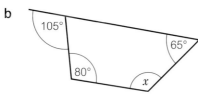

5 Work out the size of angle a.

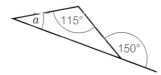

6 Make an accurate drawing of this triangle.

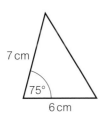

7 The table lists some properties of 2D shapes and five different
   quadrilaterals: square, rectangle, rhombus, parallelogram and kite.
   Copy the table and write a tick in the correct box for any quadrilateral
   that has each property.

Property	Square	Rectangle	Rhombus	Parallelogram	Kite
two pairs of parallel sides					
all four sides are equal					
diagonals cross at a right angle					

8 The diagram shows triangle ABC.
Work out the sizes of angles a, b and c.

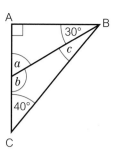

9 A general rule for a wheelchair ramp is that for every 1 cm of rise, a 12 cm length of ramp is required.
  a Draw an accurate triangle to represent this.
  b Work out the size of the angle between the bottom of the ramp and the ground.

10 The diagram shows triangle ABC.
AB = AC
  a Work out the size of angle ACB.
  b Work out the size of angle DBA.

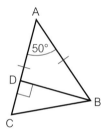

Challenge

11 A **tangram** is a puzzle made of seven shapes that fit together to make another shape.
Here is a tangram drawn on squared paper.
  a Write the name of each shape.
  b Draw your own tangram on a similar square grid.
    Try to include as many different shapes as possible.
    Label each shape from A to G.
    Write the names of the shapes.
  c Draw a tangram that includes an arrowhead, kite and pentagon.
  d Challenge a classmate to make a tangram that includes three shapes of your choice.

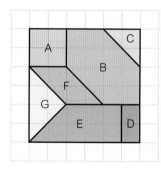

12 **Reflect** Which of these statements best describes your work on lines and angles in this unit?
  • I did the best I could
  • I could have tried harder
Why did you choose that statement?
Was it true for every lesson?
Write down one thing you will do to make sure you do the best you can in the next unit.

6.1 Place value and rounding

You will learn to:
- Recognise the place value of each digit in large numbers.
- Round decimals to 1 decimal place.

Why learn this?
Rounding numbers allows us to estimate values. For example, in 2019 the population of the world is approximately 7.53 billion.

Fluency
Round each number to the nearest 10.
- 59
- 3
- 175

Explore
What is the predicted population of the world for 2025?

Exercise 6.1

1 Write these numbers in order from smallest to largest.
123   31   321   23   231   12

2 Round each number to the nearest whole number.
a 12.3   **b** 8.7   **c** 9.25   **d** 121.9   **e** 19.5

3 What is the value of the 3 in each of these numbers?
a 123   **b** 231   **c** 321

4 a Copy the **place value table** and write each of the numbers in the cloud in the table. The first one has been done for you.

53 400 000
99 154   123 000 000
4 000 000 000

Key point

One million is written 1 000 000.
A number with 7 digits is larger than 1 million.
One billion is written 1 000 000 000.
A number with 10 digits is larger than 1 billion.
Large numbers can be read and compared by writing the digits from right to left in a **place value table**.

Billions	Hundreds	Tens	Units	Hundreds	Tens	Units	Hundreds	Tens	Units
	Millions			Thousands			Hundreds	Tens	Units
		5	3	4	0	0	0	0	0

b Write the numbers in order from smallest to largest.

c **Discussion** Ivan says '99 154 must be the largest because it begins with the largest digit'. Explain why he is wrong.

Confidence

Warm up

5 Write down the number which is
  a 10 more than 50 000
  b 1000 more than 3 000 000
  c 2 000 000 less than 30 000 000
  d 1 billion more than 8 300 000 000
  e 4 million less than 8 300 000 000

> **Key point**
>
> Digits after the **decimal point** represent fractions. You can see the value of each digit in a place value table.
>
> | H | T | U | • | $\frac{1}{10}$ | $\frac{1}{100}$ | $\frac{1}{1000}$ |
> |---|---|---|---|---|---|---|
> | | | 0 | • | 1 | | |
> | | | 0 | • | 0 | 1 | |
> | | | 0 | • | 0 | 0 | 1 |
>
> $0.1 = \frac{1}{10}$ (one tenth)
> $0.01 = \frac{1}{100}$ (one hundredth)
> $0.001 = \frac{1}{1000}$ (one thousandth)

6 **Problem-solving** A number is smaller than 1 billion but larger than 999 000 000.
  a What is the smallest whole number it could be?
  b What is the largest whole number it could be?

> **Worked example**
>
> Round 3.1428 to 1 decimal place.
> 3.1428 lies between 3.1 and 3.2
> 3.15 is half way between the two
> Since, 3.1428 is smaller than 3.15 round to 3.1
>
>
> 3.1   3.15   3.2

> **Key point**
>
> To round to 1 decimal place, look at the digit in the second decimal place. If it is less than 5 round down. If it is more than 5 round up.

7 Round each number to 1 decimal place.
  a 15.635   **b** 9.157   **c** 18.907   **d** 110.666

> **Q7 hint**
>
> Look at the number in the second decimal place to decide whether to round up or down.

8 **Problem-solving** When each of the numbers in the cloud is rounded to 1 decimal place they all give the same answer, except for one number. Which is the odd one out?

5.372   5.40
5.391   5.447   5.4111
5.3499
5.39111   5.35

9 **Real** In 2019, the population of the USA was 329 386 986.
  Round the number in millions to 1 decimal place.

10 Work out
  a $\sqrt{50}$ **b** $\frac{11^2}{5 \times 17}$ **c** $3.52 \times 1.81 - 0.467$
  d $4.9 + \sqrt[3]{75} \times 18$

  Round the answers to 1 decimal place.

11 **Real / Problem-solving** Rounded to 1 decimal place, the mass of a baby is 4.2 kg.
  What is the smallest mass the baby could be?

> **Q11 hint**
>
> Which numbers round to 4.2? Draw a number line to help.
>
>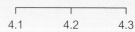
> 4.1   4.2   4.3

12 **Explore** What is the predicted population of the world for 2020? Is it easier to explore this question now you have completed the lesson? What further information do you need to be able to answer this?

13 **Reflect** In this lesson you worked with very large numbers and decimal numbers. How are they different? How are they similar?

Reflect | Explore

6.2 Ordering decimals

You will learn to:
• Write decimals in ascending and descending order.

Why learn this?
You can work out who finished first in a race.

Fluency
How many tenths are in
• 2
• 5
• 6
• 10?

Explore
Which element has the lowest boiling point?

Warm up

Exercise 6.2

1 Write these numbers in order from smallest to largest.
   a –3, 5, –2, 0, 7   **b** –2, 0, 2, –5, –3   **c** –5, –3, –8, –7

2 Write < or > between each pair of numbers.
   a –4 ☐ 2   **b** 5 ☐ 3   **c** –7 ☐ –8

Worked example

Write these **decimals** in order from smallest to largest.
6.5, 6.23, 6.55

H	T	U	•	$\frac{1}{10}$	$\frac{1}{100}$	$\frac{1}{1000}$
		6	•	5	0	
		6	•	2	3	
		6	•	5	5	

On a place value table, the numbers look like this. Write a **zero place holder** when ordering decimals with different numbers of decimal places.

6.23, 6.5, 6.55

The units are all 6. $\frac{23}{100}$ is the smallest fraction and $\frac{55}{100}$ is the largest.

3 Write these decimals in order from smallest to largest.
   0.6, 0.006, 0.06

4 **Reasoning** Carly says, '10.42 is greater than 10.5 because 42 is greater than 5.'
   Is Carly correct? Explain.

5 Write these decimals in **ascending** order.
   a 0.7124, 0.73, 0.7241, 0.724, 0.703
   b 12.874, 12.8475, 12.92, 12.9
   c –0.203, –0.291, –0.2, –0.24, –0.29
   d –0.43, –0.491, –0.45, –0.405, –0.49

Q5 Literacy hint

Ascending means increasing in value from small to large.

6 Write these decimals in **descending** order.
   a 0.3516, 0.37, 0.3105, 0.315, 0.376
   b 18.429, 18.9142, 18.49, 18.4
   c −0.13, −0.107, −0.7, −0.17, −0.73
   d −0.52, −0.514, −0.55, −0.502, −0.56

Q6 Literacy hint

Descending means decreasing in value from large to small.

7 **Reasoning** These were the top three athletes in the women's javelin at the 2012 Summer Olympics.

Athlete	Distance (m)
Christina Obergföll	65.16
Barbara Špotáková	69.55
Linda Stahl	64.19

   a Who won gold, silver and bronze?
   b Did you place the distances in ascending or descending order?
   These were the top three athletes in the women's 400 m at the 2012 Summer Olympics.

Athlete	Time (s)
Christine Ohuruogu	49.70
Sanya Richards-Ross	49.55
DeeDee Trotter	49.72

   c Who won gold, silver and bronze?
   d Did you place the times in ascending or descending order?

Q7a hint

The longest distance wins gold.

Q7c hint

The quickest time wins gold.

8 **Real** These are the qualifying times from the British Grand Prix in 2013.
In what order were the drivers placed in the qualifying heats?

Driver	Time (min : s)
Lewis Hamilton	1:29.607
Daniel Ricciardo	1:30.757
Nico Rosberg	1:30.059
Sebastian Vettel	1:30.211
Mark Webber	1:30.220

Q8 hint

The driver with the fastest time is placed first.

9 **STEM** A car part needs to measure between 0.095 cm and 0.105 cm. The first five parts off the production line measure 0.098 cm, 0.1 cm, 0.15 cm, 0.09 cm and 0.0955 cm
Which of these parts are acceptable?

10 Write < or > between each pair of numbers.
   a 2.6 ☐ 2.9   **b** 3.6 ☐ 3.54   **c** 12.043 ☐ 12.009
   d −2.14 ☐ −2.41   **e** −9.09 ☐ −9.088

11 **Explore** Which element has the lowest boiling point?
What have you learned in this lesson to help you answer this question? What other information do you need?

12 **Reflect** In this lesson you have been working with decimals.
Imagine someone had never seen a decimal point before.
How would you define it? How would you describe what it does?
Write a description in your own words. Compare your description with others in your class.

6.3 Adding and subtracting decimals

You will learn to:
* Add and subtract decimals.

Why learn this?
You can keep track of how much money you have saved.

Fluency
What is 5 230 000 as millions to 1 d.p.?

Explore
A mobile phone contract gives 2.5 GB of downloads a month. How many films can you download?

Exercise 6.3

1 Work out
  a 45 + 186
  b 387 − 35

2 Work out

  a
$$\begin{array}{r} 1\,9\,0 \\ -\ \ 7\,3 \\ \hline \end{array}$$

  b
$$\begin{array}{r} 1\,0\,0\,0 \\ -\ \ 3\,6\,7 \\ \hline \end{array}$$

3 Copy and complete.
  a 0.4 + ☐ = 1
  b 0.3 + ☐ = 1
  c 0.42 + ☐ = 1
  d ☐ + 0.67 = 1

4 Work out
  a 3 − 0.2
  b 7 − 0.4
  c 10 − 6.34
  d 100 − 8.59

5 Work out
  a 3.45 + 2.51
  b 4.56 + 7.88
  c 13.4 + 9.83
  d 2.02 + 7.9
  e 3.417 + 9.86
  f 2.91 + 0.042 + 0.39
  g 2.044 + 9.92 + 0.097

6 Reasoning Jody says, '4.3 + 2.15 = 6.18, because 2 + 4 = 6 and 3 + 15 = 18.'
Explain why Jody is wrong.

Q4a hint
Count up.

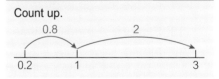

Q5a hint
Use column addition. Make sure you line up the digits correctly.
$$\begin{array}{r} 3.45 \\ +\ 2.51 \\ \hline \end{array}$$

Warm up

Confidence

7 Work out these. Use an **estimate** to check your answer.
  a 4.96 – 2.13
  b 5.11 – 4.39
  c 14.45 – 7.6
  d 3.421 – 1.27
  e 5.417 – 0.209

Q7 Strategy hint

Estimate by rounding the values to the nearest whole number to do the calculation.

8 Real / Problem-solving Varsa streams a film of 4.21 GB.
  She has a total download allowance of 7.8 GB a month.
  How much does she have left?

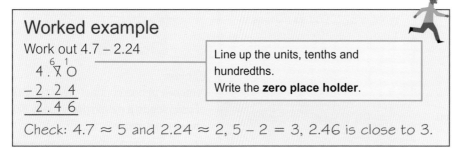

Worked example

Work out 4.7 – 2.24

$$\begin{array}{r} 4.\overset{6}{\cancel{7}}\overset{1}{0} \\ -2.24 \\ \hline 2.46 \end{array}$$

Line up the units, tenths and hundredths.
Write the **zero place holder**.

Check: 4.7 ≈ 5 and 2.24 ≈ 2, 5 – 2 = 3, 2.46 is close to 3.

Key point

You can use a **zero place holder** when subtracting decimals with different numbers of decimal places.

9 Work out these using the column method.
  a 8.5 – 3.13 + 6.9
  b 3.45 + 8.7 – 2.96
  c 4.26 – 3.94 + 8.53
  d 7.254 + 8.45 – 0.391
  e 0.231 – 0.15 + 0.892

10 Real / Problem-solving A ribbon is 12 m long. Viggo cuts off 3.92 m.
  How much is left?

11 Real / Problem-solving A plant is 0.305 m tall. In a week it grows
  0.007 m.
  How tall is it now?

12 Problem-solving Work out
  a 0.45 + 0.28 – 0.61 = ☐
  b 0.45 – 0.61 + 0.28 = ☐
  Discussion Will this always happen? Explain your answer.
  c Use this strategy to work out 0.75 – 0.96 + 0.25

13 Explore A mobile phone contract allows 2.5 GB of downloads a
  month. How many films can you download?
  Look back at the maths you have learned in this lesson.
  How can you use it to answer the question?

14 Reflect Look back at the work you have done this lesson.
  In what way is adding and subtracting decimals the same as adding
  and subtracting integers?
  In what way is it different?

6.4 Multiplying decimals

You will learn to:
- Multiply a decimal by an integer.
- Round decimals to make estimates.

Why learn this?
You can work out the total cost of vegetables by knowing the price per kg and weighing the item.

Fluency
What are the missing numbers?
- $5.5 \times \square = 550$
- $4 \div 10 = \square$
- $\square \div 1000 = 0.78$

Explore
Does multiplying always make a number bigger?

Exercise 6.4

1 Work out

   a $\begin{array}{r} 83 \\ \times\ \ 4 \\ \hline \end{array}$
   b $\begin{array}{r} 97 \\ \times 13 \\ \hline \end{array}$
   c $\begin{array}{r} 402 \\ \times\ \ 29 \\ \hline \end{array}$

2 Work out

   a $4 \times 56 = 4 \times 50 + 4 \times 6 = \square + \square = \square$

   b $9 \times 27 = \square \times \square + \square \times \square = \square + \square = \square$

   c $83 \times 7 = \square \times \square + \square \times \square = \square + \square = \square$

3 Round each number to the nearest 10 to estimate.

   a $19 \times 23 \approx 20 \times 20 = \square$

   b $34 \times 44 \approx \square$

   c $195 \times 32 \approx \square$

4 Copy and complete these number patterns:

$$7 \times 100 = 700$$
$$7 \times 10 = \square$$
$$7 \times 1 = \square$$
$$7 \times 0.1 = \square$$
$$7 \times 0.01 = \square$$

$$7 \times 200 = \square$$
$$7 \times 20 = \square$$
$$7 \times 2 = \square$$
$$7 \times 0.2 = \square$$
$$7 \times 0.02 = \square$$

$$7 \times 300 = \square$$
$$7 \times 30 = \square$$
$$7 \times 3 = \square$$
$$7 \times 0.3 = \square$$
$$7 \times 0.03 = \square$$

Confidence

Warm up

5 Work out

   a 6 × 7

   b 6 × 0.7

   c 0.6 × 7

   d 6 × 0.07

Q5 hint

Your answer will have the digits 4 and 2. Where do you put the decimal point?

6 Work out

   a 6 × 0.3

   b 8 × 0.4

   c 20 × 0.09

7 Use the multiplication facts given to work out the answers.

   a 42 × 10 = 420

     Work out

     i 42 × 0.1

     ii 42 ÷ 10

   b 37 × 10 = 370

     Work out

     i 370 × 0.1

     ii 370 ÷ 10

   Discussion What do you notice?

8 Copy and complete.

   a **i** 8 × 1 = ☐

     ii 8 × 0.1 = ☐

     iii 8 × 0.01 = ☐

   b **Reasoning** What division calculation is equivalent to × 0.01?

Worked example

Work out 8.9 × 7

Estimate: 8.9 ≈ 9, 9 × 7 = 63

$$\begin{array}{r} 8\ 9 \\ \times\ \ 7 \\ \hline 6\ 2\ 3 \\ {\scriptstyle 6} \end{array}$$

Ignore the decimal point and work out 89 × 7.

8.9 × 7 = 62.3

Use your estimate to see where to put the decimal point.

Key point

You can use the column method to multiply a decimal by a whole number.

---

9 Use the column method to work out these.

   Use an estimate to check your answers.

   a 4.6 × 8

   b 7 × 7.34

   c 6 × 24.76

   d 12.4 × 1.3

   e 3.72 × 14

   Discussion For each part, count the number of digits after the decimal point in both numbers in the question. Count the number of digits after the decimal point in the answer. What do you notice?

10 Real Omar changes 700 Egyptian pounds (E£) to US dollars ($).
The exchange rate is E£1 = $0.06.
How many dollars does he get?

11 Real / Reasoning A square tile is 9.4 cm long.
How wide is a row of 9 tiles?

12 Reasoning 4.21 × 8 = 33.68
Use this fact to work out
a 0.421 × 8
b 42.1 × 8
c 8 × 421

13 Work out
a 1 × 30
b 2 × 15
c 4 × 7.5
Discussion What do you notice about the three answers?
Explain why this happens.
d Use this strategy to calculate
  i 2.8 × 50
  ii 250 × 4.8

14 A metal rod measures 0.357 m.
Estimate the length of metal needed to make 6 of these rods.

15 Explore Does multiplying always make a number bigger?
Choose some sensible numbers to help you explore this situation.
Then use what you've learned in this lesson to help you answer the
question.

16 Reflect In this lesson you multiplied decimals using
  • column method
  • multiplication facts.
For each method, make up your own calculation to show how it
works.
Work out the answer to each calculation and show how you worked
out each step.
Explain how you chose the numbers for your calculations.

Q10 hint

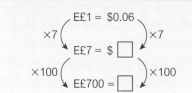

E£1 = $0.06
×7   ×7
E£7 = $ ☐
×100   ×100
E£700 = ☐

Q14 hint

Round to 1 d.p.

Explore

Reflect

6.5 Dividing decimals

Confidence

You will learn to:
- Divide decimals by a whole number.
- Solve problems by dividing decimals.

Why learn this?
You can compare different quantities of an item in a supermarket to work out which represents the best value.

Fluency
Work out
- 6×10
- 0.8×100
- 0.03×10
- 95.24×100

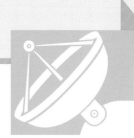

Explore
Does dividing one number by another always make it smaller?

Exercise 6.5

Warm up

1 Work out
  a $30 \div 6$ **b** $300 \div 6$

2 Work out
  a $7\overline{)903}$ **b** $6\overline{)339}$ **c** $12\overline{)348}$

Key point

You can use short or long division to divide a decimal by a whole number.

Worked example
Work out $74.8 \div 4$

$$\begin{array}{r} 1\,8\,.\,7 \\ 4\,\overline{)7^3\!4\,.^2\!8} \end{array}$$

First write the decimal point for the answer above the decimal point in the question. Then divide as normal, starting from the left.

$74.8 \div 4 = 18.7$

3 Work out
  a $58.4 \div 4$ **b** $41.52 \div 6$ **c** $198.64 \div 8$

4 Real / Reasoning A ribbon measuring 2.75 m is cut into 5 equal pieces.
How long is each piece?

5 a Copy and complete the calculation to work out $2.31 \div 4$

$$\begin{array}{r} 0\,.\,5\,\square\,\square\,\square \\ 4\,\overline{)2\,.^2\!3^3\!1\,\,0\,\,0} \end{array}$$

  b Discussion Why did you need to write the number 2.3100 in the division?

6 Work out
  a $3.42 \div 5$ **c** $19.24 \div 8$
  b $9.21 \div 6$ **d** $145.1 \div 4$

7 Reasoning $0.82 \times 7 = 5.74$

Use this fact to work out the answers to these multiplications.

a 0.082×7 **b** 8.2×7 **c** $5.74 \div 7$ **d** $5.74 \div 0.82$

8 Reasoning $0.341 \times 9 = 3.069$

Write down four facts related to this.

Q8 hint

In Q7, all the calculations were related to 0.82×7

Worked example

Work out $1 \div 6$. Round your answer to 1 decimal place.

$$6 \overline{)1.^{1}0\,^{4}0\,^{4}0\,^{4}0} \ldots \quad \begin{array}{c} 0.1\ 6\ 6\ 6 \ldots \end{array}$$

Write the 1 as 1.0000 … because you do not know how many decimal places you will need.

$1 \div 6 = 0.1666666666\ldots$ approx 1.7 (to 1 d.p.)

The digit 6 will continue infinitely.

---

9 Work out these divisions. Round all your answers to 1 decimal place.

a $1 \div 3$ **b** $2 \div 3$ **c** $1 \div 4$

d $3 \div 4$ **e** $1 \div 5$ **f** $\frac{2}{5}$

g $\frac{5}{6}$ **h** $\frac{1}{8}$ **I** $\frac{3}{8}$

j $\frac{7}{8}$

Q9f hint

$\frac{2}{5}$ can be read as $2 \div 5$

10 Real / Reasoning Farhan shares 3.5 kg of animal food equally between 6 animals.

How much does each animal get?

Round the answer to 1 decimal place.

11 Problem-solving / Reasoning Salman thinks of a number, divides it by 7 and gets 1.2.

What number was he thinking of?

12 Reasoning Chavvi works out $32.6 \div 6$ on her calculator. Her answer is 54.33333…

Use an approximate calculation to show that Chavvi must be wrong.

13 Explore Does dividing one number by another always make it smaller?

Look back at the maths you have learned in this lesson.

How can you use it to answer this question?

14 Reflect Look back at the work you did in lesson 6.4 and this lesson.

What happens if you divide a positive number by a number between 0 and 1?

What happens if you multiply a positive number by a number between 0 and 1?

Write your own 'What happens if___' question and answer it.

6.6 Decimals, fractions and percentages

Confidence

You will learn to:
- Compare and order decimals, fractions and percentages.
- Convert between percentages, decimals and fractions.
- Write one number as a fraction of another.

Why learn this?
In speed calculations, we often need to convert hours and minutes into a decimal number of hours.

Fluency
Write as a decimal
- $\frac{3}{10}$
- $\frac{7}{100}$
- $\frac{23}{100}$

Explore
What does 'up to 50% off' actually mean?

Warm up

Exercise 6.6

1 Write the value of
  a the tenths digit in 2.3
  b the hundredths digit in 34.96.

2 Convert to a decimal.

  a $\frac{4}{5}$ b $\frac{7}{8}$ c $\frac{2}{25}$

3 Copy and complete the table by finding the missing fractions, decimals or percentages.

Fraction	Decimal	Percentage
$\frac{1}{10}$		
	0.25	
		30%
	0.4	
$\frac{1}{2}$		
		75%
	1.5	
$1\frac{3}{5}$		

4 Look at the Decimal and Percentage columns in the table in Q3.
  Copy and complete these statements.
  To convert a decimal to a percentage, × ☐
  To convert a percentage to a decimal, ÷ ☐

5 Convert these decimals to %.
  a 0.72 b 0.23 c 0.09 d 1.08

Q5 hint

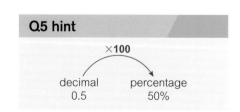

6 Lois says that $0.58 = 5.8\%$.

   a What mistake has Lois made?

   b What is the correct answer?

7 Convert these percentages to decimals.

   a 42%

   b 191%

   c 6%

   d 1.3%

   e 29.4%

Q7 hint

decimal   percentage
0.5   50%

$\div 100$

8 Write these percentages and decimals in ascending order.

   a 0.6, 6%, 0.66, 63%, 0.606

   b 80%, 0.88, 0.85, 8%, 8.8%

Q8 hint

Convert all to decimals or all to percentages to compare.

9 Problem-solving In a class of 20 students, 17 have brown eyes.

   a What fraction of the class have brown eyes?

   b What percentage of the class have brown eyes?

Q9a hint

$\frac{\square}{20}$ are have brown eyes.

10 Write each time as a fraction of 1 hour.
Simplify the fractions if you can.

   a 30 minutes

   b 15 minutes

   c 45 minutes

   d 10 minutes

   e 20 minutes

   f 5 minutes

Q10a hint

1 hour = 60 minutes

$\frac{30}{60} = \frac{\square}{2}$ hour

11 Write each time as a decimal number of hours.

   a 1 h 30 min

   b 5 h 15 min

   c 3 h 45 min

   d 2 h 12 min

   e Show that 1 hour 25 min $\neq$ 1.25 hours.

Q11 hint

Write as a mixed number first.

Q11e hint

Convert 1 hour 25 min to a decimal.

12 Write these decimals as fractions.
Simplify the fractions where possible.

   a 0.3

   b 0.8

   c 0.39

   d 1.85

   e 5.48

   f 2.529

13 Reasoning Harry says that $0.6 = \frac{6}{10}$. Sophie says that 0.6 is $\frac{3}{5}$.

   a Explain why they are both correct.

   b Write another fraction equivalent to 0.6.

Q13a hint

$0.3 = 3$ tenths $= \frac{3}{\square}$

$0.39 = \frac{39}{\square}$

Investigation

Evie uses her calculator to convert $\frac{1}{9}$ and $\frac{2}{9}$ to decimals.
She writes down:

$\frac{1}{9} = 0.111...$ $\frac{2}{9} = 0.222...$

1 Continue Evie's pattern up to $\frac{9}{9}$.

2 Write $\frac{13}{9}$ as a decimal.

14 a Convert these fractions to decimals. Write your answers to 2 decimal places.

    i $\frac{1}{3}$

    ii $\frac{2}{3}$

  b Write $\frac{1}{3}$ and $\frac{2}{3}$ as percentages.

15 Put these quantities in ascending order.

  a $\frac{1}{3}$, 35%, 0.38, $\frac{2}{5}$, 25%, 0.39

  b $\frac{7}{10}$, 73%, 79%, $\frac{17}{20}$, 0.74, 0.86

  c 0.56, 84%, $\frac{5}{6}$, 86%, $\frac{4}{5}$, 0.08

Q15 Strategy hint

Convert all the values to decimals first.

16 Copy and complete.

Fraction	Decimal	Percentage
$\frac{27}{50}$		
$\frac{5}{8}$		
$\frac{19}{25}$		

17 Convert these percentages to fractions.

  a 23%

  b 9%

  c 1%

  d 16%

  e 12%

  f 45%

Q17a hint

Per cent means 'out of 100'.

$23\% = \frac{\square}{\square}$

Q17d hint

Give your answer in its simplest form.

18 Problem-solving / Reasoning A shop has three different sale offers.

$\frac{1}{3}$ off   30% off $\frac{2}{5}$ off

Which is the largest reduction?

19 Explore What does 'up to 50% off' actually mean?
Look back at the maths you have learned in this lesson.
How can you use it to answer this question?

20 Reflect In this lesson you have converted between fractions, decimals and percentages.
Which did you find most difficult? Describe a method for this conversion.

6.7 Calculating percentages

You will learn to:
- Mentally calculate a percentage of an amount.

Why learn this?
Urban planners calculate population growth so they know how many houses to build.

Fluency
What is each percentage as a fraction?
- 50%
- 25%
- 10%
- 1%

Explore
What will the population of your town be in 10 years' time?

Exercise 6.7

1 Work out $\frac{1}{2}$ of
  a 200 cm
  b 12 m
  c 42 kg
  d 326 g

2 Work out $\frac{1}{10}$ of
  a 60 g
  b 99 km
  c 182 m
  d 4200 g

3 Work out 50% of
  a 300
  b 120
  c 90
  d 3

> **Q3a hint**
> 50% = $\frac{1}{2}$
> To find 50% of 300 work out $\frac{1}{2}$ of 300

4 Copy and complete.

  a 50% = $\frac{1}{2}$ To find 50% divide by $\square$

  b 25% = $\frac{\square}{4}$ To find 25% divide by $\square$

  c 10% = $\frac{\square}{\square}$ To find 10% divide by $\square$

  d 1% = $\frac{\square}{\square}$ To find 1% divide by $\square$

5 Work out
   a 25% of 120
   b 10% of 120
   c 1% of 120
   d 10% of 86
   e 25% of 86
   f 1% of 86

6 **Reasoning** Yoosuf says, 'To find 10% divide by 10 so to find 20% divide by 20.'
   a Explain what Yoosuf has done wrong.
   b What do you divide by to find 20%?

Q6b hint

Write 20% as a fraction.

7 **Problem-solving** In 2018, the population of the world was approximately 7 500 000 000.
   If the population increases by 10% in the next 10 years, what will the population be in 2028?

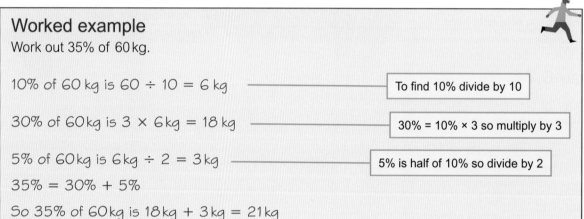

Worked example
Work out 35% of 60 kg.

10% of 60 kg is 60 ÷ 10 = 6 kg ———— To find 10% divide by 10

30% of 60 kg is 3 × 6 kg = 18 kg ———— 30% = 10% × 3 so multiply by 3

5% of 60 kg is 6 kg ÷ 2 = 3 kg ———— 5% is half of 10% so divide by 2

35% = 30% + 5%

So 35% of 60 kg is 18 kg + 3 kg = 21 kg

8 Work out
   a 10% of 360°
   b 5% of 360°
   c 30% of 360°
   d 35% of 360°
   e 25% of 360°
   f 75% of 360°
   g 90% of 360°

Q8f hint

25% × ☐ = 75%

Q8g hint

100% − ☐ = 90%

Investigation   **Reasoning**

How many different ways could you work out 85% of a number?
For example you could find 85% by:
   • finding 10%
   • finding 5%
   • finding 15% (10% + 5% = 15%)
   • subtracting 15% of the number from the original number.

Topic links: Measures

9 Work out
   a 95% of 180
   b 75% of 480
   c 80% of 320
   d 45% of 540

Q9a hint

100% − 5% = 95%

10 **Problem-solving / Reasoning** A dog weighs 15 kg.
   How much will it weigh if it loses 20% of its weight?

11 **Problem-solving / Reasoning** A dress is 130 cm long.
   It shrinks (decreases in size) by 30%.
   What is the new length of the dress?

12 **Reasoning** Which is larger?
   $\frac{1}{5}$ of £80 or 30% of £50

13 **Reasoning** Which is smaller?
   $\frac{2}{3}$ of 63 m 55% of 80 m

14 **Reasoning** a Work out
   i 1% of 540
   ii 10% of 540
   b Use your answers to part **a** to work out these percentages of 540.
   i 2%
   ii 30%
   iii 32%
   iv 68%

15 **Explore** What will the population of your town be in 10 years' time?

16 **Reflect** Write down the steps you would use to calculate 60% of a number.
   Is there more than one way?

6 Check up

Place value, ordering numbers and rounding

1 Which number is larger, 3470 or 4730?

2 Which number is smaller, 52.4 or 52.13?

3 Write these numbers in ascending order.
6.6, 6.53, 6.05, 6.535, 6.015

 4 Work out 2 ÷ 7. Give your answer to 1 decimal place.

5 Write down the number that is 10 000 more than 5 million.

Add and subtract decimals

6 Work out
  a 5.4 + 7.9
  b 3.19 + 8.7
  c 10.7 − 3.8
  d 4.8 − 2.93
  e 100 − 39.2
  f 3.129 + 2.08
  g 5.2 − 0.229

7 Leon is travelling 153.2 km.
He stops after 81.7 km.
How far does he have left to travel?

8 A carpenter has a piece of wood measuring 1.8 m.
He cuts a piece 0.95 m long.
How long is the remaining piece?

Multiply and divide decimals

9 A crate of vegetables weighs 1.352 kg.
Estimate how much 7 crates weigh.

10 Work out
  a 5.3 × 7
  b 69.2 ÷ 4
  c 8 × 9.13

11 Work out
  a 46 × 0.2
  b 0.9 × 0.9
  c 0.04 × 0.7
  d 0.03 × 0.06

12 A chef shares 1.2 kg of sugar between 8 cakes.
How much sugar is in each cake?

Fractions, decimals and percentages

13 Copy and complete this table. Write fractions in their simplest form.

Fraction	$\frac{1}{4}$			
Decimal		0.75	0.7	1.8
Percentage				

14 Will asks 25 people whether they own a tablet. 7 people say yes.
   a What fraction of people say yes?
   b What percentage of people say yes?

15 A supermarket sells 9000 different products.
   They increase this by 30%.
   a How many extra products do they now sell?
   b What is the total number of products they now sell?

16 Write these in ascending order.
   25%, $\frac{2}{5}$, 0.04, 44%, $\frac{3}{8}$, 38%

17 Copy and complete this table. Write fractions in their simplest form.

Fraction	Decimal	Percentage
$\frac{13}{40}$		
	0.245	
		17.5%

18 Work out
   a 25% of 300   b 21% of 300   c 15% of 300

19 Which is larger, $\frac{1}{3}$ of 90 kg or 35% of 80 kg?

20 Work out 95% of 6700 km.

21 **How sure are you of your answers? Were you mostly**
   😦 **Just guessing**   😐 **Feeling doubtful**   😃 **Confident**
   What next? Use your results to decide whether to strengthen or extend your learning.

Challenge

22 You start with 100 kg. You have these percentage cards.

| 10% increase | 20% increase | 25% increase |
| 10% decrease | 20% decrease | 25% decrease |

   a Which of these percentage calculations return you to your starting value?
     i 10% increase followed by 10% decrease
     ii 25% increase followed by 20% decrease
     iii 25% decrease followed by 20% increase
   b Which two cards would you use if you wanted to end with
     i 99 kg   ii 112.50 kg   iii 96 kg?
   c What is the smallest amount you could end with after using two cards?
   d What is the largest amount you could end with after using two cards?

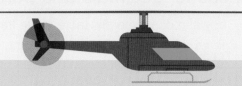

6 Strengthen

You will:
- Strengthen your understanding with practice.

Place value, ordering numbers and rounding

1 Write these numbers in order from smallest to largest.
3000   33   303   30   330   333

2 a Copy this number line. Mark on the line the number 1.33.

┼┼┼┼┼┼┼┼┼┼┼
1.3   1.4

b Which is larger, 1.4 or 1.33?

c Which is smaller, 1.4 or 1.39?

3 Write these numbers in order from smallest to largest.
a 7.2, 6.3, 6.5, 7.4
b 4.6, 4.06, 4.4, 4.44, 4.5
c 0.04, 0.33, 0.004, 0.404, 0.033

4 Which of these numbers is written to 1 decimal place?
3.24   3.5   33   3   3000   3.11

5 Round each of these numbers to 1 decimal place.
a 3.34
b 3.37
c 3.28
d 3.41
e 3.25

6 a Work out 10 ÷ 8.
b Round the answer to 1 decimal place.

Add and subtract decimals

1 Work out these. Use an estimate to check your answers.
a 15 − 1.3
b 100 − 6.4
c 200 − 102.1

2 Work out these. Use an estimate to check your answers.
a 3.5 + 6.8
b 4.7 + 2.5
c 9.4 + 4.63
d 3.1 + 7.92
e 19.2 − 6.7
f 6.03 − 4.8

Q1 hint

First find the numbers smaller than 100 and order these.
Then find the numbers smaller than 1000 and order these.

Q3c hint

Use a number line to help you.

Q5a hint

Use a number line to help you.

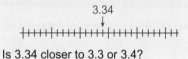

Is 3.34 closer to 3.3 or 3.4?

Q1a hint

First subtract the whole number.
Then subtract the decimal.

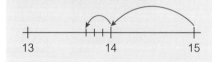

Q2a hint

$$\begin{array}{r} 3.5 \\ +\ 6.8 \\ \hline \square.3 \\ \hline {}_1 \end{array}$$

Q2c hint

Line up the decimal points.

3 Work out these. Use an estimate to check your answers.
  a 1.6 − 0.43
  b 12.9 − 5.32
  c 2.4 − 0.982

4 Sammy is 0.85 m tall. His dad is 1.7 m tall.
Work out the difference in their heights.

Multiply and divide decimals

1 Work out these multiplications.
Use an estimate to check your answers.
  a 4.3 × 2
  b 12.3 × 8
  c 10.92 × 3

2 Copy and complete these number patterns.
  a 4 × 30 = 120   4 × 3 = 12   4 × 0.3 = 1.2   4 × 0.03 = ☐
  b 7 × 60 = 420   7 × 6 = ☐   7 × 0.6 = ☐   7 × 0.06 = ☐

3 Use a mental method and the multiplication facts you know to
work out
  a 7 × 0.2
  b 40 × 0.2
  c 0.09 × 5
  d 60 × 0.03

4 Work out
  a 0.6 × 0.6
  b 0.08 × 0.6
  c 0.05 × 0.04

5 Decide whether these calculations are true or false. If they are false,
work out the correct answer.
  a 0.5 × 2 = 0.10
  b 0.8 × 7 = 5.6
  c 9 × 0.6 = 0.54
  d 3 × 0.3 = 0.09

6 Copy and complete these number patterns.
  a 300 ÷ 5 = 60   30 ÷ 5 = 6   3 ÷ 5 = 0.6   0.3 ÷ 5 = ☐
  b 738 ÷ 6 = 123   73.8 ÷ 6 = 12.3   7.38 ÷ 6 = ☐

7 Work out
  a 41.5 ÷ 5
  b 65.7 ÷ 9
  c 21.08 ÷ 4

8 41.3 ÷ 4 = 10.325
Write down the answer to
  a 4 × 10.325
  b 40 × 10.325
  c 400 × 10.325
  d 4000 × 10.325

Q3a hint

$$1.\overset{5}{\cancel{6}}\overset{1}{0}$$
$$-\,0.43$$
Write a zero
to make the
calculation easier.

Q1a hint

Use a number pattern.
43 × 2 = 86, 4.3 × 2 = ☐

Q3a hint

Use a number pattern.
7 × 2 = 14, 7 × 0.2 = ☐

Q4a hint

Use a number pattern.
6 × 6 = 36, 6 × 0.6 = ☐,
0.6 × 0.6 = ☐

Q7a hint

5)415
415 ÷ 5 = ☐
41.5 ÷ 5 = ☐

Fractions, decimals and percentages

1 Copy and complete these number lines showing percentages, decimals and fractions. Write each fraction in its simplest form.

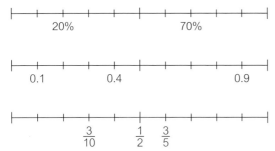

Q1 hint

First complete the percentages number line, then the decimals, then the fractions. Write the fractions as tenths and simplify.

2 Match the equivalent cards.

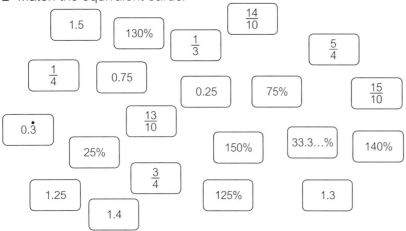

3 Write these decimals as percentages.
  a 0.24
  b 1.98
  c 1.345

Q3a hint

To convert a decimal to a percentage multiply by 100.

4 Write these percentages as decimals.
  a 27%
  b 85.5%
  c 132%

Q4 hint

To convert a percentage to a decimal divide by 100.

5 Change each decimal in Q3 into a fraction in its simplest form.

Q5 hint

H T U . $\frac{1}{10}$ $\frac{1}{100}$ $\frac{1}{1000}$

0 . 2 4

$0.24 = \frac{24}{100} = \frac{\square}{50} = \frac{\square}{25}$

6 Change each percentage in Q4 into a fraction in its simplest form.

Q6 hint

Convert the percentage to a decimal first.

7 a Write these in ascending order.
  i $\frac{3}{10}$, 23%, $\frac{4}{5}$, 0.45, 40%, 0.79
  ii $\frac{7}{20}$, 75%, 0.72, 0.6, $\frac{2}{5}$, 27%

b Write these in descending order.

$\frac{4}{5}$, 90%, 0.08, $\frac{3}{25}$, $\frac{3}{10}$, 9%

Q7 Literacy hint

Ascending means smallest → largest
Descending means largest → smallest

Q7a hint

Convert them to decimals first.

8 Convert these fractions to percentages.

   a $\frac{3}{8}$

   b $\frac{7}{40}$

   c $\frac{8}{25}$

9 Work out 1% of

   a 30

   b 150

   c 75

10 Work out

   a 10% of 300

   b 10% of 70

   c 10% of 45

   d 10% of 6.2

11 Work out

   a 10% of 200

   b 5% of 200

   c 15% of 200

12 Work out

   a 1% of 360

   b 10% of 360

   c 11% of 360

13 Work out

   a 10% of 40

   b 5% of 40

   c 35% of 40

Q8 hint

Fraction	→	decimal	→	percentage
$\frac{1}{8}$	→	$1 ÷ 8 = 0.125$	→	12.5%

Q9a hint

$1\% = \frac{1}{100}$

$\frac{1}{100} × 30 = 30 ÷ 100 = \square$

Q10a hint

$10\% = \frac{1}{10}$

$\frac{1}{10} × 300 = 300 ÷ 10 = \square$

Q11b hint

$10\% ÷ 2 = 5\%$

11c hint

Work out 10% + 5%

12c hint

Work out 10% + 1%

13c hint

Work out 10% + 10% + 10% + 5%

Enrichment

1 The value of shares can increase or decrease.

   a Copy and complete the table showing the share price of a company over a 5-year period.

Year	Value at start of year	Percentage change	Value at end of year
1	$50	30% increase	$50 × 1.3 = $65
2	$65	20% decrease	
3		20% decrease	
4		10% increase	
5		5% increase	

   b What can you say about the share price over the 5-year period?

2 **Reflect** This lesson used number lines to help solve problems with decimals.

   Did the number lines help you? Explain why or why not.

   Would you use number lines to help you solve mathematics problems in the future? Explain why or why not.

6 Extend

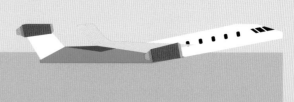

You will:
• Extend your understanding with problem-solving.

1 a Write a formula to convert percentages to decimals.
  b Write a formula to convert decimals to percentages.

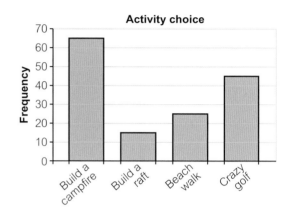

2 Problem-solving On an activity week each student selected one activity.
  a How many students took part in the activity week?
  b What percentage of students chose to build a campfire?
  c What percentage of students chose beach walk or crazy golf?
  d Round your answers to parts **b** and **c** to 1 decimal place.

3 a Use your calculator to work out these.
    Then round your answer to 2 decimal places.

	Full calculator display	Rounded to 1 decimal place
$\sqrt{2}$		
$\sqrt{3}$		
$\sqrt{5}$		
$\sqrt{6}$		

  b Why was $\sqrt{4}$ not included in this table?

4 Planners expect the population of a town to grow by 20% every 10 years.

Q4 Literacy hint
Decade = 10 years

  a Copy and complete the table to show the population at the end of each **decade**.
    Round your answers to the nearest whole number.

Year	2010	2020	2030	2040	2050	2060	2070
Population (thousands)	10	12					

  b Plot this data on a graph with 'Year' on the horizontal axis and 'Population (thousands)' on the vertical axis.
    Plot your points and join them with a smooth curve.
  c Use your graph to estimate the population in 2045.
  d Describe what happens to the population between 2010 and 2070.

5 Problem-solving a Find two possible original numbers.

Original number	Rounded to 1 d.p.	Rounded to nearest whole number
	6.5	6
	6.5	7

    b Compare your answers with someone else in your class.
Are you both correct?

6 Problem-solving Here are Carl Lewis's reaction times and race times for the 100 m sprint.

Race	Reaction time (seconds)	Race time (seconds)
1987 (Rome)	0.193	9.93
1988 (Seoul)	0.136	9.92
1991 (Tokyo)	0.140	9.86

Using this rule, Actual time = Race time – Reaction time, which was Carl Lewis's fastest race?

7 An acute angle is increased by 20%. The new angle is obtuse.
Write a possible size for the acute angle.

Q7 hint

Try some different acute angles.

8 This wooden door expands 3% in the damp (slightly wet or humid) weather. Will it still close in the doorway?

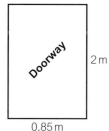 2 m
0.85 m

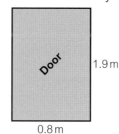 1.9 m
0.8 m

9 Jenny jogs 2 km in 30 minutes. After 6 weeks' training, she has reduced her time by 30%.
How long does she take to jog 2 km now?

10 Copy and complete this number pattern.
    a 588.8 ÷ 92 = 6.4
       588.8 ÷ 9.2 = 64
       588.8 ÷ 0.92 =
       588.8 ÷ 0.092 =
       588.8 ÷ 0.0092 =
    b Work out 58.88 ÷ 9.2. Use estimates to check your answer.

11 4.4 × 63 = 277.2
Use this number fact to work out these.
Check your answers using estimates.
    a 0.44 × 63   **b** 0.44 × 6.3   **c** 0.0044 × 630
    d 277.2 ÷ 63   **e** 277.2 ÷ 6.3   **f** 27.72 ÷ 6.3

12 Problem-solving / Reasoning A designer needs 2.5 m of fabric to make a dress.
He allows an extra 15% of fabric in case he makes a mistake.
How much fabric should he buy?

13 In an archery competition Tara scores 8, 3, 5, 9, 4 and 8.
  a Work out her mean score. Write down all the numbers on the calculator display.
  b Round your answer to 1 decimal place.

14 Work out
  a $0.75 - 0.02 \times 8$
  b $5 \times (1 - 0.3)$
  c $2 \times 0.6 + 0.4 \times 9$
  d $6^2 - 0.4 \times 7$

Q14 hint

Remember the priority of operations.

15 Let $x = 9$, $y = 0.5$ and $z = 0.7$. Work out
  a xy
  b $xy - z$
  c $x^2 + y$
  d $x - y + z$

16 **Problem-solving / Reasoning** Yash is given $10 allowance each week.
  Each week he is given 10% more of the original amount.
  How much will he get after 5 weeks?

17 **Problem-solving / Reasoning** A plant grows 10% of its **current** height each month.
  In January the plant is 120 cm.
  a How tall is it in February?
  b How tall is it in March?

Q17b hint

Work out 10% of your answer to part a.

Q18 Literacy hint

In **compound interest** the interest earned in the first year is added and then earns interest in the next year.

18 **Problem-solving / Reasoning** A bank pays 5% **compound interest** each year on money invested.
  Copy and complete the table to show how much a $10 000 investment will be worth after 3 years.

Year	Total at beginning of year	5%	Total at end of year
1	$10 000	5% of $10 000 = $500	$10 000 + $500 = $10 500
2	$10 500	5% of $10 500 = ☐	$10 500 + ☐ = ☐
3			

19 Write these in ascending order.
  0.3%, $\frac{7}{90}$, 4.51%, 0.79, 7.7%, $\frac{9}{200}$

20 The bar chart shows the percentage of adults in a country who are illiterate.

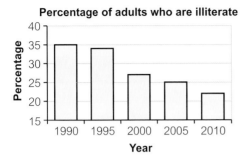

Percentage of adults who are illiterate

a In 1990 there were about 20 000 000 adults.
About how many were illiterate?

b Between 1990 and 2010, the adult population increased by 27%.
What was the adult population in 2010?

c About how many adults were illiterate in 2010?

d How many fewer adults were illiterate in 2010 than in 1990?

e What was the percentage decrease in adults who were illiterate between 1990 and 2010?

Discussion The country received a large fund from the UN during this time period. In what year does the data suggest they received the money? Explain your answer.

Q20e hint

Percentage

decrease $= \dfrac{\text{actual decrease}}{\text{original value}} \times 100$

21 5% of a number is 32.
  a What is 10% of the number?
  b What is 50% of the number?
  c What is 100% of the number?

22 Problem-solving When rounded to 1 decimal place, a number is 9.7.
Write down five possible numbers it could have been.

23 Problem-solving Ruhi thinks of a number.
To the nearest 10, it rounds to 20.
To the nearest whole number, it rounds to 17.
The number has three digits.
What is the smallest number it could be?

24 Reflect Write a definition of a decimal, in your own words.
Be as accurate as you can.
Remember to explain decimal **notation** in your definition.
Check your definition against some of the decimal numbers in this unit. Does your definition fully describe them?

Q24 Literacy hint

Mathematical **notation** means the symbols used in maths.
For example, the notation = means 'equals' and the symbol < means 'less than'.

Reflect

6 Unit test

1 a Work out 10% of 84.
  b Work out 1% of 84.
  c Use your answers to parts **a** and **b** to work out 29% of 84.

2 John has a piece of wood 2.4 m long. He cuts off a piece 0.84 m long. Work out the length of the remaining piece.

3 Copy and complete this table of fractions, decimals and percentages. Write all fractions in their simplest form.

Fraction	$\frac{3}{10}$			$1\frac{1}{4}$		
Decimal			0.25		1.2	
Percentage		40%				175%

4 An ice skater scores 74.92 in her first skate and 144.19 in her second skate. Work out her total score.

5 There are 20 questions in a test. Faye answers 17 correctly.
  a Work out the fraction of questions that Faye answers correctly.
  b Work out the percentage of questions that Faye answers correctly.

6 $2.7 \times 8 = 21.6$
  Use this fact to write down the answer to
  a 27×8
  b 0.27×8
  c 27×0.8

7 Write these decimals in ascending order.
    5.78, 5.08, 5.8, 5.287, 5.078

8 Round 4.389 to 1 decimal place.

9 Write down the number that is 30 100 more than 170 000.

10 Radi runs 100 m in 13.5 seconds.
   He reduces the time by 10%.
   Work out how long it takes him to run 100 m now.

11 Work out
   a 7×0.8
   b 0.02×5
   c $3.2 \div 5$
   d $18 \div 4$

12 A bottle of perfume costs $80.
At an airport the price is reduced by 10%.
Work out the airport price of the bottle of perfume.

13 20% of an amount is 3.2. Work out the original amount.

14 Which is further, $\frac{1}{3}$ of 60 km or 20% of 80 km?

15 Work out 32% of 56 kg.

16 Copy and complete. Write < or > between each pair of numbers.

a 22% ☐ $\frac{1}{5}$

b $\frac{3}{4}$ ☐ 81%

Challenge

17 Work out the missing digits in each calculation.

a
```
    4 ☐ . 8 3
  - 2 5 . ☐ 4
  ─────────────
    ☐ 6 . 8 9
```

b
```
    7 ☐ . 6
  - ☐ 6 . 5 4
  ─────────────
    1 7 . ☐ 6
```

18 Write some possible percentages that would give an answer of 24.

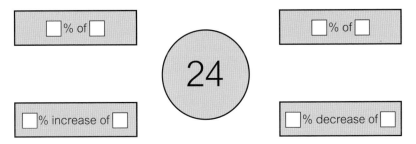

19 **Reflect** Put these topics in order, from easiest to hardest.
(You could just write the letters.)
A Writing decimals in order
B Rounding decimals
C Multiplying and dividing decimals
D Adding and subtracting decimals
E Converting between fractions, decimals and percentages
F Finding percentages of amounts
Think about the two topics you said were hardest.
What made them hard?
Write at least one hint to help you for each topic.

7.1 Writing ratios

You will learn to:
- Write and understand ratios
- Write a ratio in its simplest form.

Why learn this?
You can judge the performance of football players by comparing the ratio of goals scored to matches played.

Fluency
Simplify
- $\frac{5}{10}$
- $\frac{9}{12}$
- $\frac{30}{50}$

Explore
What is the ratio of males to females in your school? In your country? What about in the world?

Exercise 7.1

1 Find the highest common factor of each pair of numbers.
   a 10 and 15   **b** 40 and 24   **c** 63 and 72

2 Copy and complete.

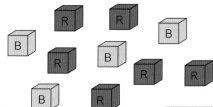

There are ☐ red cubes for every ☐ blue cubes.

> **Key point**
> A **ratio** is a way of comparing two or more quantities.

3 Write the **ratio** of red beads to white beads for each of these necklaces.

   a

   b

   c

Discussion Is the ratio 3:2 the same as 2:3?

> **Q3a hint**
> There are 3 red beads for every 2 white beads. Write the ratio 'red':'white' using numbers.
>
> red : white
> ☐ : ☐

4 Decide whether each statement is sensible.
   a The ratio of your hand length to face length is 1:1.
   b The ratio of height to width of a car is 5:1.
   c The ratio of width to height of a computer screen is 3:4.

Subject links: Science (Q8)

5 A necklace has 2 black beads for every 5 white beads.

   a What is the ratio black beads : white beads?

   b Copy these 10 white beads.

    Draw 2 black beads for every 5 white beads.
    Write the ratio black beads : white beads ☐ : 10

   Discussion Are the ratios in parts **a** and **b** the same?

Q5 Strategy hint

Sketch a diagram.

Worked example

Find the missing value in these **equivalent ratios**.

$4 : 5 = 24 : \square$

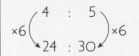

> Find the multiplier.
> Multiply each part.

$4 : 5 = 24 : 30$

Key point

The ratios 2 : 5 and 4 : 10 are called **equivalent ratios**. Equivalent ratios show the same proportion. Both sides of a ratio are multiplied or divided by the same number to give an equivalent ratio.

---

6 Green paint can be made by mixing 2 cans of blue paint with 3 cans of yellow paint. The ratio of blue to yellow is 2 : 3.

   Juanita has 4 cans of blue paint.
   How many cans of yellow paint does she need to make green paint?

7 Which of these ratios are equivalent to the ratio 1 : 2?

   a 2 : 4   **b** 8 : 12

   c 6 : 12   **d** 5 : 10

8 **STEM** 10 g of copper reacts with 5 g of sulfur.

   a Write the ratio of copper to sulfur.

   b How much sulfur is needed to react with 20 g of copper?

   c How much copper is needed to react with 25 g of sulfur?

Worked example

Write 8 : 12 in its simplest form.

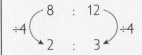

> The HCF of 8 and 12 is 4.

$8 : 12 = 2 : 3$

Key point

You can make the numbers in a ratio as small as possible by **simplifying**. You simplify a ratio by dividing the numbers in the ratio by the **highest common factor (HCF)**.

---

9 Write each ratio in its **simplest form**.

   a 5 : 20   **b** 4 : 12   **c** 6 : 30

   d 100 : 20   **e** 8 : 10   **f** 36 : 18

10 **Real** 120 students and 8 teachers go on a school trip.
    The recommended ratio of adults to students is 1 : 15.
    Is the ratio of adults to students correct?

Q9a hint

11 Simplify each ratio.
   a 4:20:36   **b** 6:24:12   **c** 25:20:45
   d 27:9:36   **e** 30:48:18   **f** 99:77:33

12 **Real** A £1 coin is made of copper, nickel and zinc in the ratio 70:5:25. Write this ratio in its simplest form.

13 **STEM** A molecule of water has 10 protons, 8 neutrons and 10 electrons.
   Write the ratio of protons, neutrons and electrons in its simplest form.

14 Simplify
   a 1 day:6 hours   **b** 15 minutes : 1 hour
   c 8 hours:2 days   **d** 2 weeks:14 days

15 The bar chart shows the numbers of boys and girls at an after-school club.

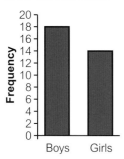

   What is the ratio of boys to girls?

16 Write these ratios in their simplest form.
   a 1:2.5   **b** $1:3\frac{1}{4}$ **c** 2:3.5   **d** $5:1\frac{1}{10}$

17 The ratio of the width to height of a photograph is 1:1.5.
   The width of the photograph is 10 cm.
   What is its height?

18 **Explore** What is the ratio of males to females in your school? In your country? What about in the world?
   Is it easier to explore this question now you have completed the lesson?
   What further information do you need to be able to answer this?

19 **Reflect** After this lesson, Layla says, 'Ratios are a bit like fractions because simplifying ratios is like simplifying fractions.'
   Do you agree with Layla? Explain
   You could use these words in your explanation: Factor, Proportion, Divide.

Q11a hint

The highest common factor of 4, 20 and 36 is ☐.

Key point

Ratios in their simplest form do not have units. To simplify a ratio involving measures, first convert the measures to the same unit.

Key point

For a ratio with fractions or decimals, first multiply both sides of the ratio to get whole numbers.

Q16a hint

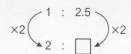

7.2 Sharing in a given ratio

You will learn to:
- Share a quantity in two or more parts in a given ratio.

Why learn this?
A smoothie recipe uses the correct ratio of ingredients to make it taste nice.

Fluency
Find three ratios equivalent to 4 : 3.

Explore
Investigate the ratio of brown-eyed people to green-eyed people.

Confidence

Warm up

Exercise 7.2

1 Write down the missing values in these equivalent ratios.
   a 2 : 5 = 6 : ☐
   b 4 : 7 = ☐ : 28
   c 3 : 10 = 15 : ☐
   d 6 : ☐ = 48 : 32

2 The ratio of students who have school dinners to those having packed lunch in Year 7 is 72 : 48. Write this ratio in its simplest form.

3 **Reasoning** Pavel and Sarah are knitting hats to sell. Pavel spends £20 on wool and Sarah spends £80. They sell all the hats for a total of £1000. Is it fair that they get £500 each? Explain your answer.

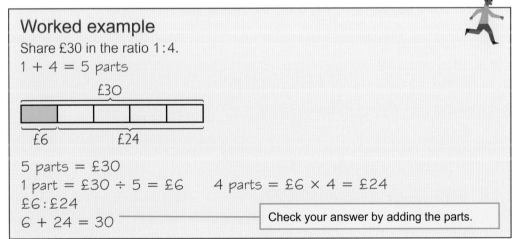

Worked example

Share £30 in the ratio 1 : 4.

1 + 4 = 5 parts

£30

£6   £24

5 parts = £30
1 part = £30 ÷ 5 = £6   4 parts = £6 × 4 = £24
£6 : £24
6 + 24 = 30 ———— Check your answer by adding the parts.

4 Share these amounts in the ratios given.
   Show how you check your answers.
   a £20 in the ratio 2 : 3
   b £60 in the ratio 4 : 2
   c £35 in the ratio 3 : 4
   d £77 in the ratio 5 : 6
   e £72 in the ratio 5 : 4
   f £120 in the ratio 5 : 7

5 Enzo and Catlina share £60 in the ratio 3 : 2.
   How much does each person receive?

6 In a class the ratio of girls to boys is 4 : 5. There are 27 students in the class. How many are boys?

7 In a tennis club the ratio of men to women is 3 : 4.
   a In 2012 there were 14 club members. How many men were there?
   b In 2013 there were 21 club members. How many women were there?

8 Problem-solving In Year 7, the ratio of girls to boys is 5 : 4.
There are 110 girls.
   a How many boys are there in Year 7?
   b How many students are there in Year 7?

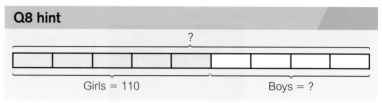

Q8 hint

Girls = 110   Boys = ?

9 Real There were approximately 60 million people in the UK in 2001.
The ratio of under-16s to over-16s was 1 : 4.
How many under-16s were there in 2001?

10 Finance / Problem-solving Jeni gives some of her earnings to charity.
The ratio of the amount she keeps to the amount she gives to charity is 9 : 1.
In 2012, Jeni earned $18 000. In 2013, Jeni earned $23 000. How much more did Jeni give to charity in 2013 than in 2012?

11 Problem-solving The Wilson family and the Jones family share the cost of a holiday cottage in the ratio of the number in each family.
The table shows the cost of the cottage and the number of people in each family for the two years they go away together.

	Number in Wilson family	Number in Jones family	Cost of holiday cottage
2016	2	3	£450
2019	4	5	£630

   a How much do the Wilson family pay in
      i 2016   **ii** 2019?
   b How much do the Jones family pay in
      i 2016   **ii** 2019?
   c Which family has the biggest increase in price from 2016 to 2019?

12 Explore Investigate the ratio of brown-eyed people to green-eyed people.
Is it easier to explore this question now you have completed the lesson?
What further information do you need to be able to answer this?

13 Reflect Look back at the questions you answered on sharing an amount using ratios.
What did you do differently in Q8 from what you did in Q7?

7.3 Proportion

Confidence

You will learn to:
- Understand the relationship between ratio and proportion.

Why learn this?
To make green paint, you can mix yellow and blue paint. Increasing the proportion of blue paint will make a darker shade of green.

Fluency
What is
- $\frac{1}{4}$ as a percentage
- 10% as a fraction
- $\frac{7}{10}$ as a decimal and a percentage?

Explore
How did the proportion of gold medals won by Team GB change from the 2008 Olympic games to the 2012 Olympic games?

Exercise 7.3

1 Convert these fractions to percentages.

a $\frac{3}{10} = \frac{\square}{100} = \square\%$ b $\frac{4}{50} = \frac{\square}{100} = \square\%$ c $\frac{3}{20}$ d $\frac{7}{25}$ e $\frac{4}{5}$

2 Write these fractions in their simplest form.

a $\frac{20}{50}$ b $\frac{12}{16}$ c $\frac{24}{30}$ d $\frac{32}{54}$

3 **Real** The Nigerian national flag has three parts.
Two parts green and one part white.
a What is the ratio of green to white?
b What is the proportion of green in the whole flag?
Write your answer as a fraction.

> **Key point**
>
> **Ratio** compares part to part.
> **Proportion** compares part to whole.
> **Proportions** can be written as **fractions** or **percentages**.

Warm up

Worked example

There are 4 male and 6 female kittens.
a Write the ratio of male to female kittens in its simplest form.
b What proportion of the kittens are male?
Write your answer as a fraction and a percentage.

a   Male : Female

$$\div 2 \left(\begin{matrix} 4 & : & 6 \\ 2 & : & 3 \end{matrix} \right) \div 2$$

b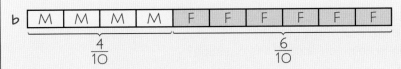

$$\underbrace{\frac{4}{10}} \qquad \underbrace{\frac{6}{10}}$$

$\frac{4}{10} = \frac{2}{5}$ — Simplify the fraction.

$\frac{4}{10} = \frac{40}{100} = 40\%$ — Write as a percentage.

4 A packet of sweets has 12 chocolates and 8 mints.

   a Write the ratio of chocolates to mints.

   b What proportion of the sweets are mints?

     Write your answer as a fraction and as a percentage.

5 For charity art exhibition, Jaime gave 12 paintings, Rob gave 8 and Fernando gave 5.

   a Write the numbers of paintings as a ratio.

   b What proportion of the paintings did each give?

6 Problem-solving A football manager is looking at recruiting a new striker. Footballer A has scored goals in 7 of the last 10 matches. Footballer B has scored goals in 13 in the last 20 matches.

   a For each footballer, write down the proportion of matches in which they scored goals.

   b Which footballer should the manager recruit? Explain your answer.

7 Problem-solving A food technician is comparing two lemon drinks.
The ratio of lemon to water in the first sample is 3 : 17.
The ratio of lemon to water in the second sample is 4 : 21.
Use proportion to explain which drink will have the strongest lemon flavour.

8 Real In the 2012 Olympic games, the Netherlands won gold, silver and bronze medals in the ratio 6 : 6 : 8.

   a What proportion of the medals were gold?

   b What proportion of the medals were bronze?

   Write your answers as a fraction and as a percentage.

   Discussion Why is it sometimes useful to write proportions as percentages?

9 Real A charity divides its budget (financial plan) like this:
35% for wages, 40% for resourcing and 25% for marketing.
Write the ratio spent on wages to resourcing to marketing in its simplest form.

10 In a wallpaper design, $\frac{3}{5}$ of the design is squares and $\frac{2}{5}$ of the design is triangles.
Write the ratio of squares to triangles in its simplest form.

11 Real A company spends its profits like this:
35% is paid out to its investors and 65% kept to improve the company.
Write the ratio of the profits paid out to profits kept in its simplest form.

Investigation   **Problem-solving**

Investigate the ratio of time you spend at school, eating, watching TV, doing homework, sleeping.
Write these as proportions.
Is this the same for other people in your class?

---

12 Explore How did the proportion of gold medals won by Team GB change from the 2008 Olympic games to the 2012 Olympic games?
What have you learned in this lesson to help you answer this question?
What other information do you need?

13 Reflect Look back at the questions you answered.
When do you think it is better to express proportions as fractions?
When would it be better to express proportions as percentages?

7.4 Proportional reasoning

You will learn to:
- Solve simple word problems involving ratio and direct proportion.
- Solve simple word problems involving ratio and inverse proportion.

Why learn this?
Architects use proportion when making scale drawings of buildings.

Fluency
- Double
  5, 6, 34, 70, 150
- Halve
  10, 48, 32, 19

Explore
How would you change the proportions of a photograph to make you look taller?

Confidence

Warm up

Exercise 7.4

1 A comic costs \$2. Work out the cost of
  a 3 comics
  b 10 comics.
  c How many comics can I buy with \$16?

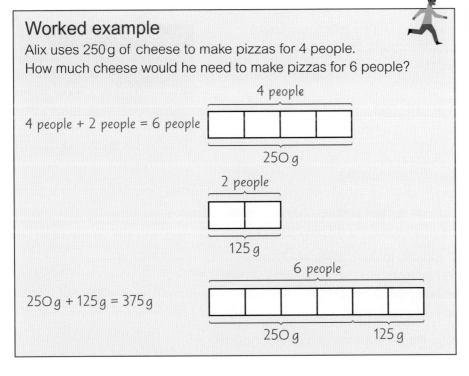

Worked example

Alix uses 250 g of cheese to make pizzas for 4 people.
How much cheese would he need to make pizzas for 6 people?

4 people

4 people + 2 people = 6 people

250 g

2 people

125 g

6 people

250 g + 125 g = 375 g

250 g   125 g

Key point

When two quantities are in **direct proportion,** as one increases or decreases, the other increases or decreases in the same ratio.

2 Two litres of lemonade costs £2.50. Work out the cost of
  a 4 litres   **b** 6 litres   **c** 1 litre   **d** 7 litres.

3 Downloading 30 songs from a music website costs £45.
  a How much does it cost to download 15 songs?
  b How much does it cost to download 45 songs?

4 Problem-solving Here is a recipe
for pancakes for 4 people.
Sofia makes pancakes for 14 people.
She has 800 g of flour, 1200 ml of milk and
10 eggs. Does she have enough ingredients?

Serves 4 people
200 g flour
350 ml milk
2 eggs

Q4 hint

Show your working. Write a sentence
to answer the question.

5 Fazia bought 6 plants for £3.60. Kunal bought 3 plants for £2.
Who got the better deal?

Worked example

It takes 2 people 20 minutes to wash a car.
How long does it take **a** 4 people **b** 1 person?

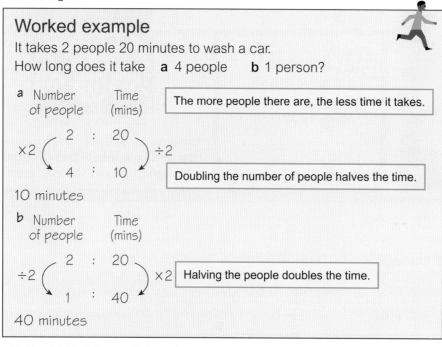

a Number of people / Time (mins)

The more people there are, the less time it takes.

×2 2 : 20 ÷2
    4 : 10

Doubling the number of people halves the time.

10 minutes

b Number of people / Time (mins)

÷2 2 : 20 ×2
    1 : 40

Halving the people doubles the time.

40 minutes

Key point

When two quantities are in **inverse proportion**, as one increases, the
other decreases in the same ratio.

6 Real / Problem-solving 6 people can paint a fence in 3 hours.
  a How long would it take 3 people to paint it?
  b How long would it take 2 people?
  c How long would it take 12 people?

Q6 Strategy hint

Use a table to set out your working.

Number of people	Time (hours)
6	3
3	?

7 Real / Problem-solving 10 men can build a house in 8 days.
  a How long will it take 20 men to build a house?
  b How long will it take 5 men to build a house?

8 It costs 12 people $400 to go mountain trekking.
How much will it cost 10 people?
Discussion There are 24 people on a roller coaster. The ride takes
3 minutes. How long will it take when there are 48 people on it?

9 Problem-solving It takes 120 minutes to drive home at 60 km/h.
  a How long will it take to drive home at 120 km/h?
  b How long will it take to drive home at 30 km/h?
  c How long will it take to drive home at 90 km/h?

10 Explore How would you change the proportions of a photograph to
make you look taller?
Choose some sensible numbers to help you explore this situation.
Then use what you've learned in this lesson to help you answer the
question.

11 Reflect In this lesson you learned about direct and inverse proportion.
Choose four questions from the lesson and explain why they were about
either direct or inverse proportion.

7.5 Using the unitary method

You will learn to:
- Solve problems involving ratio and proportion using the unitary method.
- Solve best buy problems.

Why learn this?
You can work out the best value of products by finding out how much 1 item or 100 g or 1 kg costs.

Fluency
Find the missing numbers in this multiplication grid.

×		12	8
2	18		
		108	
			12

Explore
How much does a footballer earn in 10 minutes?

Exercise 7.5

1 Work out
  a 125 cm ÷ 5   **b** 320 g ÷ 8   **c** £2.50 ÷ 5
  d 420 m ÷ 7   **e** £1.50 × 3   **f** £3.85 × 2

2 Simplify these ratios.
  a 20 m : 2 m   **b** 8 hours : 1 day   **c** 2p : £1

3 Three chocolate bars cost $2.70.
  a Work out the cost of 1 chocolate bar.
  b Work out the cost of 7 chocolate bars.
  c How many chocolate bars can you buy for $7.20?

4 6 litres of petrol cost $7.50.
  How much does 40 litres cost?

 5 80 mosquito nets cost $476.
  How much do 35 mosquito nets cost?

6 **Problem-solving** Carl earns £56 for 8 hours' work.
  a Carl works for 40 hours. How much does he earn?
  b Carl is paid double for overtime. He works 5 hours of overtime in addition to his normal 40 hours work. How much does he earn?

7 **Real / Problem-solving** A supermarket sells chocolate bars at $3.00 for a 5-pack and $4.40 for an 8-pack.
  Which is better value for money?

Key point
Using the **unitary method** means finding the value of 1 part.

Q4 hint
Work out the cost of 1 litre first.

Q6 hint
Find how much he gets paid for 1 hour first.

Q7 hint
Work out how much it costs to buy one chocolate bar first and then compare.

8 **Real / Problem-solving** Jin's car can travel 315 miles on 35 litres of petrol.
Selma's car can travel 240 miles on 30 litres of petrol.
Whose car is more economical?

Q8 Literacy hint

'Economical' means cheaper.

Q8 hint

Work out how far each car travels on 1 litre of petrol first.

9 **Problem-solving** A shop-keeper wants to charge 1.5 times as much per kitchen-paper roll for offer B than offer A. What is the cost of offer B?

Offer A
8 kitchen rolls
$2.40

Offer B
3 kitchen rolls
?

10 **Real** Here are some multipacks of crisps. Each pack is the same brand and contains the same size of smaller packs.

SMALL MULTIPACK
5 packets of crisps
£1.50

MEDIUM MULTIPACK
10 packets of crisps
£2.98

LARGE MULTIPACK
20 packets of crisps
£5.50

a Work out the price of one packet of crisps from the
  i small multipack
  ii medium multipack
  iii large multipack.
b Which is best value for money? Explain your answer.

11 **Real / Reasoning** Here are some jars of honey at different prices from different producers.

HONEY A
50 g
£1.20

HONEY B
250 g
£4.75

HONEY C
380 g
£7.80

a Work out the cost of 10 g of honey from each jar.
b Which jar of honey is the best value for money?
  Explain your answer.

12 **Explore** How much does a footballer earn in 10 minutes?
Is it easier to explore this question now you have completed the lesson?
What further information do you need to be able to answer this?

13 **Reflect** Look back at the questions you answered. In Q10, you used the unitary method to find the price of one packet of crisps from each multipack to compare value for money. What other calculations could you do to compare the value for money of the different multipacks?

7 Check up

Ratio

1 In a box there are 12 chocolates and 7 toffees.
What is the ratio of chocolates to toffees?

2 Which of these ratios is equivalent to $3:4$?
  a $4:5$ **b** $6:8$ **c** $4:3$

3 Write these ratios in their simplest form.
  a $6:15$
  b $28:32$

4 Write this ratio in its simplest form.
$22:44:55$

5 There are 210 students in Year 7. The ratio of students studying
French to students studying Spanish is $3:4$.
How many students study French and how many study Spanish?

6 Kate has blue fish and yellow fish.
The ratio of blue fish to yellow fish is $4:5$.
She has 15 yellow fish. How many blue fish does she have?

7 Dan is training for a swimming competition. In his training session he
used front crawl and back stroke styles of swimming in the ratio $7:3$.
He swam 60 lengths of back stroke.
How many lengths of front crawl did he swim?

8 Write these ratios in their simplest form.
  a $0.25:0.5$
  b $1:\frac{4}{5}$

9 10 chickens lay 12 eggs.
  a What is the ratio of chickens to eggs?
    Give your answer in its simplest form.
  b What is the mean number of eggs laid by a chicken?

Direct and inverse proportion

10 In a class of 30 drama students 18 are girls.
  a Write the proportion of girls as a fraction.
  b Write the proportion of boys as a fraction.
  c Write the ratio of girls to boys in its simplest form.

11 In a bowl of fruit there are 10 bananas, 6 apples and 4 pears.
What proportion of the fruit are apples?
Write your answer as a fraction and as a percentage.

12 The ratio of blue cars to red cars in a car park is $3:2$.
What percentage of cars are
a red
b blue?

13 It takes Paul 50 minutes to walk 2 km.
How long will it take him to walk
a 4 km
b 1 km
c 3 km?

14 3 tickets to a museum cost $19.50.
Work out the cost of 4 tickets.

15 Which is better value, 6 cartons of milk for $4.80, or 5 cartons of milk for $4.25?

16 The table shows the numbers of visitors to a museum over two days.

	Adults	Children
Saturday	120	300
Sunday	180	400

Which day had the larger proportion of children visiting?

17 It takes 6 painters 4 days to paint a large house.
How long will it take
a 3 painters
b 12 painters
c 1 painter?

18 It takes Simon 40 minutes to drive to work at an average speed of 60 mph. How long would it take him at an average speed of
a 120 mph
b 15 mph?

19 How sure are you of your answers? Were you mostly
🙁 **Just guessing** 😐 **Feeling doubtful** 🙂 **Confident**
What next? Use your results to decide whether to strengthen or extend your learning.

Challenge

20 a How many people do you think can stand in a square with sides of 1 m?
The dimensions of a football pitch are 1203 m by 50 m.
b Calculate the area of the football pitch.
c Estimate how many people can stand on a football pitch.

7 Strengthen

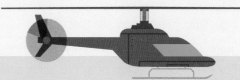

You will:
- Strengthen your understanding with practice.

Ratio

1 For each bar write down the ratio of blue to red.
Give your answers in their simplest form.

a

B	R	R

b

B	B	R	R	R	R

c

B	B	B	B	R	R	R	R	R	R	R	R

d Explain why the three ratios are equivalent.

2 a Write 2 : 8 in its simplest form.
  b Write 3 : 12 in its simplest form.

3 Match each ratio to its simplest form.

3 : 6	4 : 1
4 : 12	2 : 7
5 : 20	2 : 3
24 : 6	1 : 3
6 : 9	2 : 5
8 : 28	1 : 4
4 : 10	1 : 2

4 Write each of these ratios in its simplest form.
  a 0.1 : 0.5
  b 0.2 : 0.8
  c 0.3 : 0.6

5 Write each ratio in its simplest form.

  a $\frac{1}{3} : \frac{2}{3}$
  b $\frac{4}{6} : \frac{1}{6}$
  c $\frac{4}{10} : \frac{6}{10}$

Q2a hint

Q2b hint

What is the largest number you can divide 3 and 12 by?

Q4a Strategy hint

Multiply by 10 to get a whole number, if needed.

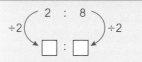

Q5a Strategy hint

Multiply by the denominator to get whole numbers, then simplify if needed.

6 Bunting has red and blue flags in the ratio 3 : 5.
A length of bunting has 20 blue flags.
How many red flags are there?

7 Jenny buys some drinks for her birthday party.
For every one carton of apple juice, she buys three cartons of orange juice. She buys 16 cartons altogether.
  a How many cartons of apple juice does she buy?
  b How many cartons of orange juice does she buy?
  c Do your answers to parts **a** and **b** add up to 16?

8 The ratio of boys to girls in a kindergarten class is 2 : 3.
There are 20 students in the class.
  a How many students are boys?
  b How many students are girls?

9 In a zoo, the ratio of female to male tigers is 3 : 1.
There are 12 tigers altogether.
How many tigers are female?

10 Ally and Billie share some sweets in the ratio of their ages.
Ally is 10 years old and Billy is 11 years old.
They have 63 sweets altogether.
How many does each person get?

11 Share these amounts in the ratios given.
  a $20 in the ratio 1 : 4
  b $32 in the ratio 1 : 3
  c $30 in the ratio 5 : 1

Direct and inverse proportion

1 a There are 3 toffees in a pack of 10 sweets.
What proportion of the pack are toffees?
  b There are 6 toffees in a pack of 10 sweets.
What proportion of the pack are toffees?
Write your answer in its simplest form and as a percentage.

2 In May there were 12 accidents on a road. Three were serious.
  a What fraction of the accidents in May were serious?
Write the fraction in its simplest form.
In June there were 15 accidents. Five were serious.
  b What proportion of the accidents in June were serious?
  c Which month had the higher proportion of serious accidents?

3 There are 10 girls and 15 boys in the school swimming team.
  a How many people are in the team?
  b What proportion of the team are girls?
  c Write your answer as a fraction.
  d Write the fraction in part **c** in its simplest form.

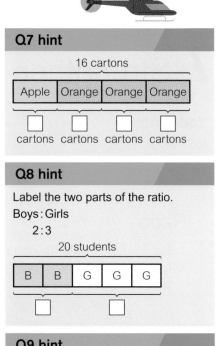

Q7 hint

16 cartons

| Apple | Orange | Orange | Orange |

☐ cartons ☐ cartons ☐ cartons ☐ cartons

Q8 hint

Label the two parts of the ratio.
Boys : Girls
  2 : 3

20 students

| B | B | G | G | G |

☐   ☐

Q9 hint

F : M
☐ : ☐
Then draw a bar model to help you.

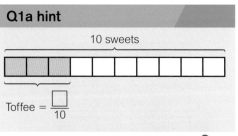

Q1a hint

10 sweets

Toffee = ☐/10

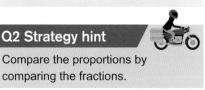

Q2 Strategy hint

Compare the proportions by comparing the fractions.

4 There are 7 apples and 3 oranges in a bowl.
   a What proportion are apples?
   Write your answer as a percentage.
   b What proportion are oranges?
   Write your answer as a percentage.

5 The ratio of cars to motorcycles in a car park is 4 : 1.
   What percentage are
   a motorcycles
   b cars?

6 **Reasoning** When taking penalties in football, Anna has a ratio of
   goals to misses of 7 : 3.
   a What percentage of penalties does Anna score?
   Bethany has a ratio of goals to misses of 1 : 4.
   b What percentage of penalties does Bethany score?
   c Who should the team choose to take their penalties?

7 2 raffle tickets cost $4. Work out the cost of
   a 4 tickets
   b 6 tickets
   c 1 ticket.

8 5 scientific calculators cost £30. How much will it cost to buy
   a 1 calculator
   b 6 calculators
   c 14 calculators?

9 In shop A, 40 pencils cost $4.80.
   In shop B, 50 pencils cost $5.50.
   a How much does one pencil cost in shop A?
   b How much does one pencil cost in shop B?
   c Which is better value for money?

10 In shop A, 3 bottles of nail polish cost £5.70.
   In shop B, 5 bottles of nail polish cost £9.
   Which is better value for money?

11 Chris can type 80 words in 2 minutes.
   How long will it take him to type
   a 40 words
   b 120 words
   c 160 words?

12 If you have fewer people, does a job take
   a more time
   b less time?

Q4a hint

How many pieces of fruit in the bowl?

Q5 hint

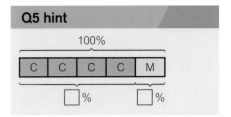

Q6 hint

Draw bar models to help you.

Q7 hint

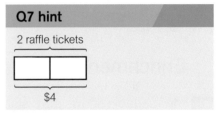

Q9 hint

Which shop has cheaper pencils?

Q11 hint

Draw a bar model to help you.
Will Chris take more or less time?

13 If you have more people, does a job take
   a more time
   b less time?

14 If you have twice the number of people, does a job take
   a half the time
   b twice the time?

15 It takes one builder 8 days to build a wall.
How long will it take
   a 2 builders
   b 4 builders?

16 It takes 2 people one day to paint a room.
How long will it take 1 person?

17 It takes four students 10 days to build a shed for the school garden.
How long does it take
   a 8 students
   b 2 students
   c 1 student?

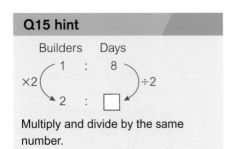

Q15 hint

Builders   Days

$\times 2 \left(\begin{array}{ccc} 1 & : & 8 \\ 2 & : & \square \end{array}\right) \div 2$

Multiply and divide by the same number.

Enrichment

1 The table shows the distances between some cities.
All the distances are in kilometres.

London			
5711	Shanghai		
5938	1764	Tokyo	
3459	11 851	10 845	New York

   a What is the distance from Tokyo to London?
     Anu is going on a business trip. She starts in London, flies to New York and then back to Shanghai before returning to London.
   b How far does she travel?
   c Each flight costs $50 plus $0.11 per km.
     Estimate the cost of Anu's trip.

Q1a hint

Read down from London and across from Tokyo.

2 One person takes 30 minutes to clean a car.
Write a maths question using this information.
Work out the answer.

3 **Reflect** The hints in these Strengthen lessons used lots of diagrams.
Look back at the diagrams in the hints.
Which diagrams did you find most useful? Why?
Which diagrams did you find least useful? Why?

7 Extend

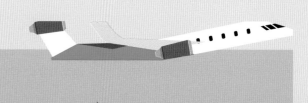

You will:
- Extend your understanding with problem-solving.

1 **Problem-solving** Karen is 12 years old. Jane is 3 years older than Karen and 3 years younger than Sarah.
Write the ratio of Karen's age to Jane's age to Sarah's age in its simplest form

2 In the UK, distances are measured in miles. 5 miles ≈ 8 km.
Convert these distances into kilometres.
a 10 miles
b 1 mile
c 8 miles
d 80 miles

Q2 hint

≈ means 'is approximately equal to'.

3 **Real** The tables show some information about the US and GB bobsled teams at the 2014 Winter Olympics.

	GB time (s)	Speed (km/h)	USA time (s)	Speed (mph)
1st run	55.26	138.8	54.89	86.8
2nd run	55.27	137.2	55.47	85.8
3rd run	55.31	137.0	55.30	85.6
4th run	55.33	138.0	55.33	86.3

	GB mass (kg)	USA mass (lbs)
Team	403	900
Sled	52	50
Total	455	950

5 mph ≈ 8 km/h
2.2 lbs ≈ 1 kg

a Compare the top speed of the GB team with the top speed of the US team.
b Work out the range of times for each team.
Which team was more consistent?
c Compare the masses of the two teams.
d Compare the total masses.
e What percentage of the total mass of the US bobsled is the bobsled itself?
f What percentage of the total mass of the GB bobsled is the bobsled itself?

4 **Problem-solving** In a classroom there are 18 desks.
There are 14 more chairs than desks.
What proportion of the furniture is chairs?
Write your answer as a fraction and a percentage.

Q4 hint

Remember to write your fraction in its simplest form.

5 The table shows the numbers of matches two football teams win, lose and draw in one season.

	Win	Lose	Draw
Team A	5	8	3
Team B	3	8	4

a Write the proportion of matches lost by each team as a percentage.

b Which team lost the higher proportion of matches?

6 **Problem-solving** In a group of 30 people, 1 in 5 people have blue eyes and the others have brown eyes.
How many more people have brown eyes?

Q6 hint
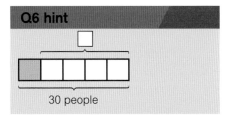
30 people

7 Jane and Claire had an equal number of stickers.
Jane gives $\frac{1}{5}$ of her stickers to Claire.
a Write the ratio of the number of Jane's stickers to Claire's stickers. Write the ratio in its simplest form.
b Claire has 12 more stickers than Jane.
How many stickers does Jane have now?
c How many stickers do they have altogether?

Q7 hint
Draw a bar model to help.
Jane
Claire

8 Simon and Mark had an equal number of video games.
Simon gives $\frac{2}{5}$ of his video games to Mark.
a Write the ratio of the number of video games that Simon has to the number Mark has now.
b Mark has 24 more video games than Simon.
How many video games does Simon have?
c How many video games do they have altogether?

9 **Reasoning** Ratio $a:b = 1:2$ and ratio $b:c = 3:4$.
What is the ratio $a:b:c$?

10 **Problem-solving / Reasoning** A shop has chocolates on offer.

OFFER A
3 for £10.50

OFFER B
5 for £17.50

OFFER C
6 for £20.40

Q10 hint
Work out the cost of one chocolate first.

a Which offer is the best value for money?
b Write your own offer, D, that is better value than A but worse value than C.

11 **Problem-solving / Reasoning** A bottle of water holds 500 ml.
A supermarket has two deals:
6 × 500 ml bottles for $3.50 and 8 × 500 ml bottles for $5.
a Work out how much one bottle costs in each deal.
b Which deal is better value for money?

12 **Problem-solving / Reasoning** Two farmers are offering different deals on their potatoes.
The first farmer offers $2.25 for 2.5 kg of potatoes, and the second farmer offers $4.50 for 7 kg of potatoes.
Which farmer would you buy potatoes from?

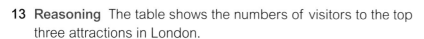

13 Reasoning The table shows the numbers of visitors to the top three attractions in London.

	2011	2012
British Museum	5.8 million	5.6 million
Tate Modern	4.89 million	5.3 million
National Gallery	5.3 million	5.42 million

a For each attraction, write the ratio of visitors in 2011 to 2012 in its simplest form.

b Has the proportion of visitors going to the British Museum increased?

14 Problem-solving In a car-park, $\frac{1}{5}$ of the spaces are reserved for cars with children.
Write the ratio of spaces for cars with children, to cars without children, in its simplest form.

Q14 hint

Work out the fraction of spaces for cars without children first.

15 Problem-solving It takes 12 people 40 days to build a bridge. How many people are needed to build the bridge in 30 days?

Investigation

Reasoning

1 Draw a square of side length 4 cm. Measure the diagonal.
2 Repeat for different squares.
3 Copy the table, and write the ratio of side length to diagonal for each square.

Side length	Diagonal length	Ratio side : diagonal
4 cm		
6 cm		
7 cm		

4 What do you notice about the ratio of the side length to the diagonal?
5 What do you think the length of the diagonal will be for a square of side length 10 cm?
6 What do you think the side length will be for a square with a diagonal of 14 cm?

16 Reflect In these lessons you were asked questions about ratios and proportions.
Are ratio and proportion the same thing or different?

Q16 Strategy hint

You could explain your answer using diagrams or real life examples.

Reflect

7 Unit test

1 In a field there are 10 goats and 3 chickens.
   Write down the ratio of goats to chickens.

2 Write each ratio in its simplest form.
   a 8:12
   b 50:20

3 Share £72 in the ratio 5:3.

4 The ratio of boys to girls in a tennis club is 3:4.
   There are 12 boys in the tennis club.
   a Work out how many girls there are.
   b Work out how many people there are altogether.

5 A 30 000 kg load is shared between two ships in the ratio 3:2.
   Work out the difference in mass between the two loads.

6 On a school trip the ratio of teachers to students is 1:9.
   Write the proportion of teachers as
   a a fraction
   b a percentage.

7 In the 2013 Wimbledon tennis final, the ratio of points won to points
   lost was 26:11 for Andy Murray and was 30:22 for Novak Djokovic.
   Calculate who won the greater proportion of points.

8 About 40% of a panda's fur is black and the rest is white.
   Write the ratio of black to white fur in its simplest form.

9 8 tickets cost $360.
   Work out how much 5 tickets cost.

10 An arts and crafts shop sells balls of wool in 100 g bundles.
   The shop has three different deals on wool.

   | **Offer A** 2 balls for $3.25 | **Offer B** 5 balls for $7.50 | **Offer C** 8 balls for $10 |

   Which offer is the best value for money? You must give a reason for
   your answer.

11 Write these ratios in their simplest forms.
   a 0.6:0.8
   b 0.02:0.09
   c 0.3:0.04

12 One month Jamie spent $\frac{1}{4}$ of his money allowance on clothes, and
   saved the rest.
   Write the ratio of the money he spent on clothes and savings as a
   ratio in its simplest form.

13 A gardener wants her flowerbed to be 60% pansies and the rest to be tulips.

   a Work out what percentage of flowerbed will be tulips.

   b Write the ratio of pansies : tulips in its simplest form.

   c She plants 150 pansies.
      How many tulips does she need to plant?

14 It takes 4 people 5 hours to build a shed.
Work out how long it takes

   a 2 people

   b 8 people.

   c Work out how many people are needed to build the shed in 1 hour.

Challenge

15 Here are six cards with ratios written on them.

3 : 5   0.1 : 0.3   1 : 4 $\frac{1}{3} : \frac{2}{3}$ 0.5 : 0.7 $\frac{1}{4} : \frac{1}{5}$

- Start with $1000.
- Choose a card and share $1000 in the ratio written on it.
  Circle the larger amount.
- Choose a different card and share the circled amount in this ratio.
  Circle the smaller amount.
- Choose a different card and share the circled amount in this ratio.
  Circle the larger amount.
- Continue these steps until you can go no further.

   a What is the smallest final amount you can find?

   b Is there a strategy you can use to try and find the smallest amount? Explain your answer.

> **Q15 hint**
>
> Use each ratio card once only.
> Only use a ratio card if it shares the amount exactly into whole numbers of dollars.

16 Reflect List five new skills and ideas you have learned in this unit. What mathematics operations did you use most (addition, subtraction and division)?
Which lesson in this unit did you like best? Why?

8.1 STEM: Metric measures

You will learn to:
- Convert between metric units of measures of length, mass and capacity.
- Solve problems in everyday contexts involving measures and conversions.

Confidence

Why learn this?
Scientists need to know how to convert between different units of measure in order to use formulae and make calculations.

Fluency
Work out
- 4 × 10
- 0.5 × 100
- 210 ÷ 100
- 300 ÷ 1000

Explore
How much do all the cars in a school car park weigh?

Exercise 8.1

Warm up

1 Which unit would you use to measure each of these?
Choose from litres, kilograms or metres.
   a the length of a tennis court
   b the weight of a person
   c the amount of liquid in a bottle of milk

2 Put these units of measure in order from smallest to largest.
   a km, mm, cm, m   b mg, tonnes (t), g, kg
   c litres (l), ml

3 Copy and complete.
   a $6\,cm = 6 \times \square = \square\,mm$ b $8\,m = 8 \times \square = \square\,cm$
   c $9\,km = 9 \times \square = \square\,m$ d $400\,cm = 400 \div \square = \square\,m$
   e $80\,mm = 80 \div \square = \square\,cm$ f $25\,000\,m = 25\,000 \div \square = \square\,km$
   Discussion When you convert between units, how do you know
   whether to multiply or divide?

4 Copy and complete.
   a $2.5\,m = 2.5 \times 100 = \square\,cm$ b $12.5\,km = 12.5 \times \square = \square\,m$
   c $88\,mm = 88 \div \square = \square\,cm$ d $160\,cm = 160 \div \square = \square\,m$

5 Copy and complete.
   a $5\,kg = 5 \times \square = \square\,g$ b $7\,l = 7 \times \square = \square\,ml$
   c $15\,000\,ml = 15\,000 \div \square = \square\,l$ d $6000\,g = 6000 \div \square = \square\,kg$

6 Copy and complete.
   a $4.2\,kg = 4.2 \times \square = \square\,g$ b $0.75\,l = 0.75 \times \square = \square\,ml$
   c $4250\,ml = 4250 \div \square = \square\,l$ d $875\,g = 875 \div \square = \square\,kg$

Key point

Metric units of **length** include the **millimetre (mm)**, **centimetre (cm)**, **metre (m)** and **kilometre (km)**.
10 mm = 1 cm, 100 cm = 1 m, 1000 m = 1 km

Key point

Metric units of **mass** include the **gram (g)** and **kilogram (kg)**.
1000 g = 1 kg
Metric units of **capacity** include the **millilitre (ml)** and **litre (l)**.
1000 ml = 1 l

7 For each pair of lengths, work out which is shorter.
 a 5 m or 400 cm   **b** 300 mm or 15 cm   **c** 6 km or 8000 m

8 Here are the heights (in metres) of five students.
 1.54, 1.5, 1.5, 1.55, 1.53
 a Write the mode. Give your answer
  i in metres   **ii** in centimetres.
 b Work out the median. Give your answer
  i in metres   **ii** in centimetres.

9 Simplify these ratios
 a 3 cm : 1 m   **b** 50 kg : 5000 g
 c 50 ml : 2 litres   **d** 2 cm : 25 mm

10 STEM A nutmeg has a mass of 10 g.
 A nutmeg tree produces 8000 nutmegs a year.
 What is the total mass of nutmegs produced by this tree each year?
 Give your answer **a** in grams   **b** in kilograms.

11 STEM / Modelling The average mass of a car is 1175 kg.
 a Write this mass in tonnes.
 b An old bridge has a safety limit of 7.5 tonnes.
  How many cars can it safely hold at one time?

12 Problem-solving Harry buys 1.5 litres of orange concentrate for his
 party. On the side of the bottle it says, 'Enough for 50 glasses'.
 Approximately how much orange juice should he put into each glass?

13 Problem-solving The diagram shows three jugs full of water.

Jug 1   Jug 2   Jug 3

3*l*   750 m*l*   500 m*l*

Using only these jugs, how can you end up with
 a 2500 m*l* in the largest jug   **b** 1750 m*l* in the largest jug?
Show your working and explain your method.

Q13a Strategy hint

Start by converting the 3 litres into millilitres, so all the units are the same.

Investigation   Problem-solving

A mechanical weighing scale uses different sized brass weights to make different totals.
With brass weights of 1 g and 2 g, you can make **total masses** of 1 g, 2 g and 3 g (1 g + 2 g).
1 Using brass weights of mass 1 g, 2 g and 4 g, what different **total masses** can you make?
2 Which brass weights can make a total mass of 15 g? In how many different ways can you do this?
3 What set of brass weights would you need in order to make **every** total mass from
 1 g to 30 g? What is the smallest set you can do this with?

14 Explore How much do all the cars in a school car park weigh?
 What have you learned from this lesson to help you answer this
 question? What other information do you need?

15 Reflect Write down the steps you used to convert from
  • metres to centimetres   • metres to millimetres   • milligrams to grams.
 Is it easier going from larger measures to smaller measures (e.g. m to cm) or
 smaller measures to larger measures (e.g. mg to kg)?

8.2 Perimeter

You will learn to:
- Find the perimeter of regular polygons with one side given.
- Find the perimeter of irregular polygons including compound shapes.

Why learn this?
Farmers have to calculate the perimeter of a field to work out the amount of fencing they need.

Fluency
Work out
- 2 × 5 + 2 × 17
- 2(3 + 4)
- 8 × 14

Explore
How much fencing is needed for an L-shaped field?

Confidence

Exercise 8.2

1 Name each of these **regular polygons**.

a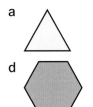

b

c

d

e

> **Q1 Literacy hint**
>
> A **regular polygon** is a straight-sided closed shape with all sides and all angles equal.

2 Work out each side length marked with a ☐ in these diagrams.

a

5 cm
6 cm
4 cm
☐
☐
12 cm

b

15 cm
5 cm
2 cm
7 cm
☐
☐
6 cm
5 cm

Warm up

3 Calculate the **perimeter** of each regular polygon using the given side lengths.

a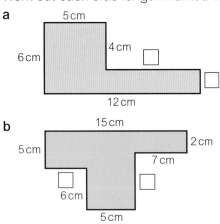
2 cm

b
6 cm

c
5 cm

d
4 cm

> **Key point**
>
> The **perimeter** is the total distance around the edge of a shape. To work out the perimeter of a shape, add up the lengths of all the sides.

> **Q3a hint**
>
> perimeter = 2 + 2 + 2 = ☐ cm
> It is quicker to multiply the side length by the number of sides.
> perimeter = 3 × 2 cm = ☐ cm

4 Work out the perimeter of each of these shapes.

a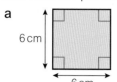
6 cm
6 cm

b
8 mm
22 mm

c
2.4 m
1.8 m

5 Work out the perimeter of each of these shapes.
Give your answers in mm.

a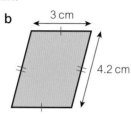
5 mm

b
3 cm
4.2 cm

c
12 mm
3.2 cm
3 cm

Q5 hint
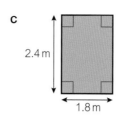
Sides are equal length

6 This shape is made from rectangles.
   a Work out the missing length a.
   b Work out the missing length b.
   c Work out the perimeter of the shape.

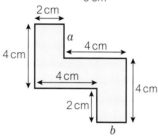
2 cm
4 cm
a
4 cm
4 cm
4 cm
2 cm
4 cm
b

7 Work out the perimeter of each shape.

a
2 cm
4 cm
3 cm
5 cm

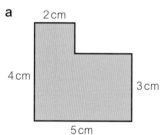

b
5 m
3 m
1 m
7 m

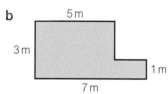

Q7 Strategy hint

Sketch the shapes.
Work out the missing lengths.
Write them on your sketch.

c
20 mm
10 mm
20 mm
40 mm
90 mm

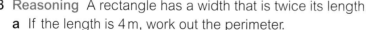

8 **Reasoning** A rectangle has a width that is twice its length.
   a If the length is 4 m, work out the perimeter.
   b If the length is x m, write an expression for the perimeter in terms of x.

Q8 Strategy hint

Draw a diagram and label what you know.

9 **Real** A farmer has a rectangular field with length 32 m and width 54 m.
   a The farmer is going to put fencing around the field. The fencing costs $80 per metre. How much will the fencing cost?
   A rectangle measuring 5 m by 7 m is removed from one corner of the field to make space for a barn.
   b Show that the remaining part of the field has the same perimeter as the original rectangular field.
   c Explain why this is.

Q9 Strategy hint

Draw a diagram of the field first.

10 Problem-solving The diagram shows a right-angled triangle.

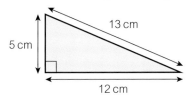

Four of these triangles are put together to make a shape, like this:

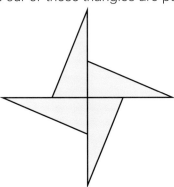

Calculate the perimeter of the shape.

Investigation

1 On a piece of centimetre squared paper, shade in
a shape made from eight squares. Here are two examples.
Rule 1: Your shape must be made from whole squares.
Rule 2: All the squares must touch side to side, not corner to corner.

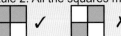 ✓   ✗

2 Work out the perimeter of your shape in centimetres.

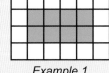

Example 1

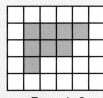

Example 2

3 Try other shapes made from eight squares and work out the perimeter of each one.
4 Which shape has the largest perimeter? Which has the smallest perimeter?

Discussion Compare your shapes with other people in your class.
Who has drawn the shape with the largest perimeter? Which the smallest perimeter?

---

11 Explore How much fencing is needed for an L-shaped field? What
have you learned from this lesson to help you answer the question?
What other information do you need?

12 Reflect What strategies have you learned this lesson? Write down
any strategies you have learned for finding perimeters of shapes.

8.3 Area

You will learn to:
- Calculate the area of squares and rectangles.
- Calculate the area of compound shapes made from rectangles.
- Solve perimeter and area problems.

Why learn this?
Carpet fitters need to calculate the area of the room when they lay carpets.

Fluency
Work out
- 25 × 6
- 3 × 4 + 7 × 8
- 12 × 8 − 2 × 10

Explore
How much will it cost to carpet a U-shaped room?

Exercise 8.3

1 Work out the perimeter of each shape.

a

7 cm
← 7 cm →

b
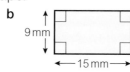
9 mm
←—15 mm—→

2 These compound shapes have been split into rectangles.
Write down the length and width of each rectangle.

a
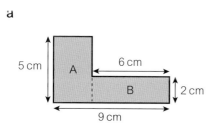
5 cm
A
6 cm
B
2 cm
9 cm

b
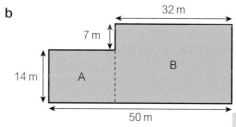
32 m
7 m
14 m
A
B
50 m

A □ cm × □ cm, B □ cm × □ cm   A □ m × □ m, B □ m × □ m

Key point
You can find the **area** of a shape drawn on squared paper by counting the squares inside it.
The **units** used for area are square units, such as mm², cm², m² and km².
 1 cm has area 1 cm².
1 cm

3 Find the area of each shape by counting squares. Give the units.

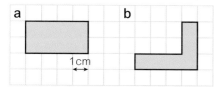
a
b
1cm

Key point
To work out the area of a rectangle or square, use
area = length × width
The length and the width must be in the same units.

4 Calculate the area of each rectangle.

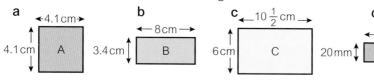
a ←4.1 cm→ 4.1 cm A
b ←8 cm→ 3.4 cm B
c ←10 ½ cm→ 6 cm C
d ←8 cm→ 20 mm D

5 Copy and complete the working to find the area of this shape.

area A $= 5 \times 3 = 15\,cm^2$
area B $= 8 \times 7 = \square\,cm^2$
total area $=$ area A $+$ area B
$\qquad = 15 + \square$
$\qquad = \square\,cm^2$

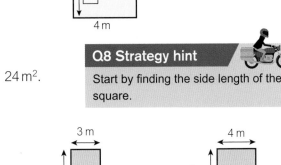

6 Work out the area of each shape in Q2.

7 **Real** The diagram shows the dimensions of a room.
Work out the area of the floor.
Discussion How many different ways are there to work out the area of the floor?

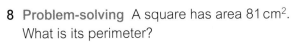

8 **Problem-solving** A square has area $81\,cm^2$.
What is its perimeter?

Q8 Strategy hint

Start by finding the side length of the square.

9 **Problem-solving / Reasoning** A rectangle has an area of $24\,m^2$.
The length and width are both whole numbers of metres.
How many possible rectangles are there with this area?

10 **Real** The diagram shows the dimensions of a room.
  a Calculate the area of the room.
  The carpet costs €20 per square metre.
  b Calculate the cost of carpeting the room.

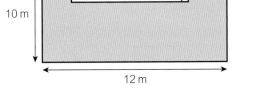

11 **Problem-solving** A regular hexagon has sides of length 10 m.
  a Work out the perimeter of the hexagon.
  A regular octagon has the same perimeter as the hexagon.
  b Find the length of the sides of the octagon.

Investigation   **Problem-solving**

A shape has a perimeter of $30\,cm^2$. All the sides are whole numbers of centimetres.
  1 How many **rectangles** with this perimeter are there? What are their **areas**?
  2 How many **L-shapes** have this perimeter? What are their areas?
  3 How many different **compound shapes** made of rectangles could have this perimeter?
  4 Which shape has the smallest area? Which has the largest area?

12 **Explore** How much would it cost to carpet a U-shaped room?
What have you learned in this lesson to help you answer this question? What other information do you need?

13 **Reflect** In this lesson, you calculated areas of rectangles and compound shapes.
What strategies did you use to calculate the area? For example, did you split up the shapes?
What information do you need to know in order to calculate the area?

Explore

Reflect

8.4 3D solids

You will learn to:
- Identify properties of 3D solids, including cubes, cuboids and prisms.
- Identify reflective symmetry in 3D solids.

Why learn this?
3D models are built to scale from 2D plans.

Fluency
What are the names of these 2D shapes?

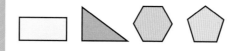

Explore
Which solid has the most planes of symmetry?

Exercise 8.4

1 Look at these solids.
  a Write the names of the solids.
  b Write the names of the 2D shapes you can see.

  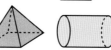

2 Copy these shapes.
Draw all the **lines of symmetry** (mirror lines) on the shapes.
The first one is done for you.

a 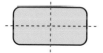   b

c   d

3 Write the number of **faces**, **edges** and **vertices** in
  a a cube
  b a cuboid
  c a triangular-based prism.

Q3 Strategy hint
Draw a sketch of each solid.

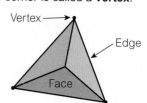

4 Write the number of faces, edges and vertices in this pyramid.

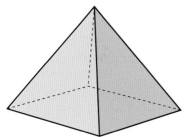

5 Problem-solving A 3D solid has 3 rectangular and 2 triangular faces. What is the name of this solid?

1 Record the number of faces (F), edges (E) and vertices (V) for each solid.

Solid	Faces (F)	Edges (E)	Vertices (V)
Cube			

2 Try to find a rule that links the number of faces, edges and vertices.

Discussion Does your rule work for a cone, sphere and cylinder?

6 Sketch a copy of each solid and draw in a **plane of symmetry**. How many planes of symmetry does each solid have?

a 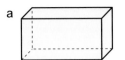 b   c 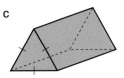   d

> **Key point**
>
> A 2D shape can have lines of symmetry. A 3D solid can have **planes of symmetry**. On either side of the plane of symmetry the solid is identical.
>
>

Discussion Which solids have an infinite number of planes of symmetry?

7 Problem-solving

a How many faces, edges and vertices does a hexagonal prism have?

b Three regular hexagonal prisms are joined together to make the shape shown.
How many planes of symmetry does this shape have?

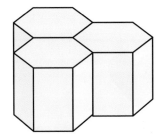

> **Q6 hint**
>
> Sketch a new copy for each plane you show.

8 Reasoning A cylinder is like a prism with a circular cross-section.

a How many lines of symmetry does a circle have?

b How many planes of symmetry does a cylinder have?

c Are there any other solids with the same number of planes of symmetry?

9 Explore Which solid has the most planes of symmetry?
What have you learned this lesson to help you answer this?
What further information do you need in order to answer this?

10 Reflect What properties of solids have you learned in this lesson?
Write down three new things you learned and one thing you want to find out more about.

8 Check up

Metric measures

1 Copy and complete.
 a 8 cm = ☐ mm
 b 2 kg = ☐ g
 c 600 cm = ☐ m

2 Copy and complete.
 a 3.2 m = ☐ cm
 b 8.7 *l* = ☐ m*l*
 c 2400 m = ☐ km

3 a Write these lengths in order from smallest to largest.
 15 cm, 100 mm, 0.1 m, 3 km, 7 cm, 0.2 km
 b Write down the mode.

Perimeter and area

4 Calculate the perimeter of this regular hexagon.

4 cm

5 Work out the perimeter of each of these shapes.
 Write the correct units with your answers.

a
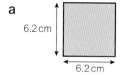
6.2 cm
6.2 cm

b
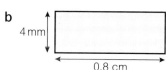
4 mm
0.8 cm

6 Work out the area of each shape in Q5.
 Write the correct units with your answers.

7 A square has area 9 m². What is its perimeter?

8 Find the perimeter of this shape.

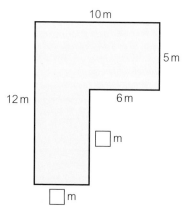
10 m
5 m
12 m
6 m
☐ m
☐ m

9 Work out the area of this shape.

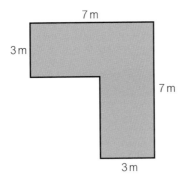

10 A rectangle and a square have the same area.
The rectangle has length 2 m and width 8 m.
What is the side length of the square?

11 How many different rectangles are there with an area of 12 cm^2,
where the length and width are both whole numbers?

3D solids

12 How many vertices, edges and faces does a pentagonal prism
have?

13 How many planes of symmetry does this cuboid have?

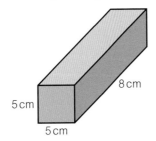

14 **How sure are you of your answers? Were you mostly**
😟 **Just guessing** 😐 **Feeling doubtful** 🙂 **Confident**
**What next? Use your results to decide whether to strengthen or
extend your learning.**

Challenge

15 A shape has an area of 9 cm^2.
Sketch and label the lengths of a possible
 a square
 b rectangle
 c L-shaped compound shape
 d U-shaped compound shape.

8 Strengthen

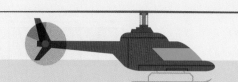

You will:
- Strengthen your understanding with practice.

Metric measures

1 Copy and complete.
  a 1 cm = 10 mm, so 6 cm = ☐ mm
  b 1 m = 100 cm, so 3 m = ☐ cm
  c 10 mm = 1 cm, so 40 mm = ☐ cm
  d 1 km = ☐ m, so ☐ km = 5000 m
  e 1 kg = ☐ g, so ☐ kg = 8000 g

2 Copy and complete.
  a 4.6 m = ☐ cm   **b** 6.5 *l* = ☐ m*l*
  c 5.25 km = ☐ m   **d** 4.8 cm = ☐ mm
  e 0.35 kg = ☐ g   **f** 5.8 m = ☐ cm

3 Copy and complete.
  a 240 cm = ☐ m   **b** 3250 m*l* = ☐ *l*
  c 9200 g = ☐ kg   **d** 4280 m = ☐ km
  e 56 mm = ☐ cm   **f** 54 cm = ☐ m

4 Here is a list of masses.
  300 g, 0.1 kg, 0.25 kg, 150 g, 200 g
  a Convert each mass to grams.
  b Calculate the mean mass.
  c Calculate the median mass.

Perimeter and area

1 Calculate the perimeter of each of these regular polygons.

  a
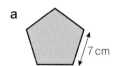
7 cm

  b
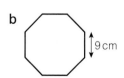
9 cm

  c

14 cm

Q1 hint

Use number lines like this to help you.

1 cm	2 cm	3 cm	4 cm	5 cm	6 cm
10 mm	20 mm	30 mm	☐ mm	☐ mm	☐ mm

Q2a hint

Use number lines like this to help you.

4 m	4.1 m	4.2 m	4.3 m	4.4 m	4.5 m	4.6 m
400 cm	410 cm	420 cm	430 cm	440 cm	☐	☐

Q3 hint

Use number lines like this to help you.

1 m .... 2 m .... 3 m
100 cm .... 200 cm .... 300 cm

Q4a hint

Use a number line like this to help you.

g: 0   100   200   300   400   500   600   700   800   900   1000
kg: 0   0.25   0.5   0.75   1

Q4b hint

To find the mean, add all the masses and then divide by how many there are.

Q4c hint

Put the masses in order first.

Q1a hint

In a regular polygon all the sides are the same length.
Perimeter = 7 + 7 + 7 + 7 + 7 = 5 × 7
= ☐ cm

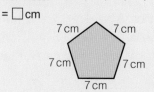
7 cm   7 cm
7 cm   7 cm
7 cm

2 This rectangle is drawn on a centimetre square grid.

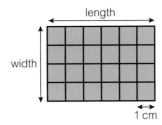

Copy and complete.
a The length of the rectangle = ☐ cm
b The width of the rectangle = ☐ cm
c The perimeter of the rectangle = ☐ cm
d The area of the rectangle = ☐ cm²

Q2a hint

Count the number of squares along the length.

Q2d hint

Work out the number of squares inside the shape.

3 Copy and complete the table showing the perimeter and area of each of these shapes.

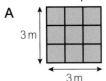

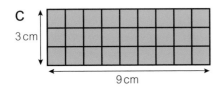

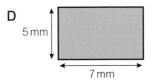

Q3 hint

To work out the perimeter, add all the side lengths together.
To work out the area, multiply the length by the width.

Shape	Perimeter	Units	Area	Units
A	☐	m	3 × 3 = ☐	m²
B	3 + 3 + 3 + 3 =			
C	☐	cm	3 × 9 = ☐	cm²
D	3 + 9 + 3 + 9 =			

4 A square has perimeter 36 cm.
a What is the side length of the square?
b What is the area of the square?

5 Copy and complete the working to find the area of this shape.

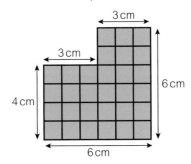

area A = 4 × 3 = ☐ cm²
area B = 6 × 3 = ☐ cm²
total area = area A + area B
= ☐ + ☐
= ☐ cm²

Q4a hint

Each side of a square is the same length, so
? + ? + ? + ? = 36
4 × ? = 36

Q5 hint

Divide the shape into two rectangles and label them A and B.

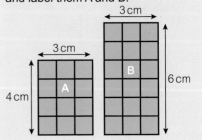

6 Work out the perimeter and area of each shape.
They have been started for you.
Copy and complete the working below.

a
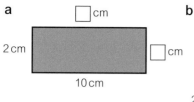
cm · 2 cm · cm · 10 cm

b
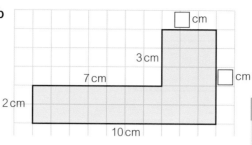
cm · 3 cm · 7 cm · cm · 2 cm · 10 cm

a perimeter = 10 + 2 + □ + □ = □ cm
area = □ × □ = □ cm²
b perimeter = 10 + 2 + 7 + 3 + □ + □ + □ = □ cm
area = □ × □ + □ × □ = □ cm²

Q6b hint
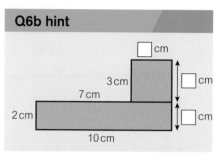
cm · 3 cm · cm · 7 cm · 2 cm · cm · 10 cm

7 Work out the perimeter and area of each shape.

a
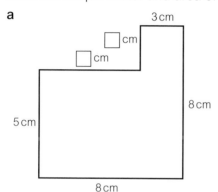
3 cm · cm · cm · 8 cm · 5 cm · 8 cm

b
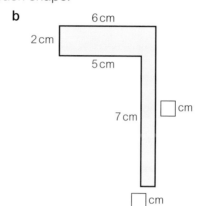
6 cm · 2 cm · 5 cm · 7 cm · cm · cm

Q7 hint

First find each missing side length marked with a □

8 This square and rectangle have the same perimeter.
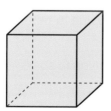
3.8 cm · 3.8 cm · ? · 4.2 cm

Work out the width of the rectangle.

Q8 hint

Work out the perimeter of the square. This is the perimeter of the rectangle too.
What calculation can you do to find the width of the rectangle?

3D solids

1 The diagram shows a cube.
Write down
  a the number of faces
  b the number of vertices
  c the number of edges.

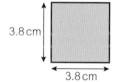

Q1 hint

Draw the cube and trace over or colour the faces, edges and vertices to help you count them.

Q2 Strategy hint

Count the edges of each shape, then the vertices, then the faces. Which is the correct shape?

2 Which of these solids has 6 edges, 4 vertices and 4 faces?

A
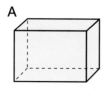
B
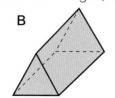
C
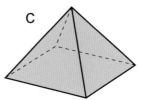
D

3 The diagrams show a cuboid divided by four planes.
Which diagram does *not* show a plane of symmetry?

Q3 hint

The two pieces must be reflections of each other in the plane of symmetry.

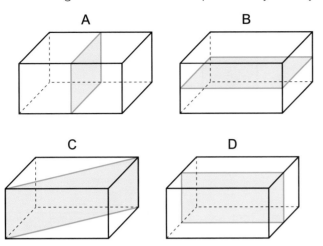

4 In this triangular prism the cross-section is an isosceles triangle. How many planes of symmetry does the prism have?

Q4 hint

How many ways could you cut it in half? Would each half be a reflection of the other?

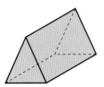

Enrichment

1 **STEM** When a hedgehog arrives at a rescue centre it is weighed and measured. Staff at the centre work out a body mass index (BMI) value for the hedgehog. A hedgehog is well enough to be released when it has a BMI value that is greater than 0.8 *and* its mass is greater than 0.65 kg.
The table shows the BMI values and weights of some hedgehogs at a rescue centre.

Hedgehog	A	B	C	D	E	F	G	H	I
BMI value	0.9	0.82	0.88	0.79	0.95	0.7	0.85	0.76	0.92
Mass (kg)	0.68	0.7	0.78	0.6	0.8	0.58	0.62	0.71	0.85

a Which hedgehogs are well enough to be released?
b Which hedgehog only needs to increase its mass to be released?
c Which hedgehog only needs to increase its BMI value to be released?

2 **Reflect** In these lessons, you drew diagrams to help you to solve problems involving shapes and solids.
Did drawing diagrams help you? Explain why or why not.
Will you draw diagrams to help you in future? Explain why or why not.

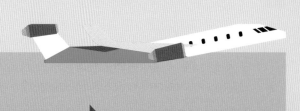

8 Extend

You will:
• Extend your understanding with problem-solving.

 1 Modelling Clare and Sarah are testing their toy rockets. Clare uses an air pump to release her rockets. Sarah uses a bicarbonate of soda reaction to release her rockets. They measure the distances that their rockets fly, and record their results in tables.

Distances covered (in metres) by Clare's rockets											
6.5	4.7	12.8	0.5	8.1	4.9	7.2	10.9	5.4	2.9	4.5	8.5

Distances covered (in centimetres) by Sarah's rockets								
1250	480	1090	1340	650	980	460	1250	990

a Work out the mean distance covered for each type of toy rocket. Give your answers in metres correct to 2 decimal places.

b Sam says, 'On average, Sarah's rockets travel about 3 metres further than Clare's rockets.'
Is he correct? Explain your answer.

c One of Clare's rockets didn't work properly. This rocket's distance was removed from the data.
  i What is the new mean for Clare's rockets?
  ii What effect does this new mean have on Sam's statement in part **b**?

d Based on the information you are given on the two methods of propulsion, do you think it is fair to say that Sarah's rockets go further than Clare's rockets?
Explain your answer.

Q1d Literacy hint

Propulsion is the force that moves or pushes something forward.

2 Problem-solving The diagram shows four regular polygons. The sum of the perimeters of the triangle and hexagon is equal to the sum of the perimeters of the pentagon and square.
Work out the side length of the square.

5.3 cm

3.6 cm

4.7 cm

3 Real A beach volleyball court is 16 m long and 8 m wide.
A rope goes around the outside of the volleyball court, 5 m from the edges of the court.
How long is the rope?

4 a A regular volleyball court has a perimeter of 54 m.
The length of the court is 18 m.
What is the area of the court?

b A rugby pitch has an area of 9800 m². The width of the pitch is 70 m.
What is its perimeter?

Q4a hint

Draw a diagram to help you.

5 The Great Pyramid of Giza has a square base.
The perimeter of the base is 921.6 m.
What is the area of the base?
Give your answer to the nearest square metre.

6 A square board game has an area of 2500 cm².
What is the perimeter of the board?

7 Give an example to show why each of these statements is wrong.
  a The perimeter of a rectangle cannot be an odd number.
  b When the length and the width of a rectangle are doubled, the
    area is also doubled.
  c Ignoring the units, the area and the perimeter of a square are
    always different.

Q7a hint

What if one side is a decimal?

8 **Finance / Modelling** A 2 km long stretch of road needs to be
resurfaced. The width of the road is 8.3 m.
  a Model this stretch of road as a rectangle.
    Work out the area of road that needs to be resurfaced in m².
  Resurfacing this road costs £30 per square metre.
  b What is the total cost to resurface this road?

9 The diagram shows a pentagonal prism.
This solid has faces in the shape of 2 pentagons
and 5 rectangles. It has 7 faces, 15 edges
and 10 vertices.

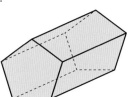

  a What shapes are the faces of these 3D solids?
    i a hexagonal prism
    ii a heptagonal prism
    iii a decagonal prism

Q9a hint

heptagon – 7 sides
decagon – 10 sides

  b Copy and complete this table for the solid in the diagram and
    described in part **a**.

Solid	Faces	Edges	Vertices	Check: F + V = E + 2
Pentagonal prism	7	15	10	☐ + ☐ = ☐ + 2 = ☐
Hexagonal prism				

  c A prism has 8 rectangles and 2 end shapes.
    What is the name of this prism?

10 **Reasoning**
  a Find the area of this shape by adding together
    the areas of A and B.
  b Find the area of the same shape again, by
    finding the area of the whole rectangle
    and subtracting the shaded area.
  Discussion Which method do you prefer? Why?

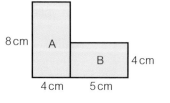

11 Problem-solving The area of this L shape is 32 cm².

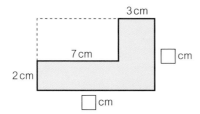

Work out its perimeter.

12 STEM Greenhouse gases slow down or prevent the loss of heat from the Earth.

The diagrams show models of two different greenhouse gases.

How many planes of symmetry does each molecule have?

a Ozone (O_3)   **b** Nitrogen trifluoride (NF_3)

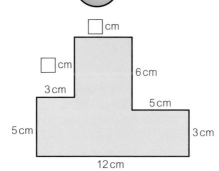

13 For this shape work out
  a the perimeter
  b the area.

14 Work out the area of each rectangle.

Give your answers in the units shown on each rectangle.

a
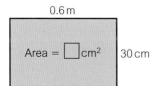
0.6 m
Area = ☐ cm²
30 cm

b
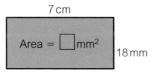
7 cm
Area = ☐ mm²
18 mm

Give your answers to parts **c** and **d** to 2 decimal places.

c
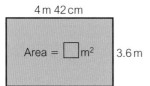
4 m 42 cm
Area = ☐ m²
3.6 m

d
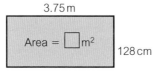
3.75 m
Area = ☐ m²
128 cm

Investigation

1 Draw these rectangles on centimetre squared paper and work out their areas.
   a 3 cm by 2 cm **b** 30 mm by 20 mm **c** 5 cm by 4 cm **d** 50 mm by 40 mm

2 Draw a 1 cm by 1 cm square.
   Copy and complete.
   area of 1 cm by 1 cm square = ☐ cm²
   area of 10 mm by 10 mm square = ☐ mm²
   1 cm² = ☐ mm²

3 Copy and complete these conversions.
   a 5 cm² = ☐ mm² **b** 9 cm² = ☐ mm² **c** 4.2 cm² = ☐ mm²
   d 300 mm² = ☐ cm² **e** 800 mm² = ☐ cm² **f** 360 mm² = ☐ cm²

4 **a** Use the same method as above to work out the connection between m² and cm², and between km² and m².
   b Convert some areas in m² to cm², and some areas in cm² to m².
   c Convert some areas in km² to m², and some areas in m² to km².

15 Each of these shapes has an area of 18 cm².
   Find the missing numbers.

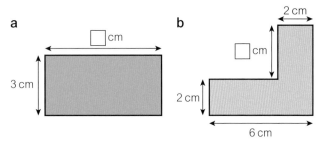

16 **Real** A bathroom wall has a height of 2.4 m and width of 3.1 m
   a Calculate the area of the wall.
   Bathroom tiles measure 25 cm by 25 cm.
   b How many bathroom tiles will be needed to tile the wall?
   What assumptions have you made to get this answer?

17 For each shape write an expression for
   i the perimeter
   ii the area.

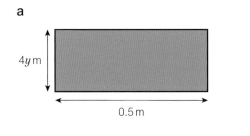

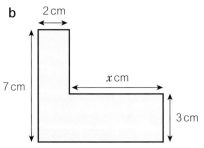

18 **Reflect** Look back at Q7. It asked you to show why some statements are wrong.
   What method did you use to show that they are wrong? In what sort of situation might you need to prove that a statement is untrue?

8 Unit test

1 Copy and complete.
  a 1000 m = □ km
  b 20 *l* = □ m*l*
  c 9000 g = □ kg
  d 20 cm = □ m

2 **a** Write these lengths in order from shortest to longest.
    3500 mm   3 m   400 cm   0.04 km   50 m
  b Write down the median length.

3 Calculate the perimeter of the square in
  a cm
  b mm.

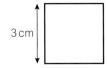

4 For each shape work out
    i the perimeter **ii** the area.

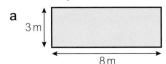

  Write the correct units with your answers.

5 For this shape work out
  a the perimeter
  b the area.

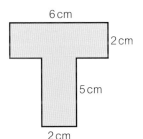

6 Which solid has more planes of symmetry, a cube or a cuboid?
  You must give a reason for your answer.

7 Write down the number of edges, faces and vertices of
  a a triangular prism
  b a square-based pyramid.

8 A square has perimeter 20 cm.
Work out the area of the square.

9 The square and the rectangle have the same perimeter.

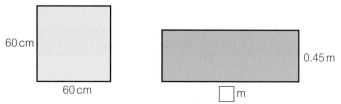

Work out
a the perimeter of the square in cm
b the perimeter of the square in m
c the length marked □.

10 Find the number of planes of symmetry of this regular hexagonal prism.

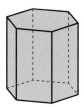

Challenge

11 A rectangle has perimeter 22 cm and area 24 cm².
The length and width are whole numbers.
Work out the side lengths of the rectangle.

12 a A rectangle has a perimeter of 12 cm.
The length and width are whole numbers.
How many possible rectangles are there?
b Work out which of these rectangles has the largest area.

13 Reflect Write these topics in order from easiest to hardest.
A Converting measures
B Perimeter
C Area
D Planes of symmetry in 3D solids
Think about the two topics you found hardest. What made them hard? Write at least one hint to help you with each topic.

9.1 Sequences

You will learn to:
- Work out the terms of an arithmetic sequence using the term-to-term rule.
- Work out a given term in a simple arithmetic sequence.

Confidence

Why learn this?
Economists spot patterns and sequences when they are predicting trends in business growth.

Fluency
What are the first five multiples of
- 3
- 8?
What is the number halfway between
- 18 and 26
- 24 and 38?

Explore
How long will it take you to count in 2s up to 1 million?

Exercise 9.1

1 Write the next three **terms** in each **sequence**.
 a 4, 8, 12, 16, ☐, ☐, ☐
 b 0.5, 1, 1.5, 2, 2.5, ☐, ☐, ☐
 c 3.1, 3.3, 3.5, 3.7, ☐, ☐, ☐
 d 1.8, 1.5, 1.2, 0.9, ☐, ☐, ☐

2 Write the missing terms in each sequence.
 a 12, 15, ☐, 21, 24, ☐
 b 1, 2, 4, ☐, 16, 32, ☐, 128
 c 1, ☐, 5, 7, ☐, 11
 d 30, ☐, ☐, 15, 10, 5

3 Look at the sequences in Q2.
 Which ones are **ascending**?

4 Are these sequences **finite** or **infinite**?
 a integers
 b positive multiples of 10 up to 100
 c prime numbers
 d square numbers smaller than 200
 e multiples of 5

5 Describe each sequence by giving the **1st term** and the **term-to-term rule**.
 a 5, 7, 9, 11, 13, …
 b 100, 90, 80, 70, 60, …
 c 15, 21, 27, 33, 39, …
 d 20, 15, 10, 5, 0, …

6 Which of these sequences are **arithmetic**?
 a 18, 17, 16, 15, 14, …
 b 1, 3, 9, 27, 81, …
 c 5, 8, 11, 14, 17, …
 d −12, −7, −2, 3, 8, …
 e 1, 0, 1, 0, 1, …
 f 1, 2, 4, 7, 11, …

Key point

Numbers in a **sequence** are called **terms**.

Key point

Numbers *increase* in **ascending** sequences.
Numbers *decrease* in **descending** sequences.
A **finite** sequence has a fixed number of terms.
An **infinite** sequence goes on forever.

Key point

You can describe a sequence by giving the **1st term** and the **term-to-term rule**. The term-to-term rule tells you how to get from one term to the next.

Key point

An **arithmetic sequence** goes up or down in equal steps. This step is called the **common difference**.

Q6 hint

Do you get to the next term each time by adding (or subtracting) the same amount?

Warm up

Topic links: Negative numbers, Types of number

7   Work out the first five terms of each arithmetic sequence.
    a 1st term = 9   **common difference = 5**
    b 1st term = 15   common difference = −3
    c 1st term = −50   common difference = −5
    d 1st term = 0   common difference = 4
    e 1st term = 9.5   common difference = 0.2
    f 1st term = −12   common difference = 0.3
    Discussion What type of sequence do you get from a positive
    common difference? ... a negative common difference?

Q7a hint

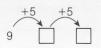

8   Describe each arithmetic sequence by writing the 1st term and the
    common difference.
    a 9, 18, 27, 36, ...   b 20, 30, 40, 50, ...
    c 3, 5, 7, 9, 11, ...   d 30, 25, 20, 15, 10, ...
    e 9, 11, 13, 15, 17, ...   f 100, 89, 78, 67, 56, ...

9   Darren starts with £1 and saves £2 each day.
    a Copy and continue the sequence to show how much money he
       will have up to 10 days after he starts saving.
       £1, £3, £5, ...
    b How many days will it be before he has saved more than £40?
    Discussion How did you work out the answer to part **b**? Is there a
    quick way to work out the answer?

10 The first five terms of a sequence are 3, 6, 9, 12, 15
    What is the
    a 10th term
    b 50th term
    c 100th term?

11 **Modelling / Reasoning** The table shows the UK population in 1950
    and 2000.

Year	UK population (to the nearest million)
1950	51 000 000
2000	59 000 000

    a Assuming that the population growth is an arithmetic sequence,
       what will the population be in 2050?
    b Do you think it is sensible to predict the population like this?
       Explain your answer.
    c The population in 2010 was actually 62 000 000.
       Does this change your prediction for the population in 2050?

12 **Explore** How long will it take you to count in 2s up to 1 million?
    Look back at the maths you have learned in this lesson.
    How can you use it to answer this question?

13 **Reflect** Think carefully about your work on sequences.
    How would you define a sequence in your own words?
    Write down your definition.
    Compare your definition with someone else in your class.

9.2 The nth term

You will learn to:
- Work out and use expressions for the nth term in an arithmetic sequence.

Why learn this?
Surveyors need a general rule to work out the materials needed for different heights of building.

Fluency
What is the 10th term of the sequence of multiples of
- 2
- 4
- 9?
- 24 and 38?

Explore
How many windows do you need for a row of 100 beach huts?

Confidence

Warm up

Exercise 9.2

1 What is the term-to-term rule for each sequence?
   a 6, 11, 16, 21, 26, …
   b 10, 7, 4, 1, −2, …

2 When $n = 3$, work out the value of
   a $2n$ **b** $3n + 2$ **c** $5n - 4$

> **Key point**
>
> n is the **term number**.
> 1st 2nd 3rd 4th...
> n is always a positive integer. You can describe a sequence by giving the **general term** (or nth term).
> The general term relates the term number, n, to the term.

Worked example

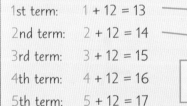

The **general term** of a sequence is $n + 12$
a Write the first five terms of the sequence.

1st term: $1 + 12 = 13$ ———— 1st term: $n = 1$
2nd term: $2 + 12 = 14$ ———— 2nd term: $n = 2$
3rd term: $3 + 12 = 15$
4th term: $4 + 12 = 16$ Replace n with the term number each time, to work out the rest of the terms in the sequence.
5th term: $5 + 12 = 17$

The sequence is 13, 14, 15, 16, 17, …
b Work out the value of the 12th term.

12th term: $12 + 12 = 24$ ———— 12th term: $n = 12$

---

3 The general term of a sequence is $4n$.
   a Write the first five terms in the sequence.
   b Work out the 15th term.

4 Work out the first five terms of the sequence for each general term.
   a $5n$ **b** $7n$ **c** $12n$
   Discussion How else could you describe these sequences?

5 Reasoning Work out

   a the 10th term in the sequence with general term $n - 3$

   b the 22nd term in the sequence with general term $2n$

   c the 50th term in the sequence $n - 20$.

   Discussion Is it easier to find a term of a sequence using the general term of a sequence or the 1st term and the term-to-term rule? Explain your answer.

6 Find the general term of each sequence.

   a 3, 6, 9, 12, 15, ...   **b** 2, 4, 6, 8, 10, ...

   c 10, 20, 30, 40, 50, ...   **d** 11, 22, 33, 44, 55, 66, ...

Q6 hint

Look at your answers to Q4. Can you see a pattern?

7 a Work out the first five terms of the sequence for each general term.

     i $n + 10$ **ii** $n - 7$ **iii** $n + 12$ **iv** $n - 1$

   b Describe each sequence by giving the 1st term and the common difference.

8 The first four terms of a sequence are 3, 4, 5, 6

Alice compares each term to its term number in the sequence.

Term number   1 2 3 4 ... n

Term   3 4 5 6 ... $n + \square$

What is the general term of the sequence?

Q8 hint

What do you do to the term number to get the term?

9 Find the general term of each sequence.

   a 5, 6, 7, 8, 9, ...   **b** 0, 1, 2, 3, 4, 5, ...

   c 10, 11, 12, 13, 14, ...   **d** 21, 22, 23, 24, 25, ...

Q9 hint

Use the method from Q8.

10 Work out the first five terms of the sequence for each general term.

   a $3n + 4$ **b** $2n + 5$ **c** $4n - 2$

   d $n + 12$ **e** $5n - 3$

   Discussion How does the common difference relate to the general term in each sequence?

11 Work out the first five terms of the sequence for each general term.

   a $n - 12$ **b** $2n - 15$ **c** $n - 8$ **d** $10n - 50$

Worked example

Work out the general term of the sequence

5, 7, 9, 11, 13, ...

First work out the common difference.

The common difference is 2, so compare it to the multiples of 2. (The general term for multiples of 2 is $2n$)

From multiples of 2 add 3 to get the sequence.

General term: $2n + 3$

---

12 Work out the general term of each sequence.

   a 4, 7, 10, 13, 16, ...   **b** 7, 9, 11, 13, 15, ...

   c 12, 17, 22, 27, 32, ...   **d** 8, 18, 28, 38, 48, ...

   e 24, 36, 48, 60, ...   **f** 8, 17, 26, 35, 44, ...

   g 9, 19, 29, 39, 49, ...

13 **Reasoning** The general term of a sequence is $10n$.
   a Is 35 a term in this sequence?
   Explain your answer.
   b Which term number has the value 60?
   c Which term will be the first one larger than 105?

14 **Problem-solving** **a** Joe says, 'The 5th term of a sequence with general term $2n + 1$ is 11'.
   Is he right?
   b What position is 23 in the sequence with general term $2n + 1$?

15 **Problem-solving** The general term of a sequence is $5n - 3$.
   Which term number is
   a 22   **b** 47?

16 **Problem-solving / Reasoning** Is 17 a term in the sequence $4n + 7$?
   Explain your answer.

17 **Problem-solving** Which of the terms in the cloud are in sequences with these general terms?
   a $2n - 3$
   b $5n - 8$

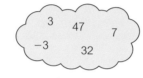

   Discussion Which terms are in both sequences?

18 **Reasoning / Modelling** The number of people reading a blog increases by 100 each day.
   a On the first day 300 people read the blog.
   How many will be reading it after 28 days?
   b Is this a good model for predicting the number of blog readers over time?

Q18a hint

Work out the general term for the sequence of the number of people reading the blog each day.

19 For an arithmetic sequence with a 1st term of -12 and a common difference of 5, work out
   a the nth term
   b the term number of the first term greater than 200.

20 **Explore** How many windows do you need for a row of 100 beach huts?
   Look back at the maths you have learned in this lesson.
   How can you use it to answer this question?

21 **Reflect** After this lesson Karen says, 'I can work out any number in a sequence using the general term.' Fiona says, 'I can tell whether a number will be part of a sequence using the general term.'
   Look back at the work you did this lesson.
   Which questions could Karen be talking about?
   Which questions could Fiona be talking about?

9.3 Pattern sequences

You will learn to:
- Generate sequences and predict how they will continue.
- Recognise geometric sequences and work out the term-to-term rule.

Why learn this?
Identifying patterns in nature can help biologists detect population growth or decline in the animal kingdom.

Fluency
- What is the term-to-term rule for 2, 4, 6, 8?
- Is this an arithmetic sequence?
- What is $2n^2$ when $n = 3$?

Explore
What is the half-life of a radioactive substance?

Confidence

Exercise 9.3

Warm up

1 Draw the next two patterns in this sequence.

$$\mathbb{N} \quad \mathbb{N} \quad \mathbb{M} \quad \mathbb{M}$$

2 a Draw the next two patterns in this sequence.
  b Write the next three terms in this sequence.
   1, 4, 9, 16, □, □, □
  c What is the name for the numbers in part **b**?
  d Look at the differences between the terms in the sequence. What do you notice?

3 This is the start of the sequence of triangular numbers.
  a Draw the next two patterns in the sequence.
  b Look at the differences between the terms in the sequence. What do you notice?
  c Work out the 10th triangular number.

  1 3 6 10

4 For each sequence in parts **a** and **b**
  i draw the next two patterns
  ii copy and complete the table
  iii write the 1st term and the term-to-term rule.

a

Term number	1	2	3	4	5
Number of lines	6	11			

b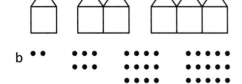

Term number	1	2	3	4	5	6
Number of dots	2	6	12			

5 The 1st term of a sequence is 2. The term-to-term rule is 'double the previous term'.
Write the first six terms in the sequence.

6 Describe each sequence by giving the 1st term and the term-to-term rule.

   a 1, 3, 9, 27, …

   b 10, 100, 1000, 10000, …

   c 1, 0.5, 0.25, 0.125, …

   Discussion Is the sequence in part **c geometric**?

7 Decide whether each sequence is arithmetic or geometric.

   a 2, 5, 8, 11, 14, …   **b** 5, 50, 500, 5000, …

   c 128, 64, 32, 16, …   **d** 0.1, 0.2, 0.4, 0.8, 1.6, …

   e 0.5, 0.3, 0.1, −0.1, …

8 For each geometric sequence in parts **a** to **d**

   i describe the sequence by giving the 1st term and the term-to-term rule

   ii write the next two terms.

   a 1, 2, 4, 8, 16, …   **b** 200, 100, 50, 25, …

   c 5, 25, 125, 625, …   **d** $1, \frac{1}{2}, \frac{1}{4}, \frac{1}{8}, …$

9 Work out the first three terms of the sequence for each general term.

   a $3n^2$ **b** $n^2 + 4$ **c** $\dfrac{n^2}{2}$

10 In the Fibonacci sequence you find each term by adding the previous two terms together.

   1, 1, 2, 3, 5, …

   a Work out the next two terms in the Fibonacci sequence.

   b Look at the differences between terms in the Fibonacci sequence. What do you notice?

> **Key point**
>
> In a **geometric sequence**, the term-to-term rule is 'multiply by ☐'.
> You find each term by multiplying the previous term in the sequence by a constant value.

> **Q10 Literacy hint**
>
> The **Fibonacci sequence** is named after the Italian mathematician Leonardo Fibonacci.

Investigation   **Problem-solving / Modelling**

A robotic rabbit is in a field. It is lonely.
It learns how to make a new robotic rabbit when it is 2 months old.
From then on, it can produce one new robotic rabbit each month.
Each new robotic rabbit works the same way, and can produce a new one when it is 2 months old.
The robotic rabbits never die.
How many robotic rabbits will there be in one year?

> **Strategy hint**
>
> Draw a diagram to show how many robotic rabbits there are each month.
>
> | 1 month | 🐰 |
> |---|---|
> | 2 months | 🐰 |
> | 3 months | 🐰 🐰 |

---

11 Explore What is the half-life of a radioactive substance?
Is it easier to explore this question now you have completed the lesson?
What further information do you need to be able to answer this?

12 Reflect Narayani and Uzma are discussing sequences. Narayani says, 'Geometric sequences get bigger quicker than arithmetic sequences.'
Uzma says, 'Not always.'
Write down a geometric and an arithmetic sequence that Narayani could have been thinking of.
Write down a geometric and an arithmetic sequence that Uzma could have been thinking of.

Explore

Reflect

9.4 Coordinates and line segments

You will learn to:
- Use positive and negative coordinates.
- Work out the midpoint of a line segment.

Confidence

Why learn this?
Air traffic controllers use the coordinates of aircraft and plot their journeys to ensure there are no accidents.

Fluency

Work out half of
- 16
- 13
- 19

Work out
- −3 + 5
- 8 + −2
- $\dfrac{-3 + 8}{2}$

Explore
How do you tell a computer to display graphics in the bottom left corner of the screen?

Exercise 9.4

Warm up

1 a Write the coordinates of points A, B and C.
  b D is the point (4, 1).
     What is the name of shape ABDC?

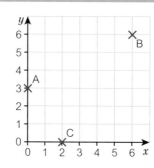

2 The length of the **line segment** AB is 4 units.
   Work out the length of the line CD.

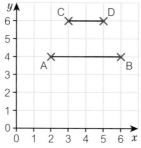

Key point

A **line segment** is part of a line.
It has a beginning and an end point.

3 Work out the distance between each pair of coordinates.
   a (0, 4) and (5, 4)   **b** (4, 8) and (4, 0)   **c** (3, 7) and (5, 7)
   Discussion How could you find the distance between (2, 7) and (2, 3) without plotting them? Does this work for (3, 1) and (5, 6)?

Q3 Strategy hint

Draw a pair of axes, plot the points and join them together.

4 Write the coordinates of points A, B, C and D.

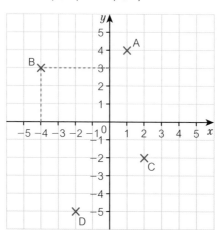

Key point

The x- and y-axes extend below 0, so you can plot points with negative x- and y-coordinates.
The point (0, 0) is called the **origin**.

Q4 hint

Look at point B. Read off the coordinate from the x-axis and then the y-axis.

5 Draw a grid with x- and y-axes from −5 to 5.
   a Plot and label these points.
      A (3, 0)   B (2, 2)   C (0, 3)   D (−2, 2)
      E (−3, 0)   F (−2, −2)   G (0, −3)   H (2, −2)
   b Join the points in alphabetical order.
      What shape have you made?

6 Work out the coordinates of the midpoint of each line segment.
   The first one has been done for you.

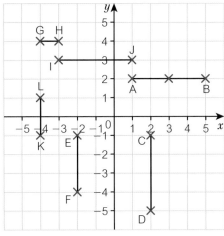

   Midpoint of AB = (3, 2)

Q6 hint

Find the point halfway between A and B. Write its coordinates.

7 Work out the midpoint of each line segment.
   a A (2, 2)   B (4, 2)   b C (1, −2)   D (1, 4)
   c E (1, 4)   F (−5, 4)   d G (−5, 1)   H (−5, −4)
   Discussion How could you find the midpoint of a line without
   plotting the coordinates?

Q7 Strategy hint

Plot each pair of points and join them. Then mark on the midpoints.

8 Find the midpoint of the line segment joining each pair of points.
   a A (2, 4)   B (2, 12)   b X (11, 4)   Y (5, 4)
   c M (2, 5)   N (6, 9)   d P (6, −2)   Q (4, 4)
   e G (−5, 2)   H (−1, −4)   f V (20, −10) W (−3, 1)

9 **Explore** How do you tell a computer to display graphics in the
   bottom left corner of the screen?
   Is it easier to explore this question now you have completed the
   lesson?
   What further information do you need to be able to answer this?

10 **Reflect** Freya, Melanie and Stef are talking about this
   line segment.
   Freya says, 'One end is at the point (2, −2)'.
   Melanie says, 'The midpoint is at (−3, 0)'.
   Stef says, 'The other end is at the point (2, 2)'.
   a Who is right and who is wrong?
   b Write a hint on reading coordinates, in your own words,
      to help the students who are wrong.
      Check your hint. Will it stop them making their mistakes?

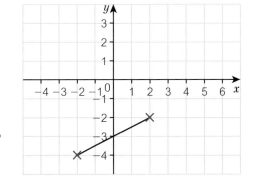

9.5 Graphs

You will learn to:
- Draw straight-line graphs.
- Recognise straight-line graphs parallel to the axes.
- Recognise graphs of $y = x$ and $y = -x$.

Why learn this?
Meteorologists plot graphs to show trends in data and predict future weather.

Fluency
Work out
- -2×4
- $-3 \times 5 + 3$
- $8 \times -2 - 7$

Explore
Do two straight lines always cross?
Can they cross more than once?

Exercise 9.5

1 Work out the output from each function machine.

a

$3 \rightarrow \boxed{\times 5} \rightarrow \boxed{+2} \rightarrow \square$

b

$-2 \rightarrow \boxed{\div 2} \rightarrow \boxed{-7} \rightarrow \square$

2 a $y = 3x$
Work out the value of y when
  i $x = 7$
  ii $x = -4$.

b $y = 2x - 3$
Work out the value of y when
  i $x = 3$
  ii $x = -2$.

3 a Write the coordinates of all the points on line A.
b What do you notice about the x-coordinates?
c Copy and complete these statements.
  i The **equation** of line A is $x = \ldots$
  ii The equation of line B is $x = \ldots$
  iii The equation of line C is $y = \ldots$

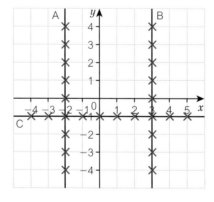

Key point

A line on a coordinate grid is called a **graph**. You can describe it by giving the **equation** of the line.

4 Look at these points.
P (5, 2)   Q (12, 5)   R (5, −3)   S (5, 0)   T (−2, 5)
Which of them are on the line
  a $x = 5$ **b** $y = 5$?
Discussion Which axis is the **graph** of $x = 6$ parallel to?

5 Draw a grid with x- and y-axes from −5 to 5.
Draw and label these graphs.
  a $x = 4$ **b** $y = 2$ **c** $y = -3$ **d** $x = -3$
Discussion Which axis is the graph of $y = 2$ parallel to?

Q5 hint

When you draw a graph it should go to the edge of the grid.

6 a Copy and complete the table of values for the equation $y = 2x$

x	0	1	2	3	4
y	$2 \times 0 = 0$				

Q6a hint

Substitute each value of x into the equation $y = 2x$

b Write down the coordinate pairs from the table.
The first one has been done for you.

(0, 0)

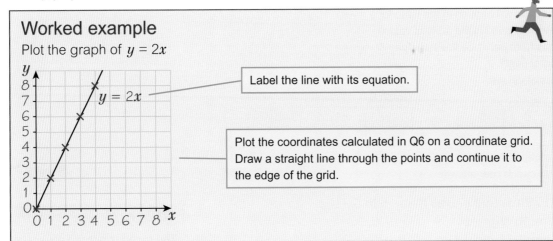

Worked example

Plot the graph of $y = 2x$

Label the line with its equation.

Plot the coordinates calculated in Q6 on a coordinate grid. Draw a straight line through the points and continue it to the edge of the grid.

7 a Copy and complete the table of values for the equation $y = x + 3$.

x	0	1	2	3	4
y					

Q7 hint

Label your graph.

b Write the coordinates.
c Draw a grid with x- and y-axes from 0 to 8. Plot the graph of $y = x + 3$.

8 a Copy and complete the table of values for the equation $y = 2x - 1$.

x	1	2	3	4	5
y	$2 \times 1 - 1$ $= \square - 1$ $= \square$				

b What is the highest y-value in your table?
c Draw a pair of axes up to this y-value. Plot the graph of $y = 2x - 1$.

9 a Copy and complete the table of values for the equation $y = 3x + 2$.

x	−2	−1	0	1	2
y					

b Draw a pair of axes and plot the graph of $y = 3x + 2$.

10 a Copy and complete the table of values for the equation $y = 4x - 3$.

x	−1	0	1	2	3
y					

Q11c hint

Draw a line from $y = -7$ across to your graph and then up to the x-axis.

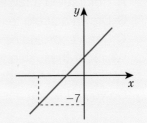

b Draw a pair of axes and plot the graph of $y = 4x - 3$.

11 a Copy and complete the table of values for the equation $y = 3 + 2x$.

x	−6	−4	−2	0	2
y					

b Plot the graph of $y = 3 + 2x$.
c Use your graph to find the value of x when $y = -7$.

Topic links: Negative numbers

Investigation

1 Make a table of values for each graph. Use the x-values 0, 1, 2, 3, 4
   a $y = x$
   b $y = 2x$
   c $y = 3x$

2 For each table in part **1**, complete the statement
   'When the x-value increases by 1, the y-value increases by ☐'

3 a Predict what you think will happen in the table for $y = 4x$
   b Check your answer by making the table of values.

4 a Plot all the graphs from part **1** on the same pair of axes.
   b Which graph is steepest?

5 Look at these tables of values.

Graph A

x	−1	0	1
y	−6	0	6

Graph B

x	−1	0	1
y	−5	0	5

   a Which graph is steeper, A or B?
   b Plot the graphs to check your answer.

12 Draw a grid with x- and y-axes from −5 to 5.
   a Plot the graph of $y = x$
   b Plot the graph of $y = -x$
   c What is the angle between the two graphs?

Q12a hint

The y-coordinate will always be the same as the x-coordinate, for example (3, 3).

13 Match the equations of the graphs to the lines.

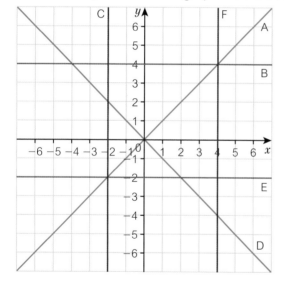

$x = -2$

$y = x$

$y = 4$

$y = -x$

$y = -2$

$x = 4$

Q12b hint

The y-coordinate will always be equal to the x-coordinate, but with the opposite sign, for example (2, −2) or (−2, 2).

14 **Explore** Do two straight lines always cross?
   Can they cross more than once?
   Look back at the maths you have learned in this lesson.
   How can you use it to answer this question?

15 **Reflect** Here are three things you have done in this lesson:
   A Completed a table of coordinate pairs.
   B Drawn a straight-line graph.
   C Read coordinates from a straight-line graph.
   Which of these things did you find easiest? What made it easy?
   Which of these things did you find most difficult? What made it difficult?
   Do you think you need more practice on any of these things? If so, which one(s)?

9.6 Working with graphs

You will learn to:
- Draw graphs that represent relationships.
- Solve problems involving coordinates and straight lines.

Why learn this?
Scientists can draw graphs to see how two variables relate to one another.

Fluency
What are the first five terms of this sequence?
- Start with 20 and add 15 each time.

Explore
Do the age and value of a car form a straight-line graph?

Exercise 9.6

1 a Write down the coordinates of of the points A, B, C and D.
   b What is the name of the quadrilateral that the points make?

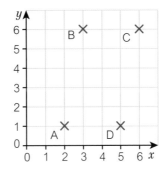

2 Copy and complete the table of values for the equation $y = x + 1$

x	0	1	2	3	4
$y = x + 1$	1			4	

3 A gardener charges £30 to come out to a house and then charges £20 per hour.
   a Copy and complete the table showing the charges.

Time (hours)	0	1	2	3	4
Cost (£)	30	50	70		

Q3b hint

Label the x-axis from 0 to 5 and the y-axis from 0 to 120. Plot the first row of the table on the x-axis and plot the second row on the y-axis.

   b Draw a pair of axes and plot the points as a graph.
   c Use the graph to work out the cost for 2.5 hours' work.

4 Rahul receives £40 from his grandmother. Each week he spends £3.
   a Copy and complete the table showing the money that Rahul has remaining each week.

Time (weeks)	0	1	2	3	4	5	6
Money (£)	40	37	34	31			

Q4b hint

Plot the first row of the table on the x-axis and plot the second row on the y-axis. Label the x-axis from 0 to 15 and the y-axis from 0 to 40.

   b Draw a pair of axes and plot the points as a graph.
   c Extend your line all the way until it meets the x-axis.
   d After how many weeks will Rahul have spent all his money? Explain your answer.

Topic links: Quadrilaterals, Graphs, Equations

Confidence

Warm up

5 The data in the table shows the amount that a spring stretches (in mm) when different masses (in grams) are placed on the end of the spring.

Stretch (mm)	0	18	36	45	54
Mass (g)	0	100	200	250	300

a Plot the points on a coordinate grid.

b Do the points form a straight line?

A mass of 400 g is placed on the spring and it stretches 85 mm.

c Plot this point on the graph.

d Reasoning What do you notice about this point compared with the other points?

Hooke's Law says that the mass and stretch will produce a straight-line graph until the elastic limit of the spring is reached.

e Reasoning Describe a range of masses that could be the elastic limit of this spring.

Q5a hint

Draw a grid with the x-axis labelled from 0 to 400 (g) and the y-axis from 0 to 100 (mm).

6 Problem-solving **a** Draw a coordinate grid on squared paper with x- and y-axes from 0 to 10. Plot the points A(2, 5), B(0, 3) and C(2, 1).

b Work out possible coordinates of a fourth point
   i D so that ABCD is a square
   ii E so that ABCE is a kite
   iii F so that ABCF is an arrowhead
   iv G so that ABCG is a trapezium.

Key point

You can describe a shape using the letters at its **vertices** (the plural of **vertex**).

7 Draw a grid with x- and y-axes from –5 to 5.

a Copy and complete the table of values for the equations $y = x - 2$, $y = -x + 2$ and $y = -x - 2$

x	–2	–1	0	1	2
$y = x - 2$					
$y = -x + 2$					
$y = -x - 2$					

b Plot each graph on the coordinate grid.

c Add each of these lines to the grid and describe the 2D shape formed. Copy and complete these statements.
   i When the line $y = x + 2$ is added, a _____ is formed.
   ii When the line $y = x + 4$ is added, a _____ is formed.
   iii When the line $y = 3x + 2$ is added, a _____ is formed.

8 Reasoning Iqra says, 'Four straight lines drawn on a grid will always form a 2D shape.'
Is Iqra correct? Draw a diagram to illustrate your answer.

9 Explore Do the age and value of a car form a straight-line graph? Look back at the maths you have learned in this lesson. How can you use it to answer this question?

10 Reflect In this lesson you have drawn lines that formed a 2D shape on to a grid.
Which did you find harder, drawing the lines or naming the 2D shape?
Write down one thing about this topic that you still do not understand. Share your answer with a classmate.

ActiveLearn Homework, Year 7, Unit 9

Subject links: Science (Q5)

Explore

Reflect

9 Check up

Sequences

1 Describe each sequence by writing the 1st term and the term-to-term rule.

   a 3, 5, 7, 9, ...   **b** 2, 20, 200, 2000, ...   **c** 20, 17, 14, 11, ...

2 For this sequence

  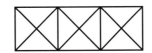

   a sketch the next two patterns

   b copy and complete the table

   c write the 1st term and the term-to-term rule.

Term number	1	2	3	4	5
Number of lines	6	11			

3 The first few terms of an arithmetic sequence are 7, 14, 21, 28, ...
What is the 11th term in the sequence?

4 Work out the first five terms of each arithmetic sequence.

   a 1st term = 12   common difference = 5

   b 1st term = 8   common difference = −6

5 Work out the first three terms and the 6th term of the sequence for each general term.

   a $3n$ **b** $n + 7$ **c** $5n - 3$

6 Work out the general term of each arithmetic sequence.

   a 5, 10, 15, 20, ...

   b 4, 5, 6, 7, 8, ...

   c 3, 5, 7, 9, 11, ...

7 Is each sequence arithmetic or geometric?

   a 1, 2, 4, 8, 16, ...

   b 1, 3, 5, 7, 9, ...

   c 20, 10, 0, −10, −20, ...

   d 240, 120, 60, 30, 15, ...

8 A geometric sequence starts 1, 5, 25, ...

   a What is the term-to-term rule?

   b Work out the 4th term.

Graphs

9 The diagram shows some points on a coordinate grid.
Write the coordinates of the points A, B, C, D, E and F.

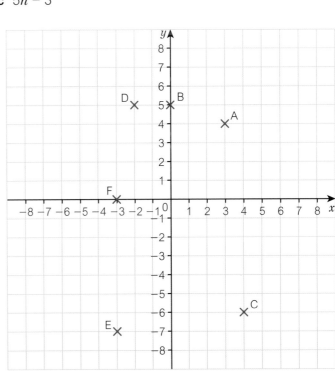

10 The diagram shows some points on a coordinate grid.
Write down the coordinates of the points A, B, C and D.

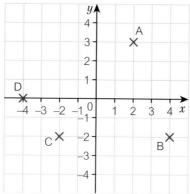

11 Draw a grid with x- and y-axes from –5 to 5.
Draw and label these graphs.
a $y = 2$ **b** $x = -3$

12 a Copy and complete the table of values for the graph of $y = 2x - 3$
b Draw a grid with x- and y-axes from −10 to 10.
Plot the graph of $y = 2x - 3$.

x	−2	0	2	4	6
y					

13 Work out the midpoint of the line segment joining
a (1, 5) and (1, 9) **b** (3, 5) and (7, 1)
c (−2, 3) and (6, −5).

14 Draw a grid with x- and y-axes from −5 to 5.
Draw and label the graphs of $y = x$ and $y = -x$

15 On a long car journey, Visha travels at 30 mph for 4 hours.
a Copy and complete the table showing the distance she has
travelled at the end of each hour.

Time (hours)	0	1	2	3	4
Distance (miles)					

b Draw a grid with the x-axis from 0 to 4 and the y-axis from 0 to 120.
c Plot the points from the table onto the grid.
d Use the graph to estimate how far Visha has travelled after 1.5 hours.

16 The diagram shows three vertices of the parallelogram ABCD.
Write down the coordinates of point C.

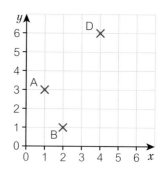

17 How sure are you of your answers? Were you mostly
😟 **Just guessing** 😐 **Feeling doubtful** 🙂 **Confident**
**What next? Use your results to decide whether to strengthen or
extend your learning.**

Challenge

18 a Work out the first three terms of the sequence with general term $7 - n$.
b How many positive terms are in the sequence?

19 The general term of a sequence is n^2.
How many terms in the sequence are less than 100?

20 Write the equation of a graph that goes through the point (3, 3).
Can you find more than one?

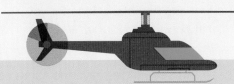

9 Strengthen

You will:
- Strengthen your understanding with practice.

Sequences

1 An arithmetic sequence starts 4, 6, 8, 10, …
  a What is the common difference?
  b Work out the next two terms.

2 a Work out the next three terms of each sequence.
     i 6, 11, 16, 21, …
     ii 30, 41, 52, 63, …
  b For each sequence, is it **ascending** or **descending**?

3 Find the first five terms of each arithmetic sequence.
  a 1st term = 5, common difference = 4
  b 1st term = 18, common difference = –2

4 Look at the sequence 5, 10, 15, 20, 25, …
  a These are multiples of ☐.
  b What is the 12th term?
  c Copy and complete this statement.
    The general term is ☐n

5 For each sequence in parts **a** and **b**, work out
    i the general term
    ii the 10th term.
  a 4, 8, 12, 16, …
  b 11, 22, 33, 44, 55, …

6 Look at the sequence in the table.

Term number	1 ⤵+☐	2 ⤵+☐	3 ⤵+☐	4 ⤵+☐	5 ⤵+☐	n ⤵+☐
Term	3	4	5	6	7	…

  a What do you add to the term number each time to get the term? Is it the same for every term?
  b Write the general term of the sequence.

7 Work out the general term of each sequence.
  a 10, 11, 12, 13, 14,…
  b 0, 1, 2, 3, 4,…
  c 15, 16, 17, 18, 19,…
  d –3, –2, –1, 0, 1, …

8 The general term (nth term) of a sequence is $n + 5$. Work out the first five terms.

Q1a hint

4   6   8   10
+☐   +☐   +☐

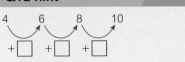

Q2b Literacy hint

Ascending numbers get bigger.
Descending numbers get smaller.

Q3 hint

1st term: 5
2nd term: 5 + 4 = 9
3rd term: 9 + 4 = ☐

Q4 hint

1st term: 1 × ☐ = 5
2nd term: 2 × ☐ = 10
…
12th term: 12 × ☐ = ☐

Q5a hint

These are multiples of ☐.
Use the method from Q4.

Q6b hint

n + ☐

Q7a hint

Draw a table to help you.

Q8 hint

1st term: 1 + 5 = ☐
2nd term: 2 + ☐ = ☐

9 Work out the first five terms of the sequence with nth term $2n - 1$
The first one has been done for you.

nth term: $\quad 2 \times n - 1$
1st term: $\quad ② \times ① - 1 = 2 - 1 = 1$

Q9 hint

2nd term: $\quad 2 \times \square - 1 = \square$
3rd term: $\quad 2 \times \square - 1 = \square$

10 These two sequences have the same common difference.
Sequence A $\qquad$ 3, 6, 9, 12, 15, …
Sequence B $\qquad$ 5, 8, 11, 14, 18, …
  a Work out the general term of sequence A.
  b What do you add to each term in sequence A to get the terms in sequence B?
  c Copy and complete the general term of sequence B.
  $3n + \square$

Q10a hint

Sequence A is multiples of $\square$.

Q10b hint

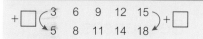

11 Which sequence in each set is a geometric sequence?
  a A $\quad$ 2, 4, 8, 16, …
  $\quad$ **B** $\quad$ 2, 4, 7, 11, …
  $\quad$ **C** $\quad$ 2, 8, 14, 20, …
  b D $\quad$ 32, 28, 24, 20, …
  $\quad$ **E** $\quad$ 32, 8, 2, 0.5, …
  $\quad$ **F** $\quad$ 32, 16, 0, −16, …

Q11 hint

In a geometric sequence the term-to-term rule is to multiply or divide by the same number each time.

12 a Work out the term-to-term rule in this geometric sequence.

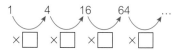

  b Work out the next two terms in the sequence.

Q12a hint

Check that the multiplier is the same each time.

Graphs

1 a Copy this grid with x- and y-axes from −3 to 3.

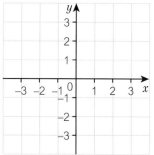

  b Plot the points (1, 2), (1, 3), (1, −2), (1, −3), (1, 0).
  Draw a line through all the points.
  c What do you notice about the x-coordinate of all the points?
  d Copy and complete this statement.
  The equation of the line is $x = \square$. It is parallel to the ___-axis.

Q1b hint

To plot the point (1, −2) move 1 to the right along the x-axis and 2 down the y-axis.

2 a Copy the grid from Q1.
  b Plot the points (4, −3) and (3, −3) and from (−5, −3), (−1, −3).
  Draw a line through all the points.
  c What do you notice about the y-coordinate of all the points?
  d Copy and complete this statement.
  The equation of the line is $y = \square$. It is parallel to the ___-axis.

3 a Copy and complete the table of values for the equation $y = x + 2$

x	0	1	2	3	4	5
y	2					

Q3a hint

Use a function machine.
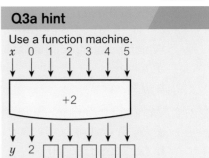

b Write each pair of coordinates from the table.
The first one has been done for you.

(0, 2)   (1, ☐),(2, ☐),(3, ☐), …
 ↑ ↑
 x y

c Copy this coordinate grid.
Plot the points.
The first one has been done for you.

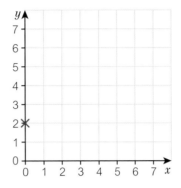

d Join the points with a straight line.
Label the graph, $y = x + 2$

4 a Copy and complete the table of values for the equation $y = 3x$

x	0	1	2	3	4
y	0				

Q4a hint

Use a function machine.
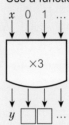

b Draw a grid with x- and y-axes from 0 to 12
Plot the points.

c Join the points with a straight line.
Label the graph, $y = 3x$

5 Virat has £20 in his bank account.
He receives £5 per week for doing jobs around the house.

a Copy and complete the table showing how much money Virat has in his bank account.

Time (weeks)	0	1	2	3	4
Money (£)	20	25			

Q5a hint

25 + 5 = ☐

b Copy this coordinate grid. Plot the points.
The first two have been done for you.

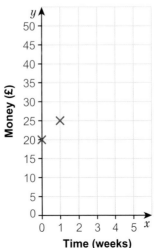

6 Look at these coordinate pairs.
(1, 1), (5, 4), (9, −9), (4, −4), (5, −5), (2, 2), (−3, −3), (−6, 6)
Which points from the list lie on the graph
  a $y = x$
  b $y = -x$?

7 Work out the midpoint of the line segment joining
  a (3, 5) and (11, 15)
  b (2, 7) and (6, 13)
  c (9, 4) and (3, 10).

8 Copy this coordinate grid and mark on the points.

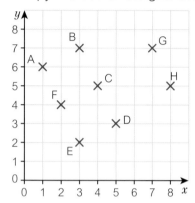

  a Connect points BGHC. What shape have you made?
  b Connect points ABCF. What shape have you made?
  c Connect points ABDE. What shape have you made?
  d Connect points ABCE. What shape have you made?

Enrichment

1 a Write five coordinate pairs that are on the graphs of
  i $y = x$ **ii** $y = -x$
  b Are there any that are on both graphs?

2 An ancient story tells of an emperor offering a reward to a clever man. The man could choose his own reward and he asked for:
'… one grain of rice on the first square of a chessboard. Then two grains on the next square, and four on the one after that. Then double the number of grains again on every square until the board is full.'
  a A bowl of rice for one person holds about 3000 grains.
  Starting at the first square, how many squares does the man need to take rice from to fill one bowl?
  b How many squares does he need to take rice from to fill six bowls?

3 Reflect Elsa says, 'The words 'term' and 'coordinates' are used a lot in these lessons. These must be important words for understanding sequences and graphs.'
Write down definitions, in your own words, of 'term' and 'coordinates'.

Q6a hint

Read the equation of the graph aloud, 'y equals x'. This means that the x- and y-coordinates are the same.

Q6b hint

Read the equation of the graph aloud, 'y equals minus x'. This means that the y-coordinate is the negative of the x-coordinate.

Q7a hint

Find the number halfway between 3 and 11, and the number halfway between 5 and 15.

Q8 hint

Choose from square, rectangle, parallelogram and trapezium.

Square   Rectangle

Parallelogram   Trapezium

Q2a hint

1 square:	1 grain of rice
2 squares:	1 + 2 grains of rice
3 squares:	1 + 2 + 4 grains of rice

Q2b hint

You could use a spreadsheet to work out the total for each number of squares.

9 Extend

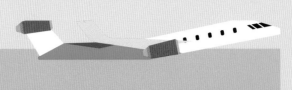

You will:
- Extend your understanding with problem-solving.

1 **Modelling** A finance director looks at the profit (financial gain) her company has made over the last three years.

Year	2012	2013	2014
Profit	£1500	£2000	£2500

Assume that the profit is an arithmetic sequence.
How much profit will the company make in

a 2015   **b** 2020   **c** 2050?

Discussion Are these predictions sensible?

2 A car hire company offers a special six-month deal. For the first month it costs £300 to hire the car. For the next five months the cost reduces by £50 each month.
How much will it cost to hire the car in

a the 3rd month   **b** the 6th month?

Discussion Why is the deal for only six months?

3 **a** Draw a grid with x- and y-axes from −5 to 5
Draw the graphs of
i $x = 4$ **ii** $x = -2$
iii $y = 1$ **iv** $y = -1$
b Work out the area of the rectangle enclosed by the four lines

> **Q3b hint**
> The area will be in 'square units'.

4 **Problem-solving** Two of the corners of an isosceles triangle are he points (−4, 1) and (2, 1).
List as many possible coordinates for the third corner as possible.

> **Q4 hint**
> Plot the two points first.

5 **Reasoning** Use a spreadsheet to follow these steps and answer the questions.
Step 1: Type a number into cell **A1**
Step 2: In cell **A2**, type the formula **=(A1+10)/2**. Press **Enter**.
Step 3: Click and drag cell **A2** down using its bottom right-hand corner, so the formula repeats itself.

a Describe in words what the formula does.
b What do you notice about the numbers in the sequence?
c What happens if you change the number in cell **A1**?
d Repeat this process with a different formula, replacing the **2** with a different number. What happens?
e Use the spreadsheet to plot a graph of the sequence generated in part **d**. Write a sentence about the shape of the graph.

6 a Copy and complete the table of values for the equation $y = 2x - 3$

x	−2	0	2	4	6
y					

b Draw a grid with x- and y-axes from −10 to 10 and plot the graph of $y = 2x - 3$.

c Copy and complete the table of values for the equation $y = 6 - x$.

x	−3	−1	0	5	10
y					

d Plot the graph of $y = 6 - x$ on your grid from part **b**.

e Write the coordinates of the point where the two graphs **intersect**.

f Copy and complete the table of values for the equations $y = 2 - x$ and $y = 2x$.

x	−4	−2	0	2	4
$y = 2 - x$					
$y = 2x$					

g Describe the shape formed by the intersections of the four lines.

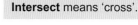

Q6e Literacy hint

Intersect means 'cross'.

7 STEM / Problem-solving In a physics experiment, Simon measures and records how much a spring stretches by, when different forces are used.

Force, F (N)	0	0.5	1	1.5	2
Extension, p (cm)	0	2.5	5	7.5	10

a Plot the graph of F against p. Put F on the vertical axis and p on the horizontal axis.

Hooke's law says that $F = $ a **constant** $\times p$.

b Work out the value of the constant.

The constant for a second spring is 0.5, so $F = 0.5p$

c Plot the graph of $F = 0.5p$ on the same grid as in part **a**.

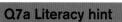

Q7a Literacy hint

A **constant** is a value that doesn't change.

Q7b hint

How much does F change by for 1 unit change in p?

8 Real / STEM A manufacturer states that a car does 60 miles to the gallon.

a Draw the graph of $d = 60f$ where $f = $ fuel used and $d = $ distance travelled.

b Use the graph to work out

   i how much fuel is needed for a journey of 150 miles

   ii how far a car can travel on 3.5 gallons.

9 Real / Reasoning A restaurant has square tables, and 4 people can sit at each one.

When 2 tables are put together, 6 people can sit at them.

a How many people can sit at 3 tables put together?

b Copy and complete this table of values.

Number of tables	1	2	3	4	5
Number of seats	4	6			

c How many people can sit at 10 tables?

d How many extra seats are made each time a table is added?

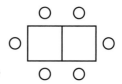

Topic links: Properties of polygons, Area, Algebraic manipulation

Subject links: ICT (Q5, Q21), Science (Q7, Q8)

e Anya says, 'The general term for the number of seats for n tables put together is $4n$, since four people can sit at each table.' Is she right? Explain your answer.

f Work out the general term for the number of seats for n tables.

g How many tables are needed for 30 people?

10 Reasoning The diagram shows some points on a coordinate grid.
Write the equation of the line that goes through the points

a A, B and C

b D, E and F

c B, G and H.

Discussion Does the graph in part **c** go through point D? Explain your answer.

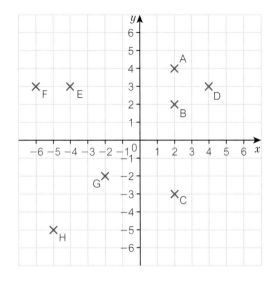

11 a Work out the midpoint of the line segment joining $(1, 5)$ and $(-4, -2)$.

b A line segment RS has midpoint, M, at $(7, 10)$.
R is the point $(5, 3)$.
What are the coordinates of S?

12 The diagram shows three vertices of a parallelogram ABCD.

a What are the coordinates of point D?

b Work out the coordinates of the midpoints of

   i AB   **ii** CD   **iii** BC   **iv** AD   **v** AC.

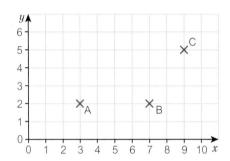

13 a Draw a grid with x- and y-axes from 0 to 5 and draw the graphs of

   i $y = x$ **ii** $x = 5$.

b **Problem-solving** Work out the area of the triangle enclosed by the lines and the x-axis.

14 Reasoning The general term of a sequence is $9n + 5$.

a Which of these numbers are in the sequence?
Explain your answers.

   i 14   **ii** 99   **iii** 860   **iv** -4

b Which number term has the value 383?

c Which term is the first term greater than 1000?

15 Problem-solving The general term of a sequence is $-2.5n - 15$.

a Is the sequence finite or infinite?

b Which term has the highest value?
What is this value?

16 Work out the next two terms in each sequence.

   a 2, 6, 12, 20, 30, ...   **b** 1, 2, 3, 5, 8, 13, ...

   c 1, 2, 5, 10, 17, ...   **d** $0, \frac{1}{2}, 1\frac{1}{2}, 3, 5, 7\frac{1}{2}, ...$

17 Work out the next two terms in each sequence.

   a 1, -1, 1, -1, 1, ...

   b 2, -4, 6, -8, 10, ...

   c $1, -\frac{1}{2}, \frac{1}{4}, -\frac{1}{8}, \frac{1}{16}, ...$

Discussion Which of these sequences are geometric?

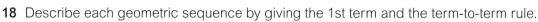

18 Describe each geometric sequence by giving the 1st term and the term-to-term rule.

   a 1, 4, 16, 64, …
            b 1, 10, 100, 1000, 10 000, …

   c 200, 100, 50, 25, …
            d 81, 27, 9, 3, 1, …

19 Work out the missing terms in each sequence.

   a 1, □, 9, 27, □
            b 0, 2, 6, 12, □, 30

   c 10, 10, 20, 30, …, 80, 130

Q19 Strategy hint

Look for a pattern between the terms. Test whether your pattern works for all the terms in the sequence.

20 The first two terms of a sequence are 1 and 3.

The sequence could be arithmetic *or* geometric.

   a For an arithmetic sequence starting 1, 3, …

     i write the next two terms
     ii work out the nth term.

   b For a geometric sequence starting 1, 3, …

     i write the next two terms

     ii describe the sequence giving the 1st term and the term-to-term rule.

21 Reasoning

   a Use a computer graph-sketching package to draw the graphs of

     i $y = x$
     ii $y = x + 1$
     iii $y = x + 2$
     iv $y = x - 1$.

   b Write the coordinates where each graph crosses the y-axis.

   c Predict where these graphs will cross the y-axis.

     i $y = x - 5$
     ii $y = x + 12$

   Check your predictions on the graph-sketching package.

22 Reasoning The first four terms of a geometric sequence are 2, 4, 8, 16, …

   a Write the 5th term in the sequence.

   b Copy and complete the table.

1st term	2nd term	3rd term	4th term	5th term
2	2×2 $= 2^2$	$2 \times 2 \times 2$ $= 2^{\square}$	… $= 2^{\square}$	… $= 2^{\square}$

   c Work out the 10th term of the sequence.

   d Write the general term of the sequence.

Investigation   **Reasoning**

1 Create this spreadsheet to work out the first six terms of the sequence where the general term is n^2.

Click and drag the bottom right corner of cell **D2** across, so the formula repeats itself.

	A	B	C	D	E	F	G
1	Term number	1	2	3	4	5	6
2	Term	=B1*B1	=C1*C1	=D1*D1			

2 Add and complete this next row to work out the differences between consecutive terms for each sequence in step **1**.

This is called the 1st difference.

3	1st difference		=C2−B2	=D2−C2			

3 Add and complete this next row to work out the differences between consecutive 1st differences.

This is called the 2nd difference. What do you notice?

4	2nd difference			=D3−C3			

4 Modify your spreadsheet to work out the 1st and 2nd differences for the sequences

   a $n^2 + 1$
     b $2n^2$
     c $3n^2$

   What patterns can you see?

5 Now try working out the 3rd differences for n^3

23 Reflect Jake says, 'Sequences and straight line graphs are all about following patterns.' Look back at the work you have done in this unit. Write three sentences that describe how what you have learned is all about 'following patterns'.

9 Unit test

1 Look at the pattern of dots.
  a Draw the next two patterns in the sequence.
  b Copy and complete the table.

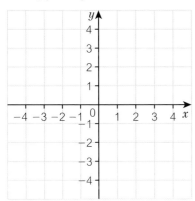

Term number	1	2	3	4	5	6
Number of dots	2	6	12			

2 The 1st term of a sequence is 64. The term-to-term rule is 'divide by 2'.
  Write the first five terms of the sequence.

3 The first five terms of a sequence are 6, 12, 18, 24, 30.
  What is the 9th term?

4 Work out the first four terms of the arithmetic sequence with
  1st term 10 and common difference −6.

5 **a** Copy the grid. Plot and label the points A(1, 3) and B(−4, −1).

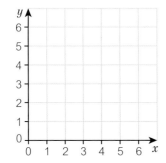

  b Draw and label the graphs
      i $x = 2$
      ii $y = -3$.

6 **a** Copy and complete the table of values for the equation $y = x + 3$.

x	0	1	2	3
y				

  b Copy the grid.
      Draw the graph of $y = x + 3$.

7 Work out the first three terms in the sequence $5n - 10$.

8 For each sequence, write whether it is arithmetic or geometric.
   a 1, 2, 4, 8, 16, ...   **b** 1, 2, 3, 4, 5, ...
   c 9, 7, 5, 3, 1, ...   **d** 2, 6, 18, 54, ...

9 Work out the general term of the sequence 6, 11, 16, 21, 26, ...

10 Point A has coordinates (4, 9). Point B has coordinates (10, 5).
Work out the midpoint of the line segment joining A and B.

11 The diagram shows four graphs.
   a Write the letter of the graph with equation $y = -x$
   b Write the coordinates of the point where lines
      B and C intersect.

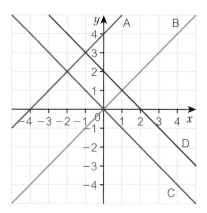

12 A geometric sequence starts 3, 9, 27, ...
   a Write the 4th and 5th terms of the sequence.
   b Work out the general term.

13 The diagram shows three vertices of the kite ABCD.
Find the coordinates of vertex D.

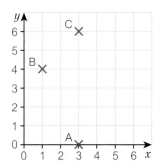

Challenge

14 Dominic makes a tile pattern from a square of
white tiles surrounded by a border of blue tiles.
   a Copy and complete the table for the number
of tiles in each pattern in the sequence.
   b Work out the general term for
     i the number of white tiles
     ii the number of blue tiles
     iii the total number of tiles.
   c Investigate similar patterns using rectangles.

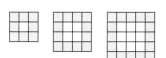

	1	2	3	4	5	6
White tiles	1					
Blue tiles	8					
Total number of tiles	9					

15 **Reflect** Write a heading 'Five important things about sequences and
graphs'.
Now look back at the work you have done in this unit, and list the five
most important things you think you have learned.
For example, you might include:
- words (with their definitions)
- methods for working things out
- mistakes you made (with tips on how to avoid them in future).

Reflect

10.1 Congruency and enlargements

You will learn to:
- Identify congruent shapes.
- Use the language of enlargement.
- Enlarge shapes using given scale factors.
- Work out the scale factor given an object and its image.

Why learn this?
Logo designers must think about what a logo will look like when enlarged from their drawing on to big advertisements.

Fluency
Work out
- 6 × 3
- 5 × 2
- 8 × 4
- 7 × 5

Explore
Does Andy Warhol use congruency in any of his art works?

Exercise 10.1

1 Which one of these shapes is not the same as the other two?

a A   B   C

b A  B 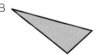 C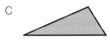

2 Copy and complete.
a 2 × ☐ = 8   **b** ☐ × 3 = 12   **c** 18 ÷ 6 = ☐   **d** 15 ÷ ☐ = 5

3 Copy each shape. Shade in the **congruent** parts of each shape in the same colour.
The first one is done for you.

a

b    **c**

Discussion Which countries use congruent shapes in their flag?

> **Key point**
>
> Shapes are **congruent** if they are the same shape and size.
> For example, these shapes are all congruent.
>
>

> **Q3a hint**
>
> The triangles are the same shape and size.
> The green rectangles are the same shape and size.

Warm up

Subject link: Geography (Q3)

4 Copy each shape. Then split it into the number of congruent shapes shown. The first one is done for you.

   a four congruent triangles

   b two congruent triangles

   c two congruent triangles and two congruent rectangles

   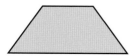

5 These two triangles are congruent.

   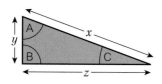 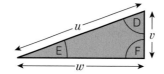

   Key point

   In congruent shapes, **corresponding sides** and **corresponding angles** are equal.

   Copy and complete these sentences.
   a Length x is the same as length ☐.
   b Length ☐ is the same as length v.
   c Angle A is the same size as angle ☐.
   d Angle ☐ is the same size as angle E.

6 **STEM** A computer programmer is working on a game where shapes fit together.
   Which shapes are congruent?

   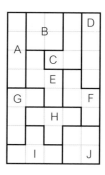

Investigation

Problem-solving

A pentomino is a shape made from five congruent squares that touch side-to-side.
The diagram shows four congruent pentominoes.
Design your own pentominoes.
How many *different* pentominoes can you draw?
How many congruent pentominoes are there for each design?

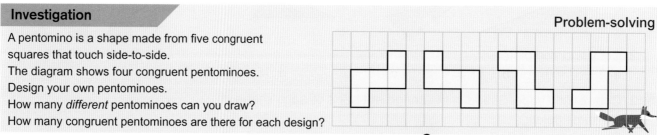

Worked example

Enlarge this shape by scale factor 2.

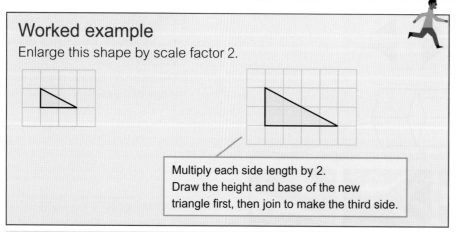

Multiply each side length by 2.
Draw the height and base of the new triangle first, then join to make the third side.

Key point

An **enlargement** is a type of transformation. You multiply all the side lengths of a shape by the same number.
The number that the side lengths are multiplied by is called the **scale factor**.

Subject link: Technology (Q6)

7 Copy each shape onto squared paper. Now **enlarge** each shape by
i scale factor 3 ii scale factor 5.

a   b 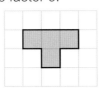 c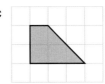

Q7 hint

For scale factor 3, multiply each side
length by 3.
For scale factor 5, multiply each side
length by 5.

8 **Real** In a school mural, all the objects in the painting need to be 15
times their real size.
a A real book is 15 mm thick. How thick is a book in the mural?
Give your answer in centimetres.
b A real plate has a diameter of 14 cm.
What is the diameter of a plate in the mural?
Give your answer in metres.

9 For each enlargement in parts **a** to **c**:
i Write the ratio of the length of a side of the **object** to the
corresponding length in the **image**.
Give the ratio in its simplest form.
ii Write the scale factor of the enlargement.

Key point

The original shape is called the
object. The enlarged shape is called
the **image**.

a object   image   b object   image

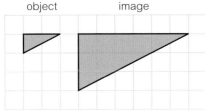   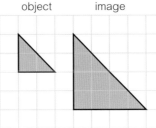

Q9a hint

i Length of object = 2 squares,
length of image = 6 squares, so
ratio is 2 : 6, which simplifies to
1 : ☐.
ii All side lengths of image are 3
times as long as side lengths of
object, so scale factor is ☐.

c object   image

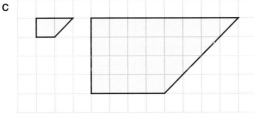

10 **Reasoning**
a Sam says, 'If I enlarge a shape by scale factor 3, the perimeter of
the image will be 3 times the perimeter of the object.'
Is Sam correct? Explain your answer.
b Ali says, 'If I enlarge a shape by scale factor 3, the area of the
image will be 3 times the area of the object.'
Is Ali correct? Explain your answer.

Q10b Strategy hint

Draw a rectangle on squared paper
and then enlarge it by scale factor 3.
Work out the area of the rectangle
and the area of its image.

11 **Explore** Does Andy Warhol use congruency in any of his art works?
What have you learned in this lesson to help you answer this
question? What other information do you need?

12 **Reflect** Scientists and graphic designers use enlargement
techniques in their work. Suggest some other careers where these
skills would be useful.

10.2 Reflection

Confidence

You will learn to:

- Recognise and carry out reflections in a mirror line.
- Reflect a shape on a coordinate grid.
- Describe a reflection on a coordinate grid.

Why learn this?
Symmetry and reflections are used a lot in science. Scientists use the reflection of light to measure distances, such as the distance between the Earth and the Moon.

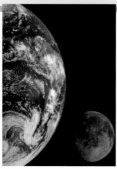

Fluency
Here is a coordinate grid.

- Which is the x-axis and which is the y-axis?
- What are the coordinates of the point A?

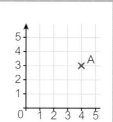

Explore
What symmetries are there in nature?

Exercise 10.2

Warm up

1 Here is a coordinate grid.
Make a copy of the grid, then plot and label these points.
A (3, 2)   B (−2, 3)   C (2, −1)   D (−1, −2)

2 The diagram shows some straight lines on a coordinate grid.
Match each line with the correct equation.
$x = -2$ $y = 1$ $x = 3$ $y = -2$ $y = x$

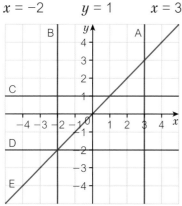

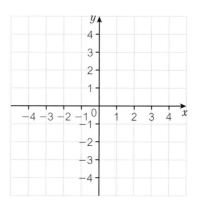

Worked example

Is the green shape a correct reflection of the white shape in the mirror line? Give a reason for your answer.

No. The green shape should be one square from the mirror line, not on the mirror line.

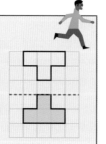

This is a correct reflection.

Key point

A **reflection** is a type of **transformation**. You reflect shapes in a **mirror line**.
All points on the image are the same distance from the mirror line as the points on the object, but on the opposite side.

Topic links: Coordinates

3 Reasoning In each diagram, decide whether the green shape is a correct **reflection** of the white shape in the **mirror line**.
If the reflection isn't correct, give a reason why.
Then copy the shape and draw the correct reflection.

a 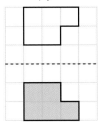 b 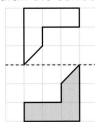 c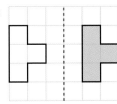

Discussion Is your body symmetrical?

4 Copy and complete each diagram to make an accurate reflection in the mirror line.

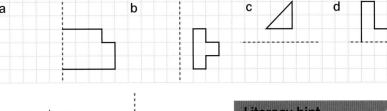

Reasoning If you reflect the capital letter A in a vertical mirror line it still looks the same.

Which other capital letters are the same when reflected in a vertical mirror line?
What about a horizontal mirror line?

A ⦙ A

Literacy hint

A vertical mirror line is ⦙

A horizontal mirror line is ------

5 a Copy each pair of shapes. Draw in the mirror line for each pair.

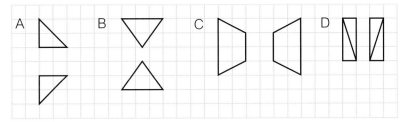

b Are the shapes in each pair **congruent**?
Discussion When a shape is reflected in a mirror line what can you say about the perimeter of the shape and its reflection?
What about the area of both?

Key point

Lines of reflection (or mirror lines) on coordinate grids can be described by their **equations**.

6 Copy this diagram.
   a Draw the image of triangle A after a reflection in the line
      i $x = 2$
      ii $y = 3$
   b Draw the image of shape B after a reflection in the line
      i $x = -3$
      ii $y = -1$
   c **i** Draw the image of triangle C after a reflection in the line $x = -3$.
      ii Reflect the combined image in the line $y = 3$.
      iii What is the name of the shape you have made? What is the area of this shape?

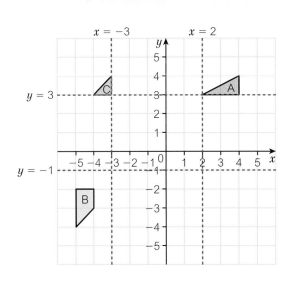

7 The diagram shows congruent shapes on a coordinate grid.
Copy and complete these statements.
The first one is done for you.

a A is a reflection of B in the line $x = -1$.
b A is a reflection of D in the line _____.
c D is a reflection of E in the line _____.
d E is a reflection of F in the line _____.
e C is a reflection of F in the line _____.

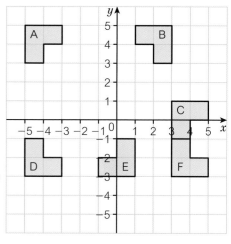

8 Copy this diagram.
Draw the images of these
shapes after reflection in
the lines given.
The first one is done for you.

a Shape A in the line $y = x$.
b Shape B in the line $y = -x$.
c Shape C in the line $y = x$.
d Shape D in the line $y = -x$.

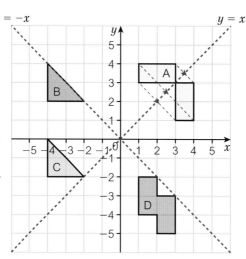

Q8 hint

When you have a diagonal mirror line
you can turn your page round so that
the mirror line is vertical.

Investigation   Reasoning

In the diagram, triangle ABC has been reflected in the line $y = x$ to
become triangle DEF.

1 Write down the coordinates of the vertices of the triangles ABC and DEF.
Put your answers in a table like this.

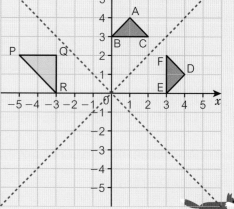

	Coordinates of vertices					
Object ABC	A	(1, 4)	B		C	
Image DEF	D		E		F	

a What do you notice about the coordinates of the object and its image?
b Draw other shapes on a coordinate grid and reflect them in the line $y = x$.
c What can you say about the coordinates of each object and its image?

2 On a new grid, label the vertices of triangle PQR and reflect it in the
line $y = -x$.

a What do you notice about the coordinates of the object and its image?
b Draw other shapes on the grid to check this is always true.

9 Explore What symmetries are there in nature?
Look back at the maths you have learned in this lesson.
How can you use it to answer this question?

10 Reflect
a Look back at Q3 and Q4.
Write down the steps you took to draw the reflected images.
You might begin with:
Step 1: I found the mirror line.

b Look back at Q8.
Write down the steps you took to draw the reflected images.

c Which steps were the same for Q4 and Q8? Which steps were
different?

ActiveLearn   Homework, Year 7, Unit 10

10.3 Rotation

You will learn to:
- Recognise and carry out rotations.
- Describe and carry out rotations on a coordinate grid.

Why learn this?
For fairground rides and moving machinery you need to be able to trace the path of an object as it rotates around a fixed point to check that it won't hit anything.

Fluency
Name these regular polygons.

Explore
What does it mean when scientists say, 'The Earth rotates about its axis'?

Exercise 10.3

1 a Match each diagram to the correct description.
 A quarter turn
 B half turn
 C three-quarter turn
 D complete turn

 i ii iii iv

 b Match these angles to turns A–D.
  i 180° **ii** 90° **iii** 360° **iv** 270°

2 Which of these arrows is **clockwise** and which is **anticlockwise**?

A   B

> **Q2 hint**
> Think of the numbers on a clock face. As you move clockwise the numbers increase.

Warm up

Worked example

Rotate this shape through a $\frac{3}{4}$ turn clockwise.

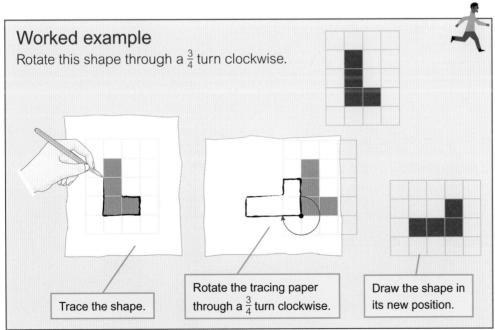

Trace the shape.

Rotate the tracing paper through a $\frac{3}{4}$ turn clockwise.

Draw the shape in its new position.

3 Copy each shape onto squared paper.
Draw the **rotation** for each shape.

a $\frac{1}{4}$ turn clockwise   **b** $\frac{1}{2}$ turn   **c** $\frac{1}{4}$ turn anticlockwise

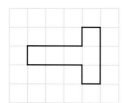 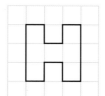 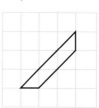

Discussion Does it matter in which direction you rotate shape **b**?
How else could you have described the rotations for parts **a** and **c**?

4 Copy each shape onto squared paper.

a   **b**

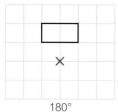

180°   270° clockwise

c   **d**

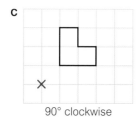 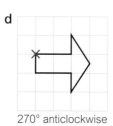

90° clockwise   270° anticlockwise

Rotate it through the angle given about the **centre of rotation** marked ×.

Discussion Are shapes congruent after a rotation?

5 The shapes marked A have been rotated about the centre of rotation ×. Describe the rotations.

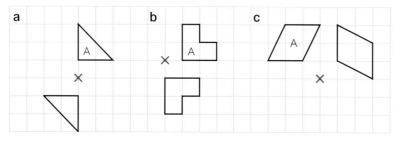

Discussion Which direction is the rotation in part **c**? Does it matter?

6 The diagram shows four flags on a coordinate grid.
Describe these rotations. The first one is done for you.

a A onto B

   90° rotation clockwise about (1, 0)

b B onto A   **c** D onto B   **d** C onto D

e A onto C   **f** C onto A

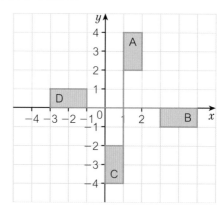

Key point

A **rotation** is a type of transformation. You rotate a shape by turning it around a point, called the **centre of rotation**. To describe a rotation you also need to give the **angle** and direction (**clockwise** or **anticlockwise**).

Q4a hint

Use tracing paper to help you.

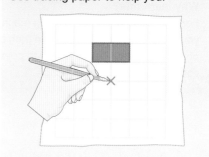

7 Write down the coordinates of the
triangle after a rotation of
a 90° clockwise about (0, 1)
b 90° anticlockwise about (0, 0)
c 180° about (0, 0).
Discussion Why do you not need
to state the direction
with a 180° rotation?

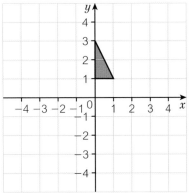

Q7 Strategy hint

Copy the grid and use tracing paper
to draw the rotations to help you.

8 Describe the rotation that takes
a A onto B
b A onto C
c B onto D
d B onto E

Worked example

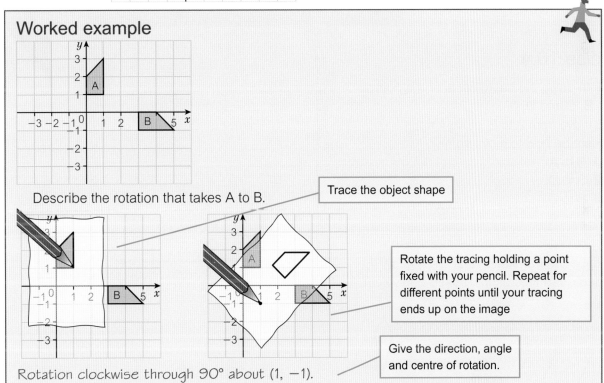

Describe the rotation that takes A to B.

Trace the object shape

Rotate the tracing holding a point
fixed with your pencil. Repeat for
different points until your tracing
ends up on the image

Give the direction, angle
and centre of rotation.

Rotation clockwise through 90° about (1, −1).

9 **Explore** What does it mean when scientists say, 'The Earth rotates
about its axis'?
What have you learned in this lesson to help you answer this
question? What other information do you need?

10 **Reflect** In the last lesson you learned about reflection. In this
lesson you learned about rotation.
Look carefully at some of the shapes you reflected and rotated in
these lessons. Can a reflection of a shape and a rotation of a shape
give the same result?

Explore

Reflect

10.4 Translations and combinations of transformations

You will learn to:
- Translate 2D shapes.
- Transform 2D shapes by combinations of rotations, reflections and translations.

Confidence

Why learn this?
With 3D modelling software, designers can use transformations to move objects around their screen.

Fluency
Which arrow points left and which points right?

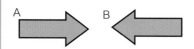

A → B ←

Explore
How many squares of a chessboard can the knight land on?

Warm up

Exercise 10.4

1 a Write down the coordinates of the points A, B, C and D.
   b To move from A to B, move 4 right. Describe how to move from
      i B to A
      ii B to D
      iii B to C
      iv C to A.

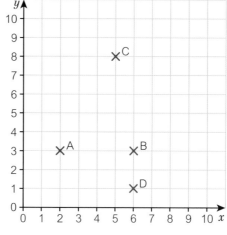

2 Describe the **translation** that takes each shaded quadrilateral onto its red equivalent.

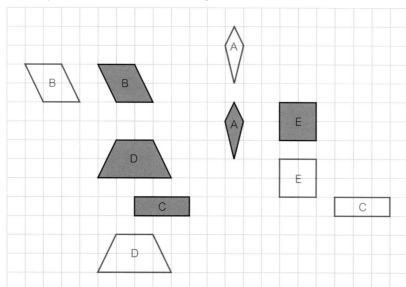

Key point

A **translation** is a type of **transformation**.
A translation moves a shape across a surface.
Describe a translation as a movement left or right, then up or down.

3 Describe each translation.
  a A to B
  b A to C
  c A to D
  d A to E
  e A to F
  f A to G
  g A to H
  Discussion When a shape is translated what can you say about the perimeter and area of both shapes?
  Are both shapes congruent?

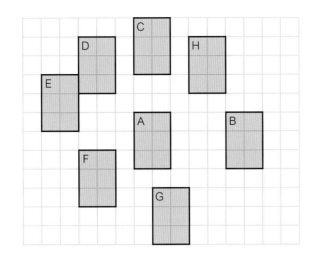

Q3 hint

Choose a vertex (corner) of rectangle A.
Count how many squares across and then up or down that you need to move that corner to reach the new position.
Describe the translation as
  ☐ squares right/left
  ☐ squares up/down.

4 Copy this grid and shape X.
  Translate shape X
  a 5 squares down.
     Label it A.
  b 3 squares right.
     Label it B.
  c 1 square right, 2 squares down.
     Label it C.
  d 1 square left, 7 squares down.
     Label it D.

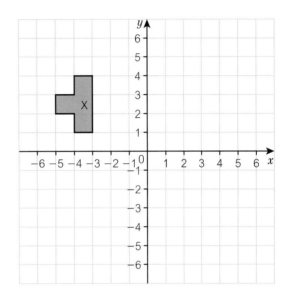

5 The diagram shows four triangles on a coordinate grid.
  Triangle A to triangle B is a translation 6 squares right and 1 square down.
  Describe each of these translations.
  a triangle A to triangle D
  b triangle A to triangle C
  c triangle D to triangle B

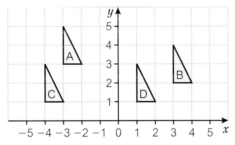

Q5 hint

When describing a translation, always give the along movement first, then the up or down movement.

Worked example

Transform the shape using this two-step transformation:
translation 3 squares left and 1 square up, followed by a reflection in the line $x = -2$.

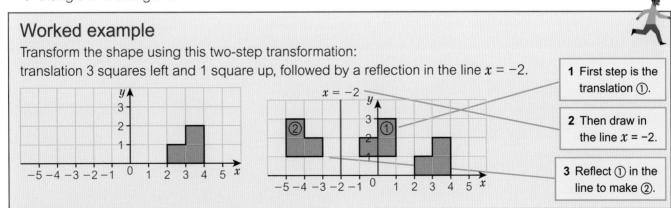

1 First step is the translation ①.

2 Then draw in the line $x = -2$.

3 Reflect ① in the line to make ②.

Topic links: Coordinates, Area, Perimeter

6 The diagram shows shapes A to H.
Write true (T) or false (F) for
each of these statements.
If the statement is false,
explain why.

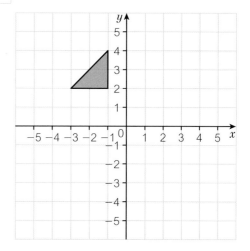

a G is a translation of B.
b F is a reflection of B.
c E is a rotation of F.
d H is a translation of C.
e G is a rotation of D.
f C is a reflection of A.
g A is a translation of B.
h B is a rotation of D.

Q6 hint

When a shape is transformed by a
translation, rotation or reflection, the
image and the object are congruent.

7 Copy this diagram four times.
On separate copies, transform the triangle using these
two-step transformations.
a Translation 4 squares right followed by a reflection
in the line $y = 1$.
b Rotation 180° about $(-1, 2)$ followed by a reflection
in the line $x = 2$.
c Rotation 90° anticlockwise about $(-1, 4)$ followed by
a translation 2 squares right and 4 squares down.
d Reflection in the line $x = -1$ followed by a rotation
of 90° clockwise about $(-1, 1)$.

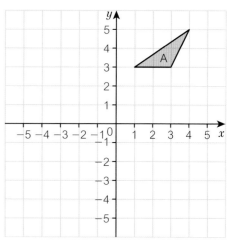

8 a Copy the diagram.
Reflect triangle A in the line $y = x$. Label the image B.
b Translate triangle B 6 left and 3 down. Label the image C.
c Rotate triangle C through 180° about the point $(-3, 0)$.
Label the image D.
d Can you describe a reflection that takes triangle A directly to
triangle D?

9 Explore How many squares of a chessboard can the knight land on?
Is it easier to explore this question now that you have completed the
lesson? What further information do you need to be able to answer
this?

10 Reflect Q8 asked you to carry out three types of transformations.
Which did you find hardest? Which did you find easiest?
Write a hint for the one you found hardest.

Explore

Reflect

10 Check up

Congruency and enlargements

1 Which pairs of arrows are congruent?

A   B   C   D   E   F

2 Copy this shape onto squared paper.
   a Enlarge the shape by scale factor 2.
   b Are the two shapes congruent?
      Explain how you know.

3 The diagram shows an object and its image after an enlargement.

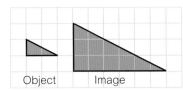

   Object   Image

   a Write the ratio of the length of a side of the object to the
      corresponding length in the image.
      Give the ratio in its simplest form.
   b Write the scale factor of the enlargement.

Reflections and rotations

4 Copy this shape onto squared paper.
   Reflect it in the mirror line.

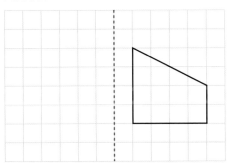

5 Copy each shape onto squared paper. Draw the rotation.

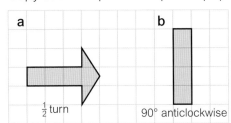

   a $\frac{1}{2}$ turn   b   90° anticlockwise

6 Copy this diagram.
Draw the image of the shape
after a reflection in the line
  a $y = 1$
   Label your reflected shape A.
  b $x = -1$
   Label your reflected shape B.

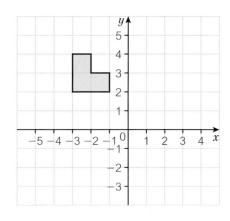

7 Use your diagram from Q6.
Draw the image of the shape after these rotations.
  a 90° clockwise about (−2, 1). Label this rotated shape A.
  b 180° about (−3, 1). Label this rotated shape B.

Translations and combinations of transformations

8 Copy this shape onto squared paper.
Draw the image of the shape after these translations.
  a 3 squares right, 2 squares down. Label this shape A.
  b 4 squares left, 1 square up. Label this shape B.

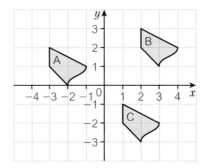

9 Describe each translation.
  a shape A to shape B
  b shape B to shape C

10 Copy this diagram and carry out these transformations
on the shape.
  a A translation 2 squares left and 1 square down followed by a
   reflection in the line $x = -1$.
  b A rotation 90° anticlockwise about (2, 2) followed by a
   translation 2 squares right and 1 square up.

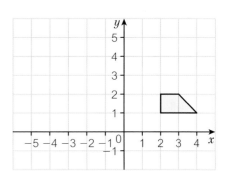

11 How sure are you of your answers? Were you mostly
  ☹ **Just guessing** 😐 **Feeling doubtful** ☺ **Confident**
  What next? Use your results to decide whether to strengthen or
  extend your learning.

Challenge

12 a Niko says that shape D can be translated
   onto shape F.
   Is Niko right? Explain your answer.
  b Idris says that shape B can be reflected onto shape H.
   Is Idris right? Explain your answer.
  c Find pairs of shapes on this grid that rotate onto
   each other. Describe each rotation fully.

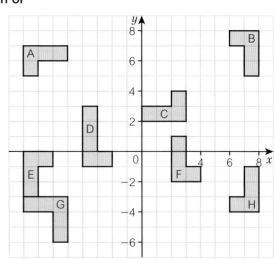

10 Strengthen

You will:
• Strengthen your understanding with practice.

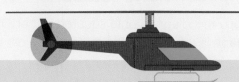

Congruency and enlargements

1 Decide whether these pairs of shapes are congruent.

a   b   c

Q1 hint

Trace one of the pair. If the tracing fits exactly over the other shape, then they are congruent.

2 Copy this shape onto squared paper.
  a **i** Enlarge the shape by a scale factor of 2.
     ii Write down the ratio of the length of the sides of the original shape to the enlarged shape.
  b **i** Enlarge the shape by a scale factor of 3.
     ii Write down the ratio of the length of the sides of the original shape to the enlarged shape.
  c **i** Enlarge the shape by a scale factor of 4.
     ii Write down the ratio of the length of the sides of the original shape to the enlarged shape.

Q2a hint

Every 1 square on the original shape (object) is worth 2 squares on the enlarged shape (image).
object : image
  1 : 2

3 Work out the scale factor of enlargement for each pair of rectangles.

a    b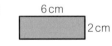

4 a Draw a shape that is congruent to shape A.

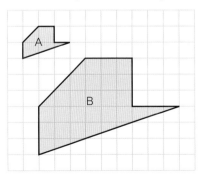

Q3a hint

3 × ☐ = 15
1 × ☐ = 5
Check that both missing numbers are the same.

  b Shape A is enlarged by a scale factor of k to give shape B. Write down the value of k.

Reflections and rotations

1 Copy this diagram onto squared paper. Draw the image when each shape is reflected in the mirror line.

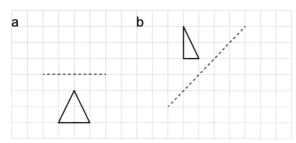

a   b

Q1b hint

Turn your book so that the mirror line is vertical.

2 a Copy this triangle onto squared paper.
  b Trace the shape. Turn the tracing a $\frac{1}{2}$ turn. Now draw the rotated shape.

  c Repeat for $\frac{1}{4}$ turn clockwise.

  d Repeat for $\frac{3}{4}$ turn anticlockwise.

  e What do you notice about your drawing for parts **c** and **d**?

Q3 hint

Write the angle and direction.

3 The red shapes have been rotated from the shaded shapes about the centre of rotation marked ×. Describe the rotations.

a 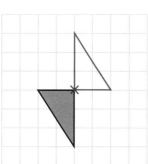   b 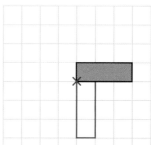   c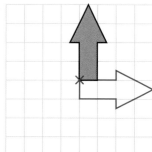

4 Copy this diagram. Draw the reflection of the triangle in the line
  a $y = 1$. Label the image A.
  b $x = 2$. Label the image B.
  c $y = 3$. Label the image C.
  d $x = 0$. Label the image D.

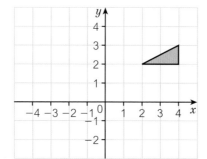

Q4a hint

Draw $y = 1$.
Check: put your finger at different points along the line $y = 1$. Do they all have a y-coordinate of 1?
Check your original shape and your reflection are the same distance from your line $y = 1$.

5 Margareta has started to reflect the rectangle in the mirror line $y = x$.
  a Copy the diagram.
  b Turn the page so the mirror line is vertical and continue the reflection.
  c Trace your completed diagram. Fold your diagram along the line $y = x$. What happens to the image and the object?

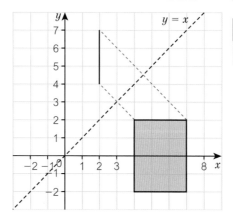

Q5 hint

Reflect each vertex in the mirror line.

6 Draw a coordinate grid with x- and y-axes from −8 to 8.
  a Plot and join the points (−2, 3), (−2, 6), (0, 6), (0, 3).
  b Draw the line $y = -x$.
  c Reflect the shape from part **a** in the line $y = -x$.

Q6 hint

Use the method from Q5.

7 Copy the diagram and draw the image
  of the triangle after these rotations.
  a 90° anticlockwise about (0, 0).
    Label your rotated shape A.
  b 90° clockwise about (2, 0).
    Label your rotated shape B.
  c 180° about (0, 0).
    Label your rotated shape C.

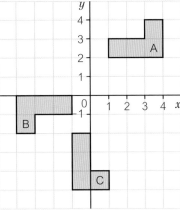

Q7a hint

Trace the triangle on tracing paper.
Put your pencil on the point (0, 0) and
turn your tracing paper 90° (quarter
turn) anticlockwise.

Q7c hint

180° is half a turn.

8 Describe the rotation that takes
  shape A to

  a shape B   **b** shape C.

Q8 hint

Rotation, centre (☐,☐),
☐° anticlockwise/clockwise.

Translations and combinations of transformations

1 The grid shows triangles A to E.
  Describe the translation that takes
  a A to B   **b** B to C
  c C to D   **d** D to E
  e E to A   **f** E to C.

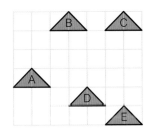

Q1 hint

Choose one vertex (corner) of the
shape. Give the number of squares
right or left followed by the number of
squares up or down.

2 Describe the translation that takes
  a A to B   **b** A to C   **c** A to D   **d** A to E.

3 Copy this diagram. Transform the shape using these transformations.
The first one is done for you.

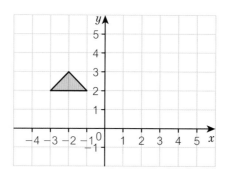

a A translation 3 squares right and 1 square up followed by a reflection in the line $y = 2$.

b A rotation 90° clockwise about $(-1, 2)$ followed by a translation 2 squares right and 3 squares down.

c A reflection in the y-axis followed by a translation 2 squares left and 2 squares up.

d A reflection in the line $y = 1$ followed by a rotation 180° about $(0, 0)$.

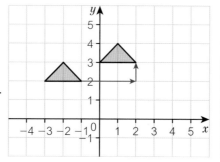

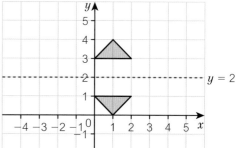

Enrichment

1 a Copy this rectangle on a square grid.
Draw the image of the rectangle after a rotation of 90° clockwise about the red dot.
Repeat the rotation of the image, 90° clockwise about the red dot.
Finally repeat the rotation of the new image, 90° clockwise about the red dot.

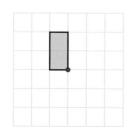

b What is the order of rotational symmetry of your combined final shape?

c Does your new shape have any lines of symmetry? Explain your answer.

2 a **Problem-solving** Copy and shade the parts of this shape that are congruent. Use different colours for each type of shape.
You will need two different colours.

b Use the parts to make two regular hexagons that are congruent to the hexagon in the middle.

> **Q2b hint**
>
> All the parts of one colour make one hexagon. All the parts of the other colour make the other hexagon.

3 **Reflect** In these lessons you have answered questions about
reflection   rotation   translation
Write a definition for each of them, using one of these descriptions:
flips over   changes position   turns around
For each definition, draw a sketch to show what the definition means.
How did your definition help you choose the shapes?

10 Extend

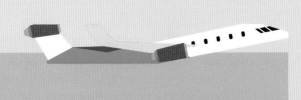

You will:
• Extend your understanding with problem-solving.

1 The diagram shows four triangles. Triangle A has been rotated 180° about the point (−1.5, 3) to get triangle B. Describe the rotation that takes
  a B onto C
  b C onto D
  c D onto A.

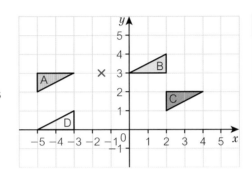

Q1 hint

Use tracing paper to find the centres of rotation.

2 The diagram shows four triangles. Describe the rotation that takes
  a A onto B
  b B onto C
  c B onto D.

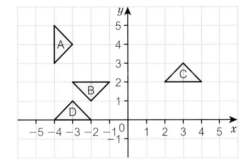

3 Describe the rotation that takes
  a A onto B
  b C onto D
  c B onto C
  d E onto F
  e F onto G.

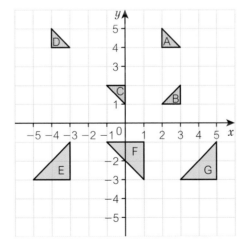

4 This is the logo for a new brand of clothing.
   Copy the logo onto a square grid.
   Enlarge the logo using a scale factor of 3.

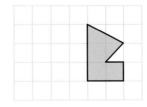

Unit 10 Transformations 242

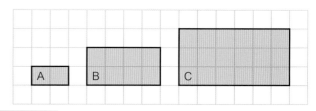

5 Reasoning The diagram shows three rectangles
A, B and C on a centimetre square grid.
B and C are both enlargements of A.

a What is the scale factor of enlargement of A to B?

b What is the scale factor of enlargement of A to C?

c What is the scale factor of enlargement of B to C?

d Copy and complete this table.

Rectangle	Perimeter (cm)	Area (cm²)
A	6	2
B		
C		

e Copy and complete this table. Write each ratio in its simplest form.

Rectangles	Ratio of lengths	Ratio of perimeters	Ratio of areas
A : B	1 : 2		
A : C			

f What do you notice about the ratios you found in part **e**?
Explain what these ratios tell you.

6 Problem-solving Ingrid drew this shape on a
centimetre square grid.
She enlarged the shape using a scale factor of 5.
Without drawing the enlargement, work out

a the perimeter of the enlargement

b the area of the enlargement.

c Draw the enlargement to check your answers to part **a** are correct.

Q6 hint

Use your answers to Q5f to help.

7 The diagram shows a white parallelogram and a
green parallelogram.
Describe the reflection that takes the white
parallelogram onto the green parallelogram.

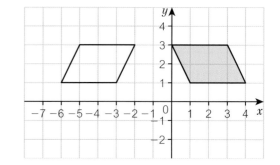

8 The diagram shows triangles ABC and DEF.
Triangle ABC has been reflected to make triangle DEF.

a Write down the equation of the mirror line.

Triangle DEF is reflected in the line $x = 6$ to become triangle GHI.

b Copy and complete this table showing the coordinates of the
vertices of the triangles.

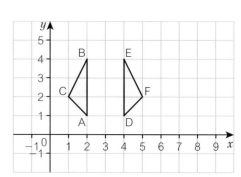

Triangle ABC	A (2, 1)	B (2, 4)	C (1, 2)
Triangle DEF	D (□, □)	E (□, □)	F (□, □)
Triangle GHI	G (□, □)	H (□, □)	I (□, □)

Triangle GHI is reflected in the line $x = 9$ to become triangle JKL.

c Without drawing triangle JKL, work out the coordinates of the
vertices of triangle JKL.
Explain how you worked out your answer.

Topic links: Perimeter, Area

9 Make two copies of this diagram.

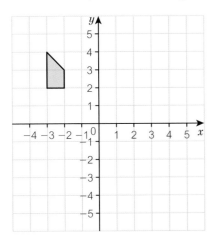

a i On the first copy, transform the object by carrying out a translation 6 right and 2 down, followed by a rotation 180° about (2, −1).

ii Describe fully the single transformation that will take the image back to the object.

b i On the second copy, transform the object by carrying out a rotation 90° clockwise about (−3, −1), followed by a rotation 90° anticlockwise about (2, −1).

ii Describe fully the single transformation that will take the image back to the object.

Q9a i hint

Draw the shape after each transformation.

Q9a ii hint

Is it a translation, reflection or rotation? Remember to give all the information.

10 **Problem-solving**

a Raji translates a shape 2 squares right and 3 squares up. He then translates the image 5 squares left and 1 square down. What single translation has the same effect as these two translations combined?

b Aya translates a shape 3 squares left and 2 squares down. What translation must she now do to the image so that the combined effect of both translations is a single translation of 7 squares left and 4 squares up?

c Explain how you can answer parts **a** and **b** without drawing and translating shapes.

Q10 Strategy hint

Draw a shape on squared paper, then carry out the translations.

11 Copy this diagram.

a Reflect the shape in the line $y = x$.

b Reflect the combined shape in the x-axis, then reflect the newly combined shape in the y-axis.

c How many lines of symmetry does your final shape have?

d What is the order of rotational symmetry of your final shape?

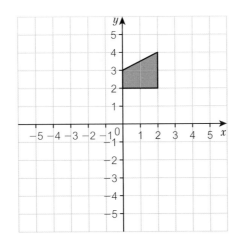

Q11a hint

Each vertex on the image needs to be the same distance from the mirror line as the corresponding vertex on the image.

12 Reasoning Copy this diagram.

a i Transform the object by carrying out a reflection in the line $y = -x$, followed by a translation 2 squares left and 6 squares down.

 ii Describe fully the single transformation that will take the image back to the object.

b i Transform the object by carrying out a reflection in the line $x = -2$, followed by a reflection in the line $y = x$, followed by a rotation 90° anticlockwise about (1, −2).

 ii Describe fully the single transformation that will take the image back to the object.

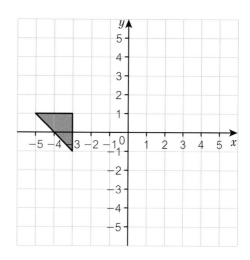

13 Real / Problem-solving A gardener plants a flowerbed measuring 3 m by 4 m.

For each square metre he needs 30 bulbs.

Flower bulbs come in bags of 50 and cost $6.99 per bag.

a What is the cost of bulbs for this flowerbed?

Another flower bed is 3 times as long and 3 times as wide.

b How many bulbs will he need for this flowerbed?

c What is the cost of bulbs for this flowerbed?

It takes him 4 hours to plant the bulbs in the flowerbed measuring 3 m by 4 m.

d How long will it take him to plant the bulbs in the larger flowerbed?

Q13 Literacy hint

A flowerbed is an area of a garden created to grow flowers.

Investigation   **Problem-solving / Reasoning**

The diagram shows kite 1.

Kite 1 is reflected in the x-axis to form kite 2.

Kite 2 is reflected in the y-axis to form kite 3.

Kite 3 is reflected in the x-axis to form kite 4.

1 Fill in the coordinates in the table.

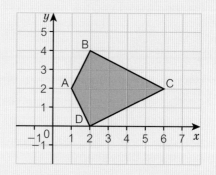

	A	B	C	D
Kite 1				
Kite 2				
Kite 3				
Kite 4				

2 What reflection would take kite 1 onto kite 4?

3 Experiment with reflecting a different shape in the line $y = x$ and then in the line $y = -x$. What do you notice?

14 Reflect Look back at the questions you answered in these Extend lessons. They were all about transformations.

List all the other mathematics topics you used to answer these questions.

Beside each one, write the type of transformation you used it for.

Reflect

10 Unit test

1 The blue arrow has been translated 3 right and 2 up. Write the letter of the correct image.

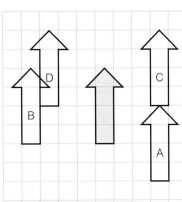

2 Write the letter of shape S after

a $\frac{1}{2}$ turn

b $\frac{1}{4}$ turn clockwise

c $\frac{1}{4}$ turn anticlockwise.

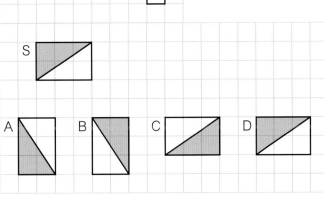

3 a Copy this shape onto squared paper. Draw the image of the shape after the translation 2 squares right, 4 squares down.

b i Draw the shape enlarged by scale factor 3.

ii Write the ratio of the length of the sides of the original shape to the enlarged shape.

4 Write down the letters representing the congruent parts of each shape.

a   **b**   **c**

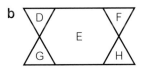
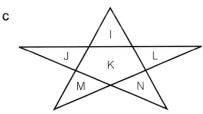

5 On this grid, Bayan reflects the white shape in the line $y = 2$ and gets the blue shape. Explain the mistake that Bayan has made.

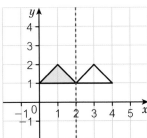

6 Copy the diagram and draw the image of the triangle after these transformations.

   a Reflection in $x = 1$. Label this shape A.

   b Reflection in $y = 1$. Label this shape B.

   c Rotation 90° clockwise about (3, −1). Label this shape C.

   d Rotation 180° about (1, 0). Label this shape D.

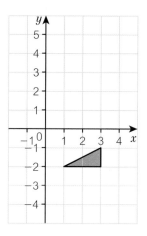

7 a Make a copy of this diagram. Reflect the shape in the mirror line. Label the image B.

   b Translate shape B 2 units right, 1 unit down. Label it C.

   c Reflect shape C in the mirror line. Label the image D.

   d Describe the translation that takes D to A.

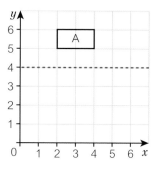

Challenge

8 The diagram shows two shapes, A and B. Describe a two-step transformation that will transform shape A to shape B.

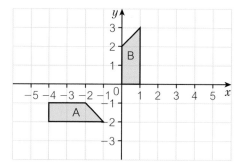

9 Split each diagram into four congruent shapes. Each shape must contain a triangle, a square, a hexagon and a circle.

   a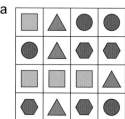

   b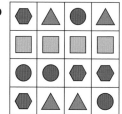

> **Q9 hint**
>
> The triangle, square, hexagon and circle can be in different places within the four congruent shapes, i.e. the outline of the shapes must be congruent, but the patterns within them do not need to be.

10 Reflect List the four transformations you have learned about in this unit.

Draw a sketch for each of them to remind you what each transformation does.

Now read this sentence carefully.

After _____ the shape and its image are congruent.

Complete this sentence with one or more transformations.

Explain your choice of word(s).

Reflect

11.1 Comparing and calculating probabilities

You will learn to:
* Use and interpret probability scales.
* Calculate and compare probabilities.

Why learn this?
Understanding probabilities helps you predict how likely it is to rain today.

Fluency
Which is more likely for each spinner: grey or white?

Explore
What chance of rain (in percentage) would make you decide to take an umbrella?

Exercise 11.1

1 Which is the bigger fraction?

a $\frac{3}{10}$ or $\frac{7}{10}$ **b** $\frac{2}{3}$ or $\frac{3}{5}$

2 Match the equivalent numbers.

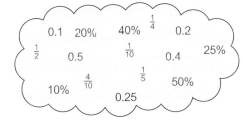

3 a Copy the probability scale.

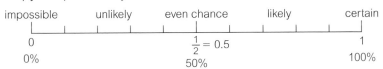

b Write the capital letter of each event in the correct place on your scale.

A Getting tails when you flip a fair coin.

B The probability of someone born in 2012 living to 100 is about 30%.

C If one of your parents is near-sighted, the probability that you will be near-sighted is about 0.2.

D The probability of two blue-eyed parents having a brown-eyed child is about $\frac{3}{4}$

E The probability of having twins is 1%.

Q1 hint

Write the fractions as equivalent fractions with the same denominator.

Key point

All probabilities have a value between 0 and 1. You can use words, fractions, decimals and percentages to describe probabilities.

Topic links: Comparing and converting fractions, decimals, percentages

4 Each of these **fair** spinners is spun once.

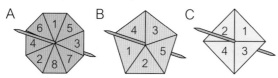

For each spinner
a write all of the possible **outcomes**
b write the total number of possible outcomes.

5 A fair 6-sided dice is rolled once.
What are the **successful outcomes** for each event?
a The dice lands on an even number.
b The dice lands on a number less than 5.
c The dice lands on a prime number.
d The dice lands on a prime number or an even number.

Worked example

Find the probability that
this spinner will land on red.

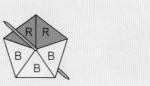

Probability that spinner lands on red = $\frac{2}{5}$

There are two successful outcomes: red, red.
The total number of possible outcomes is 5.

---

6 Rakesh spins this fair spinner once.
a What is the probability that it lands on
  i blue   **ii** white
  iii red?
b Write your answers as decimals.
c Write your answers as percentages.
d Describe each probability using words from the probability scale in Q3.

7 A bag contains 2 chocolates, 3 toffees and 5 chews.
Lin takes a sweet from the bag without looking.
Find these probabilities. Write your answers as decimals.
a P(chew)   **b** P(toffee)   **c** P(chocolate)

8 In class, 14 students have brown eyes, 4 students have blue eyes and
2 students have green eyes. A student is chosen at random.
Work out
a P(brown eyes)   **b** P(blue eyes)   **c** P(green eyes)

9 a A bag has 16 red counters and 11 blue counters. Are you more
likely to pick a red or blue counter at random from the bag?
b Bag A has 8 red counters and 11 blue counters. Bag B has 8 red
counters and 5 blue counters. Are you more likely to pick a red
counter at random from Bag A or Bag B?

Q4 Literacy hint

Fair means that the pointer on the
spinner is equally likely to stop at any
position.

Key point

An **outcome** is an end result. For
example, one outcome of flipping a
coin is Heads.

Q5 Literacy hint

Successful outcomes are the
outcomes you want.

Key point

Probability of an event happening
$= \dfrac{\text{number of successful outcomes}}{\text{total number of outcomes}}$
This formula only works if the
outcomes are equally likely.

Key point

P(X) means 'the probability that X
happens'.

Q9 Strategy hint

Calculate the probability of each
event as a fraction.

10 Each of these fair dice is rolled once.

  a Which event is more likely?

   i The number 3 with dice B or the number 3 with dice C.

   ii An even number with dice A or an even number with dice B.

A   B   C

6 sides   5 sides   10 sides

  b Which dice has the greatest probability of showing a square number?

11 STEM When it rains, the probability of a thunderstorm is $\frac{4}{5}$ in Kampala and 66% in Singapore.

In which city is a thunderstorm more likely?

Investigation   Problem-solving / Reasoning

Michael puts red, purple, yellow and orange counters in a bag.

He picks a counter at random.

The probabilities of getting each of the colours are:

P(red) = $\frac{1}{6}$ P(purple) = $\frac{1}{5}$ P(yellow) = $\frac{2}{15}$ P(orange) = $\frac{1}{2}$

1 What is the smallest number of counters that there could be in the bag?

2 How many counters of each colour are in the bag?

---

12 Real / Problem-solving

  a A single-wheel lock (with numbers 0–9) can be opened by the number 2. What is the probability that a stranger can open the lock in one attempt?

  b A different lock has two wheels of numbers.

   i How many possible combinations are there?

   ii What is the probability that a stranger can open this lock at the first attempt?

  c If the lock has three wheels, what is the probability that a stranger can open it at the first attempt?

13 Problem-solving Each of these fair dice is rolled once.

A   B   C

8 sides   10 sides   12 sides

  a Which event is less likely?

   i A square number on dice A or a square number on dice B.

   ii A prime number on dice A or a prime number on dice C.

  b Which dice has the greatest probability of showing an even number?

14 Explore What chance of rain (in percentage) would make you decide to take an umbrella?

Choose some sensible numbers to help you explore this situation. Use what you've learned in this lesson to help you answer the question.

15 Reflect Will is rolling a fair 6-sided dice. He says, 'It's harder to roll a 6 than a 3.'

Use what you have learned in this lesson to decide if Will is correct. Explain.

11.2 More probability calculations

You will learn to:
- Calculate more complex probabilities.
- Find the probability of an event not happening.

Why learn this?
A roadside repair service can use probabilities to help decide on the spare parts to carry.

Fluency
A bag contains 3 red, 2 blue and 5 green sweets. One is picked at random.
What is the probability it is
- red
- blue
- green?

Explore
What is the probability of a car breaking down because of a flat tyre or flat battery?

Confidence

Exercise 11.2

1 Work these out. Give each answer as a single fraction in its simplest form.

a $\frac{3}{10} + \frac{1}{10}$

b $1 - \frac{3}{10}$

c $1 - \frac{1}{12}$

Q1b hint

$1 = \frac{10}{10}$

2 Work out

a $1 - 0.7$

b $100\% - 33\%$

3 Copy and complete this probability scale.

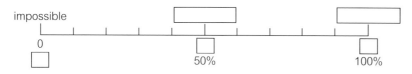

4 a Work out the probability that this spinner will land on blue or red.

b **Reasoning** Louis says, 'P(blue or red) is the same as P(not yellow).' Is Louis correct? Explain.

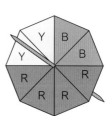

5 At a disco, there are 3 red, 2 green and 1 yellow laser lights.
A computer turns one on at random.

a How many possible outcomes are there?

b Work out

  i P(yellow)

  ii P(red or yellow)

  iii P(green or red)

  iv P(red or green or yellow)

  v P(not red)

  vi P(not red or yellow)

Warm up

6 Reasoning Persephone puts all the letters from her name into a box.

P   E   R   S   E   P   H   O   N   E

She then picks one of the letters at random.

Find the probability that she picks

a a vowel

b a consonant

c a letter that is neither a vowel nor a consonant.

Q6 hint

In the English alphabet AEIOU are vowels. The other letters are consonants.

7 The table shows information about the eye colour of Year 8 students.

	Blue	Brown	Green	Hazel	Total
Girls	20	32	7	25	84
Boys	17	29	6	24	76
Total	37	61	13	49	160

A student is picked at random.

a What is the probability that the student is

  i a girl with green eyes

  ii a boy with blue eyes?

b Who is more likely to be picked: a boy with hazel eyes or a girl with brown eyes?

8 Problem-solving The table shows the probabilities of events A, B and C.

Event	A	B	C
Probability	0.3		

The probabilities of events A and C are equal.

Work out the probability of event C.

9 Reasoning An ordinary 6-sided dice is rolled once.

a List all the possible outcomes.

b What is the probability of each possible outcome?

c What is the sum of all their probabilities?

d Copy and complete the rule:
  The sum of the probabilities of all
  possible outcomes is ☐

e Show that the rule works for this fair spinner.

Discussion Why does this rule work?

10 Problem-solving A fair 10-sided spinner has four colours.

P(red or blue) = $\frac{3}{5}$ P(not yellow) = $\frac{4}{5}$

Draw a picture of how this spinner might look.

11 STEM The computer sound cards made on a production line are either thrown away, repaired or passed. 4% are scrapped, 8% are repaired. What is the probability that a sound card is passed?

Q11 hint

The sum of the probabilities of all possible outcomes is ☐%

12 Problem-solving A variety of sweetcorn plant produces 1, 2 or 3 cobs.
The probability of a plant producing 3 cobs is 0.4. 1 cob and 2 cobs are equally likely.
Work out the probability of a plant producing 2 cobs.

Q12 hint

	1	
0.4		
3 cobs	2 cobs	1 cob

13 a The probability of a spinner landing on green is $\frac{1}{6}$
What is P(not green)?

b The probability of rolling an odd number with a fair dice is $\frac{3}{6}$
What is the probability of rolling an even number?

c The probability of it raining today is 0.1.
What is the probability of it not raining today?

Discussion Can the probability of an event not happening be 1?

Q13 hint

How can you write a probability of 1 as a percentage?

14 The probability that a baby is born on the due date is 5%.
What is the probability that a baby is not born on the due date?

Investigation   **Reasoning**

This fair spinner is spun once.
1 What is the probability it will land on
   a 2
   b not 2?
2 Add the probabilities together. What do you notice?
3 Copy and complete this rule:
   Probability of an event happening + Probability of the event not happening = ____
Discussion When you know the probability of an event happening, how can you find the probability of it not happening?

---

15 Explore What is the probability of a car breaking down because of a flat tyre or flat battery?
Is it easier to explore this question now that you have completed the lesson? What further information do you need to be able to answer this?

16 Reflect Sami works out that the probability of this spinner landing on an even number is $\frac{1}{2}$ and the probability of it landing on red is $\frac{2}{3}$
Use what you have learned in this lesson to explain why the probabilities don't add up to 1.

11 Check up

Calculating probabilities

1 This spinner is spun once.
List all the possible outcomes for the spinner.

2 This fair spinner shown is spun once.
a List all possible outcomes.
b What is the probability of each possible outcome?
c What is the sum of all their probabilities?

3 A bag contains 3 red, 2 blue and 5 green sweets.
One sweet is picked at random.
Calculate the probability that it is
a red
b blue
c green?

4 These number cards are shuffled and turned upside down.

The top card is turned over.
a List the possible outcomes.
b What is the probability that the top card is
 i 1
 ii odd
 iii not 3?

5 A fair 6-sided dice is rolled once.
Work out
a P(prime number)
b P(square number).

6 A bag contains some sweets with different coloured wrappers.
A sweet is taken from the bag at random.
a The probability of a toffee is $\frac{3}{8}$.
What is the probability that it is not a toffee?
b The probability of a chocolate is $\frac{1}{2}$.
Which is more likely: a toffee or a chocolate?
c What is the probability of picking a toffee or a chocolate?

7 The probability that a new smartphone will develop a fault in the first 12 months is 0.1
What is the probability that it does not develop a fault?

8 On a spinner, P(blue) = $\frac{1}{3}$
Work out P(not blue).

Probability problems

9 An ordinary 6-sided dice is rolled once.
Jaswinder says, 'The probability of getting an odd number is the same as getting a prime number.'
Is she correct?
Explain your reasoning.

10 A car park contains 3 red cars, 6 blue cars and 2 black cars.
Danilo says, 'There there are twice as many blue cars as red cars.'
Jana agrees and says, 'This means that the probability of choosing a blue car is twice the probability of choosing a red car.'
Is she correct?
Explain your reasoning.

11 Complete the probability table for this spinner.

Colour	Red	White	Blue
Probability			

12 A fair 7-sided spinner has 1, 2, 3 as the only possible outcomes. The probability of the spinner landing on 1 is twice the probability of it landing on 2, which is twice the probability of it landing on 3.
Draw a picture of how this spinner might look.

13 How sure are you of your answers? Were you mostly
☹ **Just guessing**   😐 **Feeling doubtful**   ☺ **Confident**
What next? Use your results to decide whether to strengthen or extend your learning.

Challenge

14 a Use the numbers 2 and 3 to fill in the sections of these two spinners.

Spinner 1   Spinner 2

   b The two spinners are spun and their results are added. Make a table to show the totals.
   c Work out the probability of getting a total of 4.
   d Draw a tree diagram to show the results of the two spinners.
   e Use your tree diagram to find the probability of spinning two 3s.
   f Make up the rules of a fair game for two players using the totals of the spinner results. Each player must have their own rule for winning.

11 Strengthen

You will:
- Strengthen your understanding with practice.

Calculating probabilities

1 Ruairi spins spinner 1 and Kulvinder spins spinner 2.

Spinner 1   Spinner 2

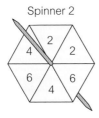

a Find the probability that
  i Ruairi spins a 1
  ii Kulvinder doesn't spin a 1.
b Kulvinder says, 'I am more likely to spin a 2 than Ruairi is.'
  Is Kulvinder correct? Explain your answer.

2 Each of these spinners is spun once.

Spinner A   Spinner B

a Which spinner is more likely to land on blue?
b Which spinner is more likely to land on red?
c Work out P(grey) for each spinner.
  What do you notice?

Q2a hint

Compare the probabilities.

For spinner A, P(blue) = $\dfrac{\square}{4} = \dfrac{\square}{8}$

For spinner B, P(blue) = $\dfrac{\square}{4}$

3 These numbered counters are placed into a bag.
One is picked at random.

a How many possible outcomes are there?
b How many of the possible outcomes are 2?
c Write the probability of picking a 2 as a fraction.
d Work out the probability of picking
  i 1 or 2
  ii 6
  iii an even number
  iv a number less than 4.

Q3a hint

How many counters are in the bag in total?

Q3c hint

$\dfrac{\text{number of 2s}}{\text{total number of counters}}$

4 This fair spinner is spun once.

It is a fair spinner because it is equally likely to land on any edge.
a How many possible outcomes are there?
b Work out
   i P(blue)
   ii P(red)
   iii P(blue or red)
   iv P(red or yellow)
   v P(not blue)
   vi P(not yellow).

5 Misha rolls an ordinary dice, numbered 1 to 6. Draw a probability scale and mark on it the letter of each event.
The dice lands on
A the number 5
B an odd number
C the number 9
D a number greater than 2
E a number less than 7.

6 **Real** Gordon is a goalkeeper.
The probability that he saves a penalty is 0.3.
What is the probability that Gordon will not be able to save a penalty?
Discussion Can the probability of something happening be 0?
Can the probability of something happening be the same as the probability of it not happening?

7 Astronomers predict that there is a 45% chance of a solar storm tomorrow.
What is the probability that there will not be a solar storm tomorrow?

8 **STEM** The computer hard drives made on a production line are either scrapped, repaired or passed. 5% are scrapped, 7% are repaired.
What is the probability that a hard drive is passed?

9 The probability of a certain type of coin landing on heads is 0.55.
Is the coin fair?
Explain your reasoning.

Q4a hint

How many edges are there?

Q4b i hint

What fraction of the spinner is blue?

Q4b v hint

$P(blue) = \frac{1}{6}$
$P(not\ blue) = 1 - \frac{1}{6} = \frac{\square}{\square}$

Q5 hint

Decide if each event is impossible, unlikely, even chance, likely or certain.

Q6 hint

To find the probability of something not happening, subtract the probability of it happening from 1.

Q7 hint

Subtract the probability of the event happening from 100%.

Q8 hint

The sum of the probabilities of all possible outcomes is $\square$%.

10 Problem-solving For this spinner P(red) = $\frac{3}{8}$ and P(blue) = $\frac{1}{8}$

What is the probability of the spinner not landing on blue or red?

11 The numbers on the faces of a 10-sided dice are

5   100   20   10   1   1000   15   50   20   1

Lochan rolls the dice once.

a What is the probability (as a fraction) it will land on

   i the number 1

   ii a 2-digit number

   iii a number greater than 1

   iv a multiple of 10?

b Write your answers to part **a** as decimal probabilities.

c Write your answers to part **a** as percentage probabilities.

Probability problems

1 The probability of being struck by lightning is roughly 1 in a million.

a Write this probability as

   i a fraction

   ii a decimal.

Sarka says, 'There is no way I will ever be struck by lightning.'

b Discuss Sarka's statement with a classmate. Do you agree with her? Give a reason for your answer.

2 At a light show, there are 4 red, 3 green and 1 yellow laser lights.
A computer turns one on at random.
What is the probability it is

a green or red

b red or yellow

c yellow

d red or green or yellow?

3 Shah places 12 coloured marbles in a bag. Three are green, four are blue and the rest are yellow.
Shah thinks that the probability of randomly picking a yellow marble is the same as the probability of randomly picking a green marble.
Is he correct? Explain your answer.

4 Design a spinner with a prime number of sides.
Colour the spinner so that
P(blue) = P(green) = P(red).

5 Reasoning Ollie says, 'The probability of a football team winning is $\frac{1}{3}$ because winning is only one out of the three possible outcomes – win, lose, draw.' Explain why Ollie is wrong.

Enrichment

1 A fair dice has n sides. Each side is numbered either 1, 2 or 3.
P(1) = 0.2, P(2) = 0.4 and P(3) = 0.4.
Work out the smallest possible value of n.

2 **Problem-solving** **a** Write six numbers to label a blank 6-sided dice
so that the probability of rolling an even number is unlikely.
b Write ten numbers to label a blank 10-sided dice so that there is an
even chance of rolling a number greater than 3.

3 **a** Sketch five 8-sided fair spinners like this.

b Fill in the sections with any numbers between 1 and 8, so that
- Spinner 1 has P(5) = $\frac{1}{2}$
- Spinner 2 has P(less than 3) = $\frac{1}{4}$
- Spinner 3 has P(not a 6) = $\frac{3}{8}$
- Spinner 4 has P(2 or 7) = $\frac{5}{8}$
- Spinner 5 has P(at least 4) = $\frac{3}{4}$

4 **Reflect** In this Strengthen lesson you have answered probability
questions involving
- comparing probabilities
- probability problems.
Which types of question were easiest? Why?
Which types of question were hardest? Why?
Write down one thing about probability you think you need more
practice on.

11 Extend

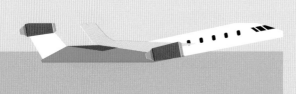

You will:
• Extend your understanding with problem-solving.

1 **Reasoning a** When you drop a matchbox, is it equally likely to land face up or end up?

b Monsur says, 'A matchbox has six faces. The probability of it landing on one face is $\frac{1}{6}$.' Explain why he is wrong.

2 Order these events from least likely to most likely.

	Event	Probability
A	I will walk to school in the morning.	0.15
B	I will get the bus to school in the morning.	$\frac{1}{2}$
C	I will ride a bicycle to school in the morning.	30%
D	I will get the train to school in the morning.	$\frac{1}{20}$

3 Design a set of counters so that
P(yellow) = P(red) = $\frac{1}{4}$ and P(blue) = $\frac{1}{8}$.
There are 3 times as many green counters as blue ones.

4 Write a set of 10 number cards so that
• P(square number) is very unlikely
• P(6, 8 or 10) is even chance
• P(multiple of 4) is very likely
• P(even number) is certain.

Q4 Strategy hint

You can use the same number on more than one card.

5 **Modelling** A fair spinner with an odd number of sides has sections coloured red and blue. The probability of landing on red is one quarter of the probability of landing on blue.
Work out the smallest number of sides the spinner can have.

6 **Problem-solving** A single counter is placed on a table.
A spinner is spun to decide where to place the next counter.

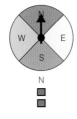
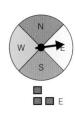
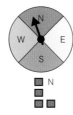
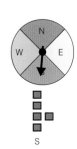

Match each spinner to the counter pattern that it will produce.

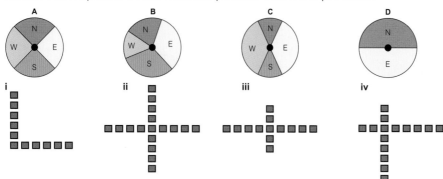

7 Problem-solving Each of these cards has a different number between 1 and 20 written on it. A card is picked at random. The probability of picking a prime number is $\frac{3}{4}$

Write the three possible numbers that could be written on the hidden card.

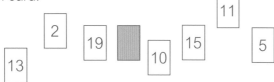

8 Reasoning This table shows the probability of picking different colour counters from a bag.

Colour	Red	Blue	Green	Black
Probability	0.2		0.1	

There are twice as many blue counters as red ones in the bag.
Work out
a P(blue) **b** P(black).

9 Problem-solving Abdullah needs to fill a bag with counters.
He has four different colours.
How many of each colour could he use so that

$P(green) = \frac{1}{20}$ $P(blue) = \frac{1}{4}$ $P(red) = \frac{1}{5}$ $P(orange) = \frac{1}{2}$

Challenge

10 A weather forecasting service predicts that the chance of rain tomorrow is 0.5 and that the chance of sunshine is 0.7.
Discuss this prediction with a classmate.
Has the weather forecasting service made a valid prediction? Give a reason for your answer.

11 Reflect Look back at the questions you answered in this section.
a Which question are you most confident that you have answered correctly?
What makes you feel confident?
b Which question are you least confident that you have answered correctly?
What makes you least confident?
c Discuss the question you feel least confident about with a classmate.
How does discussing it make you feel?

11 Unit test

1 An ordinary dice numbered 1 to 6 is rolled once.
Work out the probability of rolling
a a 1
b a number less than 4
c a number that is not a square number.

2 Giovanni puts the letters of his name in a box and then picks one letter at random.
a Find the probability that the letter that Giovanni picks is a vowel.
Riccardo does the same thing using his own name and a new box.
b Find the probability that the letter that Riccardo picks is a consonant.
c Who is more likely to pick a vowel, Giovanni or Riccardo?

3 These cards are shuffled and placed face down.

The top card is then turned over.
a List the possible outcomes.
b Work out the probability that the top card is
  i 6
  ii odd
  iii not 4.

4 Copy this diagram of an 8-sided spinner.
Colour the sections so that

$P(\text{blue}) = \frac{1}{4}$ $P(\text{red}) = \frac{3}{8}$

$P(\text{green}) = \frac{1}{8}$ $P(\text{yellow}) = \frac{1}{4}$

5 Each of these spinners is spun once.
a Write down which spinner is more likely to land on
  i yellow
  ii blue.
b Deron says that both spinners have the same probability of landing on blue.
Is Deron correct? Explain your answer clearly.

Spinner 1   Spinner 2

6 A box contains a mixture of milk, dark and white chocolates.
A chocolate is taken at random from the box.
a The probability of taking a milk chocolate is $\frac{1}{3}$
Find the probability that the chocolate taken is not a milk chocolate.
b The probability of taking a white chocolate is $\frac{1}{6}$
Find the probability that the chocolate taken is a dark chocolate.

7 Arthur has a fair 5-sided dice numbered from 1 to 5.
He says, 'the probability of rolling a prime number is greater than the probability of rolling a square number'.
Is Arthur correct? Explain your reasoning.

8 A money box contains 30 coins. Five of the coins are 10p, eight are 20p, twelve are £1 and the remainder are 50p coins.
A coin is selected at random.
a Find the probability that a £1 coin is selected.
b Find the probability that the value of the coin chosen is greater than the mean value of the coins in the money box.

9 Copy this diagram of a net of a cuboid-shaped dice.

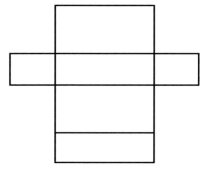

Write numbers on the sides so that
P(1) = P(4) > P(2) = P(5) > P(3) = P(6)

10 The table shows the probability of picking different coloured socks from a bag.

Colour	Blue	Grey	Black	White
Probability		0.4		0.3

There are half as many blue socks as there are black socks.
Copy and complete the probability table.

Challenge

11 The probability that a computer microchip is faulty is 0.22 when the production process is working properly.
A company employee found that six microchips were faulty out of a batch of 20.
Is the production process working properly? Explain your answer.

12 Reflect
Discuss the test with a classmate.
Which question are you most confident that you answered correctly? Why?
Which question are you least confident that you answered correctly? Why?

Index